TIME FOR DRAMA

Open University Press

English, Language, and Education series

General Editor: Anthony Adams

Lecturer in Education, University of Cambridge

This series is concerned with all aspects of language in education from the primary school to the tertiary sector. Its authors are experienced educators who examine both principles and practice of English subject teaching and language across the curriculum in the context of current educational and societal developments.

TITLES IN THE SERIES

TIME FOR DRAMA

A Handbook for Secondary Teachers

Roma Burgess and
Pamela Gaudry

Open University Press

Milton Keynes · Philadelphia

Open University Press
Open University Educational Enterprises Limited
12 Cofferidge Close
Stony Stratford
Milton Keynes MK11 1BY, England
and
242 Cherry Street
Philadelphia, PA 19106, USA

First Published 1985 by Longman Cheshire Pty Limited
this edition published 1986

British Library Cataloguing in Publication Data

Burgess, Roma
 Time for drama : a handbook for secondary
 teachers. — (English language and education
 series)
 1. Drama — Study and teaching (Secondary)
 I. Title II. Gaudry, Pamela III. Series
 808.2 PN1701

 ISBN 0–335–15249–X

**Library of Congress Cataloging in Publication
Data**
 Time for drama.
 (English, language, and education series)
 Bibliography = P. Includes index
 1. Drama in education. I. Gaudry, Pamela.
 II. Title. III. Series.
 PN3171.B87 1986 792'.07'12 86–12677
 ISBN 0–335–15249–X

Printed in Great Britain by St. Edmundsbury Press,
Bury St Edmunds, Suffolk

CONTENTS

General Editor's Introduction

Drama is possibly one of the most feted, and least understood elements in the English curriculum. Indeed, there are many who would deny that it belongs within that curriculum at all and who would argue for its place as a separate curriculum element in its own right. Still others have argued the case for 'drama across the curriculum', the role of drama in history and geography teaching for example. Here, perhaps, is the source of much of our difficulty in thinking about drama in the secondary school, the need to focus on what is at once a subject (or part of one) and a methodology of wide application.

This has led to a similar confusion in the many books that have been written on drama in the school. They vary from those that seek to provide a serious theoretical focus, most notably in recent years in the work of Gavin Bolton, or those that give a glimpse of the brilliant practitioner at work (as in the case of Dorothy Heathcote) to those that are simply practical tips for the classroom practitioner. What many of us have felt was needed for some time was a book that could combine a wealth of classroom experience and understanding alongside an adequate theoretical understanding of what was being achieved in the process. It was, therefore, with considerable excitement that I first read the present volume. Its two Australian authors seem to have achieved a remarkable success in making this blend of theory and practice, and (more importantly still) have drawn eclectically upon a wide range of traditions in their analysis. Since drama in education was first considered seriously many of the issues have tended to be discussed in a partisan way making much of such dichotomies as 'theatre versus drama', 'subject versus method', or 'process versus produce'. Much of this debate has ranged shrilly in British, and more recently, American publications, and it may take writers from outside this tradition to be able to stand back from the fray and appreciate the issues in a wider perspective.

This book is, therefore, non-partisan but not uncommitted. The authors insist that there is more in common between drama and theatre than that which differentiates them, that both are concerned with content and with a unique way of exploring, experiencing and understanding the human condition.

It is appropriate that the book begins with an overview of models for drama and an attempt to define 'the drama event'. Many classroom teachers will turn first to Part III and the very practical illustrations for actual drama lessons across the whole age range of the secondary school. Many of these lessons could stand by themselves or be integrated into the wider English curriculum, especially where this is organised on thematic lines. But the best use of these 'model lessons' will be found when there is a clear understanding of the theory on which they are based. It is to be hoped, therefore, that all users of the book (and it is essentially one to be used) will take as much note of Parts I and II as they do of Part III.

Under the coming impact of the GCSE examination in the United Kingdom, there is likely to be even more interest in the role of drama in the senior secondary school in connection with syllabuses both for English and for Drama in its own right. The final chapters of the present volume will provide much help for those concerned with work at this level in the school. But all those involved in English teaching are likely to find its pages both stimulating and illuminating.

Anthony Adams

Preface

In the early to mid-seventies, we completed our teacher training in drama and began teaching in Melbourne. At that time the emphasis on 'drama as doing' denied teachers the opportunity to engage in any significant consideration of the nature of learning in drama, or of the teacher's role in achieving that learning. Teachers spent most of their time searching for ideas which would maintain a constant hive of activity in drama classes. There appeared to be no coherent criteria for the selection of activities, and role-taking may or may not have occurred. Teachers felt inadequate if they failed to provide cathartic, fun experiences for their students. To cope with the demands for new activities, teachers found themselves going to many different sources, often to feel let down by the lack of satisfying material.

This book attempts not only to satisfy teachers' needs for activities but also to provide a comprehensive consideration of the dramatic process. This consideration exposes the need for drama to be a separate subject discipline with adequate time allocation if significant learning is to be achieved.

The book is divided into three parts. Part One establishes a definition of drama, Part Two examines the role of the teacher in the classroom and Part Three provides lesson plans for various age groups. Each part informs the other; Parts One and Two provide the essential framework for implementing the lessons in Part Three.

The teaching of drama requires a continual process of reflection, evaluation and refinement if we are to teach with clarity and confidence. We hope that this book will help teachers in this important process.

Acknowledgements

To John McLeod, for his insight into the dramatic process, for his vision of drama as paramount to learning, for his professional support and his valued qualities as a friend; to Kate Donelan, for her endless enthusiasm for drama and her sound theoretical and practical expertise, which she has been willing to generously share over the years; to Helen Collins and Tony Tartaro, whom we have been privileged to work with on professional projects and whose capacity for pleasure transformed the most mundane professional tasks into 'dramatic' events; to Brian Hogan, whose outstanding abilities as an educator and leader continually challenge and motivate those with whom he has contact; to Russel Davies, whose quiet strength and practical wisdom have influenced our thinking in this book; to John Deverall, whose ability to objectify and articulate aspects of educational drama has significantly contributed to this work; to Gwyneth McCubbin and Norman Price, whose passionate commitment to artistic and educational excellence is inspirational; to Lindy Kemp, Myrna McCrae and Peggy Sterkin, for their ideas, friendship and constant professional integrity; to Gaby Werffeli and Beth Hall whose year-long visits were dominated by the endless process of this book; to David Musker, for his ability to shoulder added burdens and remain caring and considerate; and to Judy Carlson, for her comments on 'The School Play'.

Thanks also to our many students whose work and responses primarily inform the ideas of this book; to the colleagues with whom we have interacted; and to the drama educators whose written ideas will be found throughout the book and whose works we trust you will make time to read.

And, finally, untold love and thanks to Max Burgess, Peter Fullerton and Janet Williams, who in their unique ways have made this book possible.

PART ONE:

The Drama Event

1 Drama in Education: an Overview

With any relatively new subject discipline, various methodological and theoretical approaches will seek to inform classroom practice. Many drama teachers have become advocates of one particular methodology or theory and this has led, subsequently, to large variations in teaching practice. A common, coherent framework for the teaching of drama has not existed.

Approaches to Drama

The 'Drama versus Theatre' Debate

Education for personal development, for the acquisition of improvisation skills or for problem solving highlights the confused state of drama in the face of seemingly opposed philosophical movements. This was further manifest in the lively debate which took place in the 1970s: that of the process/product debate or 'drama versus theatre' polarisation. The supposed distinction between drama and theatre determined the approach drama teachers had to their work. Burgess, Collins, Gaudry and Tartaro in *Drama and Theatre: A Shared Role in Learning*, state that:

'. . . "drama" came to be perceived as synonymous with "personal development", "self expression" and "interpersonal communication". It was the development of these qualities through the process of dramatic activity which was deemed to be educationally significant; the product, performance, was not.

'Theatre not only came to be viewed as an extra-curricular activity, but its contribution to the child's personal development was seriously questioned by drama teachers. Words such as "actors", "audience" and "making a play" were a source of embarrassment to teachers and "doing a school play" was anathema indeed.' (p. 3)

This polarisation of opinion posed some difficulty for the drama teacher. Historically, drama meant 'acting on a stage'. Teachers risked incurring the wrath of other staff members when they refused to be involved in the production of *Showboat* or *Annie Get Your Gun*. Unfortunately, it was difficult to express any clear explanation for this stance, beyond claiming that it was detrimental to the educational development of the child. In their constant search for what to do with 7E, 8B or the other eighteen drama classes for the week, teachers tended to think of drama more in terms of how it was applied rather than how it worked. Even now questions asked about what drama is are often answered in general terms which state that drama is communication, personal development, theatre skills, or simply, 'It's Life'! Such responses may reveal the teachers' goals, certainly they reflect diverse methodological influences, yet they give no clues as to the basic nature of drama. The nature of theatre and its relationship with 'drama as personal development' was never fully explored, and for many teachers this conflict has yet to be resolved.

The range and diversity of the role of drama for personal development and the extent to which theatre imbues the curriculum can be illustrated by examining statements from particular drama programmes in several different schools.

School 1 — a large middle-class girls high school

Drama aims to effect a marriage between skills and content. The programme exposes the children to a wide variety of skills involved in the dramatic medium within the parameters of a prescribed content.

'It is envisaged that the children will become familiar and reasonably proficient with these skills as a necessary part of pursuing the content involved.

'It is unnecessary to teach the skills separately before beginning to teach the content, therefore eliminating skills lessons which may be superficial and time-consuming.

· 'The programme is group-centred and caters for a performance basis if desired.

The drama programme aims to engender self-awareness through the development of student initiative and responsibility; to develop personal expressive/creative abilities, and to encourage responsibility in the initiation and execution of tasks.

'Evaluation of the students' progress is a subjective appreciation by the teacher.

Obviously one can record the acquisition of skills, but it is decidedly more difficult to determine to what extent a student has used her imagination and creative abilities to complete a task.

'Drama's major aim is to encourage a positive and co-operative spirit in group activities. In most other subjects the children do not normally get the opportunity to plan and execute tasks in group situations, but are restricted to performing individual and taking responsibility only for themselves.

There is a distinct difference between the overt curriculum, that of skills acquisition, etc., and the hidden curriculum — that of developing a positive and confident self concept, with the former facilitating the acquisition of the latter.'

In this example, the acquisition of specific theatre skills occurs within the context of activities designed for personal development.

School 2 — a large inner-city high school with a substantial migrant population

Drama is run as a child-centred activity. The main aim of the drama programme is to increase the students' social skills. Some of the areas are helping the students learn how to solve problems in a non-aggressive manner, learning to work within a group, clear verbal expression, extended physical expression and confidence in their . . . language.'

Obviously, this approach is purely a 'personal development' one with an emphasis on problem-solving activities.

School 3 — a large suburban technical school

GENERAL AIMS OF THE DEPARTMENT

'1 To provide learning situations which maximise the expressive, creative and imaginative potential of each student.
'2 To encourage students to analyse the world in which they live, in order that they may more clearly identify:
   (a) 'themselves' — their self-concept:
   (b) their responsibilities, both personal and social;
   (c) their values systems.
'3 To encourage students to take an active role in the society in which they live, by developing social and aesthetic awareness.
'4 To equip students with a wide range of practical, *transferable* skills. To develop confidence and competence in:
   (a) intuitive thinking processes;
   (b) perception and reflection;
   (c) critical analysis and appraisal;
   (d) decision making.
'5 To foster an appreciation for the arts and an awareness of its potential in recreational and vocational realms.
'Dramatic skills, while forming an important part of the

working process, are not taught as ends in themselves, rather, they are seen as tools designed to assist the student to pose and seek solutions to questions of personal, inter-personal and universal significance. The drama programme has a pronounced social bias or orientation; the primary concern is for value clarification and student self-actualisation.'

Here we see a limited 'theatre' contribution with the focus clearly on personal development.

School 4 — a small independent senior school
'The drama course aims to provide opportunities for the stu-dent to understand the art form of drama. The students will develop individual expressive talents. The course comprises a study of theatre history and the evolution of various acting styles, stage design and construction, theatre technology, light-ing, and voice production. All students will be involved in at least two major theatrical performances each year.'

This course is clearly designed for the training of actors with a strong emphasis on technical knowledge and design skills. Personal development aims are not made explicit in the course; although they may be a by-product, they are not specifically the objectives of this work.

These statements reflect the most common methodological approaches to the planning of drama. But, as John Deverall highlighted in his teaching at Melbourne College of Advanced Education, other approaches also focussed on the use of drama as a method of teaching in other subject areas and as a form of therapy in both educational and broader social set-tings. John identified four general classroom approaches to student development through Drama. He labelled these ap-proaches 'Personal Development', 'Therapy', 'Learning Me-dium' and 'Art Form'. The following analysis uses these labels as categories for a discussion of teaching methods and strategies in drama.

Personal Development

This approach to drama confidently asserted the need for drama activities to focus on the feelings and attitudes of in-dividuals and the skills of social interaction and communi-cation. Personal development and the creative self-expression of the student were the major teaching objectives. Drama was seen as the most effective means to this end and the goals were claimed to be sufficiently important to deserve consider-ation by curriculum committees. Drama on the timetable would develop the individual's self-confidence and interper-sonal communication skills. Spontaneous self-expression and personal development, it was argued, were denied by the rigidity, rigour and personal restriction accompanying other subjects.

Although some members of staff were sceptical about the freedom associated with self-expression, improving self-confidence and communication skills was justifiable in educational terms and perhaps even essential. Drama earned its place on many timetables, either as a subject in its own right or as a period a week set aside in the English syllabus, particularly at junior secondary level. The teacher assumed a nurturing, pastoral role in this learning process, and any notion of product or quality of work was regarded with unease, if not outright rejection. As was mentioned earlier, doing plays and performing them was seen as anathema to drama. Teachers were preoccupied with setting up activities which were fun to do and offered a cathartic release from the rigidity and boredom of desks and 'academia'.

Drama lessons were characterised by endless games and a multitude of sensory, relaxation, concentration and movement exercises. Some improvisation games were also used, but the emphasis was on participation rather than product. Tolerance, sensitivity and group co-operation were explicitly identified as learning objectives. Role play was not seen as essential to the drama. Leslie Button (1982), highlights the role drama has to play in the pastoral curriculum of the school. He states:

> 'In the pastoral context, communication skills underlie caring, concern and interest in the other person . . . It is possible to focus directly on empathy through simple (trust) exercises . . . In the early stages there needs to be a good deal of emphasis on listening . . . role play is used . . . to explore personal behaviour, group behaviour and to practise new approaches . . . Our aim should be to help young people to build up their own social competence . . . so they can cope with life's problems as they arise.'

Clearly the learning objectives in this sense are concerned with social adaptation and socialisation. Simple co-operation tasks are used to achieve this end. Books of games and 'getting to know you' activities are guaranteed a market in this approach. In-services and meetings of drama teachers become the hunting ground for new games and activities that could result in fresh stimulus for the class.

In the personal development application of drama, reading about drama-in-education was usually considered unnecessary and even harmful. To engage in an analysis of the learning in specific activities was labelled as intellectual and therefore anti-drama. Particular writers in drama became the target of a great deal of antagonism because they were grappling with the question of what the 'specifics' of drama were. An oft-heard statement by drama teachers was,

> 'As the authors are not working in the field, they can't possibly understand the difficulties experienced in the classroom'.

This was untrue, as many authors were, and indeed still are, practitioners in their own right. Regardless of this, their work is constantly dismissed as being distant and theoretical and therefore irrelevant to the classroom teacher.

For this reason, the drama writers' work did not reach a large target audience; moreover in some instances it was regarded as a direct threat to the integrity and accountability of the methods employed by the classroom teacher.

To conclude, social issues and the exploration of personal feelings and attitudes were central to the drama curriculum, although in many schools no drama curriculum or specific syllabus was ever asked for. Indeed, writing out such details was a denial of the essential need for spontaneity in drama.

Therapy

Closely associated with the personal development approach to drama is the recognition of the therapeutic benefits of the subject. In this approach it is implicitly assumed that the participants in drama are in need of curative treatment and the drama teacher holds the skills of the therapist. In its mildest form this manifests itself in a spontaneous openness and freedom of response which is rejuvenating and cathartic. Many of the games and exercises used in drama achieve this end; they evoke joyous involvement and often a good healthy laugh; the 'social health' of the group can be improved. Theatre games and improvised drama also offer the possibility for a cathartic release of energy and emotion. Other activities are geared to the stimulation of dull and ailing senses. Perhaps a less desirable orientation is that which manifests itself in quasi-psychodrama. Here personal dilemmas are played out in the drama or individuals use the group structure to 'constructively' explore the annoying or negative behaviour of one of its members.

So far we have been discussing the usual school situation. If we turn now to the area of special education, the use of drama as therapy assumes its rightful place. In dealing with physically or mentally handicapped students, for example, the application of drama has a specific and identifiable role to play in the therapeutic development of individuals. In these cases, drama takes on a specialist function and the teacher also needs to be aware of the para-medical nature of the application of drama. The need for the acquisition of special skills in therapy is essential. Special education courses now being run by tertiary institutions are evidence that this need is being catered for. Such training should equip teachers with knowledge related to specific areas so that appropriate and effective drama strategies can be adopted.

Learning Medium

As vehemently as some claim the *raison d'être* of drama to be personal development, others assert that drama should exist to service the learning in other areas of the curriculum. This stance is a strong affirmation that drama is a method of teaching capable of stimulating and achieving powerful learning. The commercial availability of packaged simulation games aimed to teach a broad spectrum of subjects highlights this faith in drama to get the point across.

When this utilitarian application of drama is adopted the drama teacher often becomes a resource for other teachers in the school, particularly in the humanities departments. The content is drawn from the topics being studied and the drama focusses quite clearly on the pursuit of specific learning. Perhaps it should be stated that we are not discussing drama activities adopted in other classrooms, most frequently in English, in order to develop the social health of the group or their personal communication skills. The prime objective of the drama when it is applied as a learning medium will be to have the students leave the drama knowing more about a particular issue or event than when the lesson began. The teacher manipulates the drama structures so that this learning can be highlighted. Reflection and discussion play a major part in the drama; the learning must be made explicit.

A misunderstanding of how to apply drama as a learning medium sometimes occurs. In an English classroom recently, the teacher wanted to set up drama which would allow the students to act out a factory situation. Workers would carry out boring and repetitive tasks under the constant supervision of bosses whose responsibility lay in increasing the productivity of the workers. What clouded the issue and changed the entire learning focus was the imposition of a game structure over the basically sound drama already set up. A theatre status game was used to inject interest and fun into the drama. Whilst the situation was being played out, the workers were to find moments where they could snatch the bosses' hats from their heads and thereby alter their status. The preoccupation with such a strategy obviously does not allow a focus on the learning objectives. There is a confusion as to what learning is inherent in the activities themselves. The role taking and experience of the dramatic situation in this instance were subsumed by the skill needed to play the game. Reflection revolved around the successful strategies adopted by individuals to get the hats!

Related to this function of drama is the emphasis, once again, on drama as a process used to service a teaching goal which is not in itself dramatic. This emphasis has, in the past, added more strength to the process/product debate mentioned earlier. There can be no doubt that some most effective teaching occurs in drama when this clear learning goal is pursued. This should not, however, deny the drama its own integrity. Heathcote's work firmly reminds us that the quality of expression is an indication of the quality of learning likely to occur. If the class does not see a sincerity, for example, in the work of the students, Heathcote may choose to stop the drama and/or change its direction. This occurred when she was working with a group of American children on 'The Building of a Nation'. The group's insincere expression of grief over a death indicated the need for teacher intervention in the drama if the learning goal was to be achieved. Unless the drama quality is seen as significant, neither the learning nor the medium will be of much value.

Art Form

Historically, much of what occurred in drama was play reading. The value of acting out scenes was clear, students enhanced their understanding of the text and at the same time developed self-confidence and skills in expressive communication. Rehearsal and performance of the play intensified and broadened the learning still further. Personal and social development were seen as an important learning bonus, but in this approach to drama, the play and its performance were the methods used to achieve these goals. One can still find some very strong drama programmes in schools which are the heritage of innovative English teachers who saw the need to capitalise on this learning and introduce drama into the curriculum as a separate subject. Although in some programmes the learning focus moved quickly to an emphasis on games and exercises for personal development, there were others which specifically taught theatre skills and expended their energies in the preparation and performance of plays.

Many teachers still see the theatre product as the prime function of drama. Some schools are even changing the name of the subject Drama to 'Theatre' or 'Performing Arts' so that the orientation is quite explicit. In these programmes, even when a less formal improvised drama occurs to develop skills, performance is the real stimulus for activity undertaken in the classroom. Time is spent developing characterisation skills through movement, improvisation and voice exercises. Students may create their own scripts, but just as often, the text is the focus of the lesson. Practice in creating theatrical scenes and images is constant. Units of work may also develop skills in related technical and design areas such as make-up, mask, costuming, set design and lighting. In this approach to drama, finding appropriate material is often a problem. Drama consultants are constantly being asked for good plays for years 7, 8, 9, 10 and so on.

Performance in drama festivals and competitions offers a wider perspective for learning about the art form and can be a motivation for groups to devise their own material for performance. The 'winners and losers' syndrome or the 'good and bad' aspects of competitions can change the focus of the learning.

In contrast with drama as a learning medium, the art form approach to drama is not primarily concerned with the learning inherent in specific content, an approach not usually associated with the production of *Showboat*. Instead, its focus is the execution of the drama, the quality of its expression and its effect on an audience.

Commonality in Drama

If we reflect for a moment now on the commonalities that exist between the learning areas and their associated activities, it is possible to understand why there is confusion when it comes to planning drama curricula. When personal development, self expression and interpersonal communication were the desired objectives, the activities adopted were most often games and exercises which bore no relation to role taking and imaginative, dramatic situations. Instead, participation in drama involved the students in activities which were stimulating, invigorating and fun. The individual's experiences were essentially egocentric and introspective.

Much of what has been said about drama for personal development also holds true for the therapeutic application of drama in the classroom. Many of these activities promoted a release of personal energy and emotion, external to participation in dramatic situations.

When drama was used as a learning medium the focussing occurred somewhat differently. The students' participation in the dramatic situation provided the content and learning focus for the drama. The meaning of the drama lay in the significance of the students' interaction within dramatic situations.

Similarly, when drama was primarily concerned with the art form, interactions within dramatic situations provided the focus and meaning of the drama.

What emerges from this search for commonalities in the teaching of drama is, once again, the disparate nature of activities and learning goals. Trying to establish a foundation from which to plan curricula is a daunting task. It is little wonder that objective onlookers and newcomers to drama teaching encounter many difficulties.

2   The Drama Model

If we are to arrive at a common understanding that will responsibly inform our planning and teaching in drama it is going to require a moment's patience and objectivity. In the first instance, it will be helpful to distance ourselves from drama-in-education philosophies, teaching goals and classroom activities; these hold more potential for confusion than for the clarity and commonality of understanding that we seek. Secondly, we need to put aside our classroom blinkers, especially those with tinted anti-theatre lenses, because it is the dramatic and artistic experience of theatre that provides us with insights rich in meaning and implications. Now, before you impatiently close the book, remember the blinkers and then consider the following fundamental aspects of drama.

Drama-in-Theatre

Drama is a series of imaginary events based on life and acted out by people who tacitly agree to adopt role behaviour appropriate to the created situation. Playwrights, directors, actors and technicians work imaginatively and artistically from their experiences of life to create the artificial and symbolic life of the play. Whilst it is the interaction of characters and events which holds the audience's interest in the play, it is the individual's experiences of the real world, combined with a capacity for thoughtful reflection, that results in the creation of personal symbolic meaning.

How Meaning is Created

There can be no doubt that the interaction of characters creates the life of the play; the essence of that life, however, is the development and expression of role. In developing a character, the actor creates personal meaning through a role relationship between the 'me' and 'not me' (Winnicott 1971), and expresses this in concrete artistic images which seek to communicate. Although the actor's personal knowledge and experience of life informs this development of character, his understanding and command of the meaning inherent in the art form allows him to competently express and communicate the fullness of that character. If the event of the play is to be significant, then both actors and audience depend on this quality of dramatic expression. While watching the actors at work in the drama, the audience identifies and empathises with the characters as they are expressed. Individual members of the audience establish passive role relationships between the self and the characters. Any personal meaning evolving from this relationship will be expressed in passive, abstract thought rather than the concrete actions of the characters.

At this point it will be useful to look in detail at this creation of meaning through role relationships. To do this we will borrow from an example developed in a recent research paper (1982) by the writers with teaching colleagues, Helen Collins and Tony Tartaro.

Creating the Role

When an actor is playing the role of a character, he is simultaneously aware that he is himself (the 'me') and that he is playing at being someone else (the 'not me'). He does not give up his 'self' to become the other, but rather projects onto the role, extending his notion of self to incorporate that of the role — the character. This is illustrated in Figure 1.

Let's imagine an actor is to play the role of Macbeth. What this actor has experienced and feels subjectively about leadership, duty, courage, power, love, ambition and honour will be tested against what he knows of these concepts from his

Figure 1: The notion of self and role

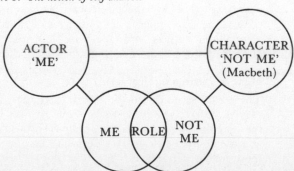

objective observations of the world. Shakespeare's script will also be part of the actor's range of objective knowledge. An oscillation occurs in the relationship between the subjective and objective realities (the 'me' and 'not me') until a reconciliation of the two allows for the creation of personal symbolic meaning. This abstract internal meaning is then expressed in the concrete words and actions of the actor in role as Macbeth. This is illustrated in Figure 2.

Figure 3 (page 16) offers an approximation of one particular moment in the actor's performance. When Macbeth woodenly

Figure 2: Creation of role

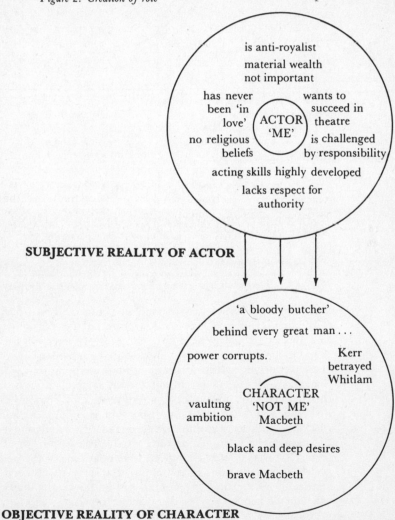

is anti-royalist

material wealth
not important

has never
been 'in
love'   ACTOR   wants to
succeed in
theatre

no religious   'ME'   is challenged
beliefs   by responsibility

acting skills highly developed

lacks respect for
authority

SUBJECTIVE REALITY OF ACTOR

'a bloody butcher'

behind every great man . . .

power corrupts.   Kerr
betrayed
Whitlam

CHARACTER
vaulting   'NOT ME'
ambition   Macbeth

black and deep desires

brave Macbeth

OBJECTIVE REALITY OF CHARACTER

Figure 3: Role relationship and the creation of meaning

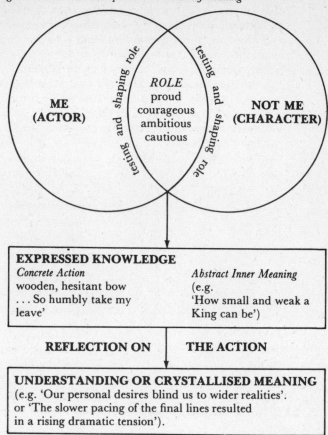

EXPRESSED KNOWLEDGE
Concrete Action
wooden, hesitant bow
. . . So humbly take my
leave'

Abstract Inner Meaning
(e.g.
'How small and weak a
King can be')

REFLECTION ON   THE ACTION

UNDERSTANDING OR CRYSTALLISED MEANING
(e.g. 'Our personal desires blind us to wider realities'.
or 'The slower pacing of the final lines resulted
in a rising dramatic tension').

Note: This illustration isolates one particular moment in the play.

and hesistantly bows his farewell to Duncan, these concrete
symbolic actions may represent 'an internal abstract meaning
of "How small and weak a king can be!"' Inherent in the act
is the potential for a change in personal understanding. The
actor is working with meanings related to the human condition and with knowledge about the art form. It may be that
the actor is fully aware of the significance of both levels of
meaning and in thought or discussion is able to articulate
this. It is just as possible however, that the particularity of
the moment will simply become part of the larger life of the
play. Essential to this change of understanding is the actor's
ability to be conscious of the moment and to reflect upon the
experience of it. Some individuals are better at this than others. During rehearsal it is the director's task to work closely

with the actor/s to bring about this change of understanding. The quality of the actor's development will be closely related to the director's skills in handling this process.

The symbolic creation of meaning is inextricably linked with the product of its expression. The elements of the art form, namely rhythm, focus, climax, sound, dynamic, conflict, symbol, space and contrast, are utilised in the expression of role and playing through of the dramatic situation. Performance explicitly uses these elements for their symbolic effect on an audience. If the individual's expressive act is going to communicate meaning effectively then the actor must be aware that feeling and expressing meaning does not automatically guarantee its communication to others. Command of technical skills and knowledge of how to apply them allows the actor to be more responsive and expressive within the creative process. Members of an audience then have a greater opportunity to become involved in the role relationships and creation of personal meaning. To use the example of Macbeth again, a somewhat cynical individual in the audience may express this personal meaning in thought as, 'self-gain forms the basis of all human interactions!' Alternatively, someone else may be aware of the subtlety and contrast of movement which carries the inner private thoughts of humans.

Whatever the meaning, those who participate in the process are fully aware of the conventions and artifice that constitute the theatrical event. Their expectations and behaviour are a direct response to the nature of that event; they are involved in a dramatic process which is expressive, experiential and communicative. To misunderstand the process is to have the experience and miss the meaning!

Drama in Education

In the classroom students act out imaginary situations based on life. They work imaginatively and artistically from their experiences of life to create the artificial and symbolic life of the drama. The interaction of characters and events holds the students' interest in the drama, but their real-life experiences are essential to the creation of personal symbolic meaning. Participation in this dramatic process involves the students in experiential, expressive and communicative modes of action.

Drama in education then, is merely the educational, rather than theatrical, application of the dramatic process. Participation in the process however, will vary depending upon the mode of dramatic action adopted and emphasised. The major influence on the selection of a particular mode of action will be the individual's changing ability to use role and create meaning. John Seely (1976) suggested that the mode of dramatic activity varies according to the changing use of role. His classification of three basic models of role behaviour: exploratory, illustrative and expressive, has made a significant contribution to our understanding of how drama works in the classroom.

Individual Development and Dramatic Action

Young children readily adopt roles. They become totally absorbed in the action and these actions remain sincere and spontaneous. At this stage of dramatic development, especially with younger students, the play is not clearly separate from the real world. The children are largely unaware of an audience and as Slade (1954) states:

'. . . they have no need for spectators because the play exists only for the self; it is egocentric and private.'

Indeed, awareness of an audience will destroy the child's focus and break the role. These role relationships are used to explore new experiences in an attempt to make sense of the real world and develop confidence in dealing with it.

With the onset of puberty, adolescents enter a very self-conscious and confused stage of their development. The identity confusion that occurs at this time makes for a sensitivity and vulnerability within the group. There is a keen desire to use role as a means of communication but this conflicts with a hyper-awareness of 'the me' in building role and expressing character to an audience. Comedy and caricature offer some security in this dramatic presentation that is not always possible in the more absorbed and naturalistic expression of roles. Students use the drama to test out their ideas and opinions through the communication of their roles to others in the group. As Seely states (page 21):

'They (the students) imitate other people's behaviour in order to back up some analytical point they wish to make: this type of person behaves in this way, they say, and here's an example to prove it' (p. 21)

In middle and later adolescence, the concern with communication is intensified and the safety of comedy and exaggeration assumes less importance. Students are able to take on a range of roles with much greater ease and the individual pushes for a more sophisticated expression of role. Individuals now have a stronger sense of self ('the me') and can readily extend themselves into the world of the other (the 'not me') without too much personal threat. They are involved in the same twofold process as the actor in theatre: creating personal meaning and finding a way to clearly and dramatically communicate this. Seely relates this type of communication to the theatre of Bertholt Brecht.

> 'Rather than analysing aspects of behaviour in interpersonal relationships, the speaker is concerned to communicate both factual information about an event and comment on its general social significance. This is close to the expressive form of adult theatre but (as Brecht makes clear) it is a form of theatre in which *what* is communicated is important to both actors and audience'. (p. 22)

At this stage a more intense interest in the elements of the art form is present as students seek to become effective communicators to wider audiences. They are very aware of their need to consciously manipulate expressive symbols for the purpose of effectively communicating meaning.

Controlling Dramatic Action

Involvement in drama engages the individual in a development of understanding about the human condition and the elements of the art form. Drama explores aspects of human endeavour and it does so by consciously manipulating the elements of the art form. It is our capacity to identify with these situations from our own experiences of life that results in us being entertained and challenged in our perceptions of life.

Because the dramatic situation and the interaction of characters within it are artificial, the artistry with which the drama is created is essential to its meaning. To put it simply, the way in which the drama is presented is what the drama means. Participation in the dramatic process must then involve us in an experience that affords knowledge about life and about art.

Richard Courtney (1980), draws a distinction between the intuitive knowledge obtained whilst participating *in* dramatic action and knowledge gained through talking, reflecting and writing *about* the drama. This distinction is useful in reminding us that dramatic activity itself must be significant and meaningful if it is to contain knowledge that can be experienced. Any reflection on the experience should crystallise, and make explicit, meaning that has been encountered in the dramatic action. This explicit knowledge will then be tested and utilised in further dramatic action. As Courtney points out (page 72),

'Although both kinds of knowledge are important in the class-room, knowledge IN is paramount. It leads to knowledge ABOUT. Thus, throughout all school life, curriculum design should be based on experiential knowledge. Discursive knowledge should arise from direct dramatic action.'

If experience and intuitive knowledge are overemphasised, however, there is a danger that the learning process will be devalued and retarded. Reflection on the event outside the experience of it is of paramount importance. It cannot be assumed that the individual's expressive act is the be-all and end-all. Liv Ullmann (1979) highlights something of this process when she discusses her rehearsal of the part of Grusha for a production of *The Caucasian Chalk Circle*, in Oslo in 1962 (pages 56–7).

'When I was twenty-two, Peter Palitzseh, a German director, came to our theatre in Oslo. He taught me that everything we portray on the stage ought to be shown from two sides. Be illustrated in both black and white. When I smile, I must show the grimace behind it. Try to depict the counter-movement — its counter-motion. I learned to work more con-sciously. (These concepts are more fully discussed in chapter 8.) I remember the opening scene of the *Chalk Circle*. At the first reading I thought I was to play a woman in a heroic situ-ation. Her name was Grusha.

'Revolution had come to the village where she lived in poverty. Everyone had fled the murder and fire that followed in the wake of war. While she herself was running away she found an infant abandoned by its mother. She stopped without knowing what she would do with the little bundle wrapped in silk and velvet, precious materials that she had never touched before.

My interpretation was to sit down and look tenderly and softly at the baby. Sing to it, pick it up, and take it with me. "Think a bit deeper", the director said. "Show her doubts: surely she must have had some? Her cowardice; don't you feel it? And what about her ambivalence in the face of this new respon-sibility? The audience will sympathise with you anyway. Even if they don't grasp everything you are trying to illustrate, they will recognise you as acting in a way they themselves might have acted. No spontaneous nobility. Not necessarily symbol-ising goodness all the time".

'My interpretation became this:

The woman is sitting with the baby, but puts it down as she realises what a hindrance it will be on her flight. She stands up and walks away. Stops. Doubt. Turns back. Reluctantly sits down again. Looks at its little bundle. Looks away. Then, finally, she picks it up with a gesture of resignation and runs on . . .

'I, who for years had kept Stanislavsky's book on the art of acting on my bedside table, now began to look for other ways. Partly, I found a new technique which seemed right for me . . . Less feelings, more concentration on giving expression to the feelings.' (pp. 56–7)

By focussing attention on this artist at work in the dramatic process we can see the complementary relationship between involvement of feelings in the experience, the reflection upon the experience, and the growth in understanding that is achieved. The actress is extended in her understanding of the human condition as experienced by her character; she also learns how to control the artistic medium which expresses this understanding. Ullmann seeks to become involved in the experience of the situation, but at the same time is conscious of the artifice of it. She recognises the need for a balance between the subjective and objective realities of the role and the dramatic situation. She must at the same time be participant and spectator in the dramatic event. 'Less feelings — more concentration on giving expression to the feelings.'

Feeling and Meaning in Dramatic Action

Role relationships in drama use a quality of feeling that is different from that which we experience in our everyday interactions. The spontaneous actual emotions of real-life situations are replaced in dramatic action by emotions which may recall real life feelings, but which change to become 'imaginative and artistic fiction'. (Stanislavsky 1936, page 121). These imagined feelings are controlled and expressed in such a way that a sense of truth is created out of them. Participant actors and audience recognise this artistic truth with its quality of sincerity and so believe in the drama that is happening.

Knowing about this feeling quality and being able to use it to create dramatic truths is one aspect of understanding that must evolve from participation in the dramatic process. Stanislavsky points out that many actors, when they become involved in the drama, lose this capacity to discriminate between what is artistically true and false. Within the drama, it would seem, they become so involved in the making of it that they are unable to pay due attention to *how* it is being made. Yet these two processes must consciously co-exist for expressive meaning to occur.

The essential factor in this expression of emotion is the sense of truth that is recognised in the concrete, physical actions of the drama. The hollow, falsified emotion of poorly imagined and/or imitated activity devalues the dramatic experience and deprives it of meaning.

Elements of the Art Form and Meaning in Dramatic Action

In attempting to create artistic truths and build dramatic tension, playwrights, actors, directors and technicians exploit the elements of the art form. By manipulating these elements they are able to add truth and significance to the drama. This heightened artistic meaning elevates the quality of the dramatic experience as well as the quality of its expression. The prime purpose of using these elements relates to the drama. This heightened artistic meaning elevates the quality of the dramatic experience as well as the quality of its expression. The prime purpose of using these elements relates to the desire to consciously create symbolic meaning. As was obvious in the example used by Liv Ullmann, the extent to which the actor is aware of this manipulation of artistic elements will vary. In drama in education the developmental stage of the students and the specific teaching focus of the lesson will be major factors influencing the degree to which this manipulation is made explicit. What is felt within the dramatic experience will first require attention by the director; how this is expressed will follow from there.

Before we briefly consider these elements and how they manifest themselves in the drama, it is important to realise that there is an inter-dependent relationship between them. The use of one may call into action the effect of others.

Rhythm is essentially related to the notion of time, intensity and repetition. It can be heard in the exhausted traveller's slow dull knocking on the door; the landlord's rapid resounding banging as he tries to wake his tenants; the judge's deliberate, evenly spaced repetition of, 'You are charged with disloyalty, you are charged with dishonesty, you are charged with irresponsibility . . .'

Focus is the converging or concentration of energy. Caesar's blood-stained toga which Antony holds before the Roman crowd illustrates this manipulation of the element of focus. The use of teacher-in-role in classroom drama is also a clear example of an effective strategy for achieving focus. For example, the teacher as Professor Brainstorm inspects the apprentices' invention, their time machine. The use of objects such as the mysterious sealed casket in *The Merchant of Venice*, or the curious looking box placed before the class by the 'visiting archeologist', also act as focussing agents. A specific setting for the drama may also provide this focussing of energy, for example, the convicts crowded in a hulk awaiting transportation to Australia.

Space is the expanse of the working area and the movement and grouping patterns adopted within it. For example, convicts in a work-gang widely distanced from each other as they build the road, or a large group of factory workers forced to argue their grievances from the factory floor whilst the four executives stand in the office overhead (the raised rostra at the end of the room/stage).

Dynamic is often the result of other elements combining to create the energy of the drama. This can be achieved through surprise or sudden changes in the action of the drama, the juxtaposition of comic/tragic events, or the accumulation of particular dramatic force does much to gather involvement and focus the energy of the participants.

Symbol is any object, and sometimes sound, light, or movement which is used explicitly to add a reverberation of meaning to the drama. 'The sun's coming up', when spoken by the Grand Master at the witches' coven, needs no further explanation. The gun or cross are objects readily understood for their depth of meaning.

Climax occurs where a drawing together of actions and meaning forces resolution or a change in the direction of the drama. (This is often the place where Heathcote will stop the drama for reflection, in order to crystallise its meaning.)

Contrast is actually the manner in which certain elements such as sound, movement or rhythm are manipulated. Differences are juxtaposed so that the variation is emphasised and therefore significant. Robert Bolt's Common Man, in *A Man for All Seasons* (1960), offers contrast of a different nature. By stepping aside to comment colloquially upon the actions and theatricality of the play's events there is a dynamic contrast in the dramatic style itself.

Sound Between the extremes of silence and the loudest of sounds there exist endless possibilities for portraying meaning. Obviously the very range and subtlety of the language used by the actor to express character is one example of the manipulation of this artistic element. Ticking clocks, door bells, footsteps and music are sounds which may be technically added to build dramatic tension.

Conflict is a state of tension that arises because of contrasts or inconsistencies in the behaviour or values of different characters. It is the subtle antagonism and irreconcilability of the conflict which provides greater potential for creating dramatic tension than the direct clash or quarrel between opposing views. Macbeth's plotting to kill Duncan and then his inability to carry out the deed are examples of personal conflict effectively used to build dramatic tension. Inexperienced actors and students too readily resort to direct verbal and physical clashes as a means of dealing with differences and as a way of expressing conflict.

It is significant that these artistic elements are not seen as ends in themselves. Rather they are a means to an end, which has to do with offering new perspectives on the human condition and the individual's struggle to find order and meaning within it (see chapter 7).

Human Development in Drama

The primary function of drama in theatre and drama in education is to provide a context whereby individuals may participate in the experience and contemplation of issues of human concern. Both manifestations of the dramatic process serve to increase personal understanding and extend awareness of one's relationship with the wider world. The nature of role-taking and dramatic action hold the potential for personal meaning to be created. Drama is always about something and as characters live through the dramatic moments of the play, actors and audience participate in a symbolic and meaningful event.

Because the event depends upon the conventions of interpersonal interaction and group support, there is a secondary type of learning which occurs at the personal, social level. Being sensitive, aware and tolerant of others, developing personal confidence in expressing thoughts and initiating ideas in the planning and making of the drama are interpersonal qualities that are vital to the dramatic process. We are aware that one actor's poor performance can significantly reduce the impact of a piece of theatre; this holds true for the classroom as well. Dramatic action relies on the active and positive support of each participant if the play is to evolve. It is as fundamental as transgressing a rule in football, tennis or any other game.

In fact, some drama theorists (most recently Watkins, 1982) would claim that drama's *raison d'être* is at base linked to this personal, social aspect of dramatic action. However, to focus on the learning that occurs because of 'we're all part of a team playing a game' approach, unfortunately distorts the issue, and diverts attention from the artistic and symbolic nature of the drama. Personal and social skills will be developed as a result of participation in drama. This is a positive by-product of the dramatic process, although a great deal of the development in this respect will occur outside any involvement in dramatic action. Gavin Bolton (1979) states his reservations about the emphasis on this kind of learning in drama (pages 123–4).

> 'I am not sure that I can accept some current practice that appears to connive at a low-level standard of drama on the grounds that the all-important social needs are being met; and it seems to me that it should be a rare occurrence for social improvement to be the only goal when clearly sensible structuring could concurrently meet a number of additional requirements related to meaning ... and aesthetic form.' (pp. 123–4)

3 Fundamentals of the Drama

To this point we have described the fundamentals of the dramatic process, analysing role relationships and the creation of meaning. Role relationships are seen as central to the dramatic process and dramatic action as experiential, expressive and communicative in nature. Dramatic meaning was intrinsically related to human development and the art form. Drama in education applied this process within the classroom.

Figure 4 illustrates the fundamentals of the drama in education process.

Figure 4: Fundamentals of the drama

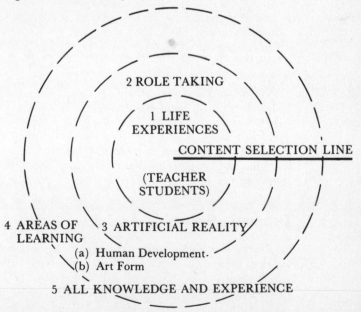

2 ROLE TAKING

1 LIFE EXPERIENCES

CONTENT SELECTION LINE

(TEACHER STUDENTS)

4 AREAS OF LEARNING   3 ARTIFICIAL REALITY

(a) Human Development.
(b) Art Form

5 ALL KNOWLEDGE AND EXPERIENCE

At the centre of the diagram lie the personal experiences and knowledge brought to drama by the participants, primarily the students, and teacher. This small circle of experience (the subjective reality) is contained within the large outer circle of all knowledge and experience (the objective reality). The middle circle shows the dramatic medium by which these two areas of experience are brought into a creative relationship with one another. Role relationships and the artificial reality of this dramatic medium act as an expressive filter for both subjective and objective experiences and knowledge. A line drawn as the radius of the circle constitutes content selection. Drama lessons can be planned from content chosen from any point along this line — from the students' own experiences, from the dramatic medium itself (characterisation, improvisation, theatre history, or movement skills, for example), or from the vast, known experiences of all knowledge. Inherent in the dramatic medium is a creative tension which gives rise to specific learning. This tension evolves from the juxtaposition of real life experiences with the artificial experience of the drama. Specific learning relates to (a) the art form, and (b) human development. From here we can now extract the four basic components of drama.

The Components of Drama

1 Life experiences and knowledge which provide the **dramatic content**.
2 An artificial reality based on life which forms the **dramatic situation**.
3 Individuals using role relationships which constitute the **dramatic action**.
4 To ensure that the dramatic event can indeed happen and be meaningful we also need individuals who agree to participate in the dramatic event 'as if' it were real — to abide by the **conventions of drama**.

So, what implications do these components have for the planning and teaching of drama?

Dramatic Content

In drama in theatre the playwright's knowledge and experiences of life's events provide the raw material or **content** from which the play will be created. The personal sensitivity and richness of insight associated with that content selection determines much about the play's quality and inherent meaning. Not all playwrights, for example, are capable of giving us the richness of meaning contained in *Oedipus Rex* or *Hamlet*. We cannot deny however, that many plays offer far too little in terms of interest or significance. Neither the content nor the way in which it has been manipulated provide sufficient interest or challenge for others to participate in it. In such instances the playwright will simply need to learn from his efforts and consider more fully the raw material and the form with which he works.

In drama in education the teacher must look to the playwright to gain insight into setting up drama, for both share the function of providing the important framework for the dramatic process. What the teacher offers the students as stimulus for their work is akin to dramatic content selected by the playwright for the drama; it must be substantial enough to create interest and personal meaning. Unlike the artist/playwright, the teacher is firstly a professional educator, and secondarily a drama teacher. Teachers assume the added responsibility of ensuring that the content provides opportunities for the students to maximise learning. Thus the content must not only be capable of involving and extending the students, but it should also suggest dramatic situations with which the developing students will be able to cope. The previously cited example of Heathcote's students attempting unsuccessfully to deal with grief in the drama is one instance in which the content gave rise to a dramatic situation with demands clearly beyond the capabilities of the students.

Choice of content therefore, will have a direct bearing on the quality of drama in the lesson and its potential to extend the students' experiences. Carefully selected content and a teacher who has confidence in manipulating it will build a firm basis for the expressive act and the learning associated with it.

If the dramatic content is selected from events close to the students' subjective experiences, it may prove difficult for individuals to move into dramatic action in which feeling responses are appropriate. Some content used to explore social issues places students in situations which are 'too close to home' emotionally for them to enter fully the artificial reality of the drama. On the other hand, dramatic content selected from events too remote from the student's personal experiences may also result in dramatic action that has no ring of truth or dramatic integrity. Content which evokes intense and complex emotional responses too frequently destroys dramatic action in the classroom. 'Disaster drama' that explores topics such as nuclear holocausts, shipwrecks, deaths and a multitude of other sensational events requires a great deal of skill and sensitivity by the teacher/playwright if the student actors are to engage in meaningful dramatic activity.

It must be the teacher's responsibility to understand the dramatic process and manipulate content in such a way that it provides the appropriate base for dramatic engagement. Understanding something of the student's subjective reality and the kind of issues that interest them will mean the teacher has a greater chance of providing appropriate dramatic content. There is a great deal of confusion in teachers' and students' minds about the quality of emotional input needed for the drama. There is just as much doubt, too, about the type of content likely to achieve this. One thing is certain: the teacher must be constantly in search of content material that is broad in its range of experence and varied in its form of presentation. To rely on the experiences that students and teacher carry with them as the sole means of structuring drama is a very random and superficial way of approaching the dramatic process. Complexity and richness of content that makes firm links with the experiences of the participants is essential to the making of good drama.

Contrary to popular belief, drama is not contentless, it is **content dependent**; but because the individual's experience must lie at the centre of drama, curriculum content will not be prescriptive. This does not mean, however, that choice of content can be ignored as immaterial. Teachers, like playwrights, pay homage to the importance of content when they associate themselves with the artificial world of the play. Drama must be about something! **Dramatic content** must be capable of tapping into the experiential reality of students in order to move beyond it.

Dramatic Situations

If we consider for a moment the artificial world of the play, it is impossible to avoid wondering at the imagination and artistry of a work such as *Oedipus Rex*. It is also somewhat daunting when we talk in the same breath about drama teachers. Obviously, if we're seeing ourselves as needing to be something of a Sophocles, Shakespeare or Beckett, we're all failures before we begin. What does seem to be within our grasp however, is an understanding of the basic principles that inform the structuring of the drama.

In the first instance the dramatic situation is an imaginative context arising out of perceptions of the events of real life. Contrivance of this imagined and artificial life uses the elements of the art form, as distinct from the actual feelings and desires that govern real-life situations. Secondly, a dramatic event (the play or classroom drama) is comprised of a number of dramatic situations which give focus to the dramatic content and offer new insights into its meaning. To this end, the dramatic situations must maintain a sense of unity and direction. Participation in one dramatic situation should stimulate awareness and build resources for involvement in the next. This interlinking and interdependent relationship between situations is vitally important in establishing artistic unity and meaning. Thirdly, the creative tension that evolves from the merging of two opposing realities (real life and dramatic life) is further heightened by conscious manipulation of the elements of the art form so that particular dramatic situations are elevated in their significance.

And finally, in heightening the dramatic significance of given situations, the nature of the characters who people the drama is of prime importance. The selection of the particular context — the setting of the drama — is one thing; the personal situation of the character is another. So it is that a would-be assassin plays host to his proposed victim in lavish and warm surroundings. The resulting dramatic tension is subtle and immediate. A new perspective on the dramatic content is evident.

Dramatic situations must therefore be contrived to this artistic and meaningful end! A playwright can not assume that a *pot-pourri* of dramatic situations can be placed before an audience and trust that the rest will take care of itself. On the contrary, the playwright must shoulder the responsibility of providing a work which will invite, challenge and involve others in its experience. Teachers must shoulder this same responsibility. They cannot assume that their students will make meaningful connections between dramatic situations consisting of superficial and disparate experiences. Nor can students be expected to intuitively understand how to contrive dramatic situations in order to explore content with satisfaction. These are functions which the teacher must be prepared to fulfil. At times this will mean that a relatively detailed scenario, which hones in on specific experiential learning, will be contrived; at others, bare but significant dramatic situations will be needed. The playwright offers a model for this particular teaching function.

Dramatic Action

Dramatic actions are the concrete, physical expression of role; they give dramatic form to abstract thoughts and feelings and are therefore symbolic and meaningful. Dramatic actions arise out of dramatic situations and bring life and interest to the dramatic event. Dramatic action may be totally spontaneous and improvised or time may be spent planning and rehearsing the drama. Usually, classroom drama is minimally rehearsed or totally spontaneous. Performance of scripts is more often intensely rehearsed, especially for formal theatre.

Dramatic action is built around the willingness of actors to express personal feelings honestly and to accept and develop new responses in relation to the actions of others. Without this supportive building the drama will lack unity and substance.

Artistic sincerity and truthfulness of dramatic action is also of prime importance to the integrity of the drama. It is for this reason that a director works closely with actors in preparing them for performance. Drama teachers should nonetheless be interested in the sincerity and truthfulness of dramatic action. But whereas the director has one clear goal of performance is mind, the goals of the teacher vary, modifying the orientation of the action and the criteria by which the quality of the drama is judged. Dramatic action is experiential, communicative and expressive in nature. In pursuing specific learning goals, drama teachers are able to emphasise one particular orientation of the dramatic act, thus changing the kind of thought and feeling processes required in the particular drama experience.

Experiential Dramatic Action

An experiential emphasis in the drama stresses the importance of the individual's experience within the role. What is understood about the feelings, actions and ideas confronted during the dramatic action is both the meaning and the purpose of the drama. The making of personal meaning, or learning about the self and the world, is more important than finding an artistic form which will communicate images and meaning to an audience. Dramatists often claim that this type of action is closely related to the child's dramatic playing. What the teacher looks for in the work of the students is absorption and commitment.

Experiential dramatic action is usually of an improvised form, although it is true that the same focus can also be achieved in drama that is rehearsed. Living through the drama experientially and spontaneously offers maximum potential for individuals to test the effect of their responses upon the direction and outcome of the drama.

Communicative Dramatic Action

When communication to others is emphasised in the drama a more distant spectator stance is needed in the making of the drama. This objectivity forces a new perspective on dramatic action.

Whether the action is spontaneous or planned is of little consequence, since the processes of thought and feeling are now modified by the external reality of an audience. Ideas and feelings must be shaped in such a way in the drama that they represent meanings to onlookers rather than directly expressing experience.

Despite the desire to communicate personal meanings that are held to be important, the public and social nature of the experience imposes a further external consideration on the students. Not only must the drama clearly represent ideas, but it must be such that it will be favourably received by the audience. Personal and social realities that operate within the group will be a major influence on the way ideas are given dramatic form. Being 'King' or 'Clown' within the drama may have more to do with the nature of peer-group relations than the dramatic representation of personal experiences and ideas.

Communicative dramatic action leads to a consciousness of how the drama looks, rather than how it feels. When the appearance of the drama is emphasised, an understanding of the art form elements and the dramatic skills of individuals are called into focus. Maintaining a relationship between the meaning of the drama and its communication is important if integrity of dramatic action is to be preserved. If awareness of audience is what gives rise to the shape of the drama, then the learning is clearly of quite a different nature. How to exploit drama for one's own gains may be the major lesson learned.

The quality of sincerity and truth in communicative dramatic action is related to the way the meaning is represented. Concrete images must be 'truthful' enough to evoke artistic belief in them. Drama that is primarily a response to the social reality of its audience more often carries a quality of precociousness and play acting — control of the artistic medium disappears.

Expressive Dramatic Action

Emphasis on expressive action demonstrates a consciousness of the elements of the art form as the rules of the medium through which the individual's inner thoughts and feelings will be projected and expressed. Feeling and form are fashioned together so that the relationship between the individual's subjective and objective realities, between real life and artificial life, is consciously realised. In expressive dramatic action, there is little likelihood that the presence of an audience will carry sufficient influence to distort meanings carried by the drama. In fact, new and varied experiences are sought which test and challenge the individual's developing capacity for expressive action. Performance of existing dramatic works, often scripts of complex symbolic meaning, move the students into realms of thinking and feeling not previously encountered in their drama.

Analysis and criticism of dramatic literature and theatre is an important adjunct to the learning processes of expressive action. The social, cultural and artistic levels of meaning in this realised form are an important extension of the students' dramatic development. The critical and appreciative perspective on drama furnishes the students with an abstract knowledge about the drama. Knowledge within the drama is balanced and enriched by this critical appreciation. Of course the reverse is also true; knowledge from within the drama gives richness and balance to knowledge about drama. Both processes are essential to full artistic knowledge.

In emphasising a particular orientation of action, the drama teacher is guided by the needs of different student groups. Their changing capacity for role taking influences the extent to which any aspect of dramatic action can be effectively used. Whatever orientation is emphasised however, the teacher will need to help the student find appropriate involvement in the action. The role of director offers a model for this teaching function.

Conventions of the Drama

Ultimately drama asks participants to straddle the forces of reality and unreality. This is the constraint that focusses and gives artistic life and significance to the drama. This is a world where, in Stanislavskian terms, we behave 'as if things were really happening'. It is the realm of children's make-believe, of Dorothy Heathcote's 'big lie', and of what is frequently referred to as the 'willing suspension of disbelief'.

Participation in a dramatic event, then, requires individuals to make a conscious commitment to behaving in a manner which allows the creative act to happen. For some, young children for example, this setting aside of the normal rules of reality in order to live through an imagined reality is not an issue; perceptions of what is real and what is not are readily incorporated into the wider scheme of things. Many individuals, however, are shy of actively committing themselves to an unreality such as drama. It is easy enough to 'con' someone by behaving in a fictitious way (the white lie), but it is much more difficult, indeed pointless, if you know that someone recognises your act as fictitious. To change the tone of the interaction, both parties must agree to behave in a like manner; both must agree to participate in the 'con' ('the big lie'). The instant this agreement is made, different meanings accrue to the situation; the fictitious become part of a new reality, an artificial reality lived through in the present. In this sense, Warren Lett (1982), denies the validity of notions of make-believe in drama.

> 'This is not a make-believe reality, it is an actual phenomenological experience of self in making ... although the external is imaginary, the experience is actual'. (p. 15)

Many students in the classroom find the present reality of the experience very threatening. In fact, self-consciousness dominates the experience, making participation and commitment extremely difficult.

To help overcome this difficulty teachers need to know how to provide personal security for their students in a potentially threatening situation. Helping the students understand what is required of them in the making of drama is fundamental. Knowing 'the rules of the game' (Courtney, 1980) offers security and control for both students and teachers. The making of drama cannot be seen as a mysterious process that defies the existence of any guidelines and accepts any interaction as valid. Such guidelines must be intrinsic to the nature of drama and not simply extrinsic rules set to aid general classroom control. A consideration of role taking, improvising and the creation of meaning will give rise to these 'rules of the game'.

An audience in drama must also participate appropriately in the dramatic event. In theatre, for example, members of an audience understand that they must tacitly agree to be passive participants in the role relationships. Their responses are constrained and focussed by the nature of the dramatic event. If a member of the audience were to invade the acting space, dramatic communication and symbolic meaning would be destroyed. Conversely, if the theatrical event is designed to use audience responses and the audience do not respond, self-consciousness will predominate amongst the participants, again destroying the drama. In both situations, inappropriate responses result from a confusion about how to behave within the event.

Classroom audiences also need to have access to these conventions of drama. Because the teacher understands what is required if specific learning objectives are to be met, it will be up to him/her to explicitly teach students about this aspect of drama. It is a part of classroom drama that requires clear, firm and sensitive leadership.

4 Classifying Drama Activities

When we speak of doing drama, certain elements have combined to bring about a creative tension which carries the potential for symbolic learning. The dramatic event itself is the way of knowing; reflection on the drama occurs to make the learning explicit.

In the drama classroom, however, teachers use a range of activities which fall outside this description of drama. Many of the games and exercises referred to in chapter 1 are examples of non-drama events used to develop personal skills as varied and complex as communication, co-ordination, spontaneity, imagination and self-knowledge. Some activities are also used specifically to develop the expressive skills of voice, movement and improvisation. When these games and exercises are analysed in terms of inherent symbolic meaning and 'as if' qualities of emotional involvement, they cannot be classified as drama *per se*.

On the other hand, some activities move participants into areas where the pursuit of quite specific technical and art form skills is called for. Puppetry, dance and mime, for example, demand that individual skills be used in expressive forms quite different from that of 'acting'. If such forms, therefore, are to be used with a satisfactory level of personal control and expressive confidence, new awarenesses and knowledge have to be acquired.

In using any of the above activities, decisions about drama objectives, their priorities and how much time to devote to them, have to be made. It makes sense that a drama-in-education curriculum ought to use the majority of its time to achieve learning through involvement in drama, rather than other vaguely associated tasks. It follows then, that whatever the activity of the classroom, its relationship with drama needs to be understood. It is one clear way that we have of knowing where we are in terms of curriculum planning and the development *through drama* of our students.

The nature of activities and the purposes for which they are used can be classified as either 'complementary', 'preparatory' or 'fringe' in their relationship with drama.

Complementary Drama

Activities which are complementary in their relationship with drama have the potential to directly enhance the expressive quality and meaning of the drama, yet in themselves may not constitute participation in the dramatic event. These activities, however, are an essential part of any drama class and may often be very time-consuming. Verbal and written language tasks and activities to develop skills in theatre crafts are the most obvious examples of complementary drama.

Oral Language

Words are the most accessible currency for communicating ideas, clarifying thoughts and sharing experiences in relation to the drama. Students need to talk about the making of the drama, about the significance of interactions within it and certainly about new meanings that may have evolved as a result of the experience. In addition, both teacher and students rely on statements and questions as essential aids in building belief in characters and situations. Regardless of the particular objectives of the drama, discussion, questions, statements and instructions are required as an adjunct to it. This is not to say, however, that any talk which happens is automatically capable of servicing the drama and its learning. All talk is constrained by the focus of the drama and the clear intention of using words as a way of improving the expressive experience of the drama and its meaning. The responsive leadership of the teacher is extremely important in this sense. Stopping discussions which have strayed too far from the focus of the drama is not in itself some kind of awful authoritarianism. Statements which are clearly 'red herrings' or tenuous in their relationship with the drama will not improve the quality of work or the individual's learning. Instead of complementing the drama, the discussion simply takes on a life and meaning quite separate from the dramatic event. Talk in drama is clearly linked with knowing through the experience of the drama.

Written Language: Reading, 'Riting, Research

These 3 r's of classroom activity are other valuable aids to the making of good drama. Sometimes the teacher may simply read a story or poem at the beginning of a lesson to motivate interest and/or broaden the objective experiences of the group. Alternatively, the drama itself may stimulate students to do their own reading and research. The use of well-chosen resources provides a rich input which complements the learning by ensuring that things not already known have a chance to deepen and extend the drama experience. In this way, if both teacher and students engage in research, a range of personal, social, historical, political, cultural and theatrical perspectives can be gained. Tasks may range from simply cutting out a newspaper item on a particular issue to the detailed study of an aspect of political power. What remains important is the need for its dramatic experience to be central to the tasks and the learning. Writing activities may be adopted to help plan the drama, deepen commitment or perhaps advance the action. Brainstorming, for example, provides a useful way of allowing students to share ideas and explore avenues for the focus of the drama. This beginning provides a more representative and realistic basis for negotiating what the drama will be about. When the drama is about to begin, students may be asked to write down important details of their character as a foundation for establishing and sustaining role. During the drama, a deeper commitment to role and situation is gained when students, as specific characters, are asked to write letters, reports or diary entries, for example. Individual characters or groups within the drama may find themselves writing legends, or perhaps rules and laws which advance the plot of the drama and govern the actions of the participants.

Of course it is feasible that other writing may occur in relation to reading and research activities. Teachers at times prescribe tasks for students to do before specific drama experiences. One group of year 10 students, who were doing drama about competition and sport, were required by their teacher to attend a junior sporting event and write about an incident which they felt threw some light on the subject. These detailed observations added real insight into the content they were exploring, and at the same time provided a concrete basis for some satirical drama.

Recently, log books and drama diaries have gained popularity with teachers as writing activities. These are designed to complement the learning in drama via the process of reflection. Students are usually required to record the activities of the lesson, comment on their participation in them and evaluate the effectiveness of the drama in stimulating learning. Because of the difficulty of these demands, students at junior secondary levels are often only required to record what happened, taking turns at writing up and reading out the description of the lesson. Whilst there is no doubt that at times such activities can be a real help in complementing the action and learning in drama, it is equally true that a closer examination of the task may reveal little or no such relationship. If the writing is to be a meaningful exercise, a great deal of careful guidance is needed from the teacher.

Theatre Crafts

Activities which develop knowledge and skills in theatre crafts do not depend on role relationships as the medium of learning, yet the application of these skills may have a direct bearing on the quality of the drama. Work related to makeup, mask, costuming, set design and lighting fall into this category.

At times, aspects of these crafts are used to motivate students, focus energy and gain commitment to the drama. Different coloured green lights can certainly help build belief in the magic forest or tropical jungle. The cloak of the king or the white coat of the professor may provide an important step in the process of establishing roles and characters. When used in this way, however, interest and involvement in the drama can just as easily be weakened or destroyed. A preoccupation with these drama crafts may overshadow all other considerations. A group of year 7 students, for example, who were allowed to used the costume box to help build a drama about Keystone cops, completely lost the focus of their work because the fun of dressing up and seeing what their friends looked like provided a stronger motivation for action than being Keystone cops. Despite such occurrences, though, these theatre aids can work effectively to complement the drama if they are used with careful restriction. Very self-conscious and disparate social groups of students often feel less personally threatened by the drama when their involvement is supported by the use of these aids.

If the development of skills in theatre crafts becomes an end in itself, however, and participation in drama happens only at this technical craft level, then clearly the individual's learning will not be directly related to knowing through role relationships within the dramatic event. Rather than these activities being classified as complementary drama, they will have assumed a learning status of their own as 'theatre arts', 'theatre crafts'. Only when these skills and knowledge are used to enhance the direct experience and meaning of the drama can these crafts be seen as complementary drama.

Preparatory Drama

A multitude of simple games and exercises come under this heading. Ostensibly the activities are used to develop those skills and awarenesses that many teachers feel are necessary before the group can begin doing drama. Interpersonal communication for example, concentration, imagination, spontaneity, group trust and co-operation, and the expressive skills of voice language, movement, improvisation and characterisation. Activities are usually short term and they can be repeated several times, if not endlessly. Fun and simplicity are important selection criteria although some 'drier' skill drill is sometimes considered to be 'necessary'. Like medicine, it may not be very pleasant, but it is good for you! Role relationships, if present at all, bear only a tenuous link with an 'as if' reality. The function of the activities is clearly one of *preparation*, and any relationship with the quality and meaning of drama is tangential.

Skill Development

Many of the activities referred to in drama for personal development and therapy are standard approaches for preparing students for doing drama. There are exercises of all kinds, designed to isolate the senses, the mind, the muscles, the limbs; games that range from the stillness and concentration of Assassin, to the physical, energetic Tag and the interpersonal intimacy of Musical Knees; blindfold activities which seek to develop trust and communication within the group; relaxation and 'mind trips' to develop imagination and instruction games to sharpen responses and develop spontaneity. Drama books are available offering a range of ideas for developing instant programmes based on the notion that these activities are essential to any drama programme, yet clearly we are still a long way from dramatic learning.

Improvisation games and exercises designed to develop expressive skills appear to move closer to drama, but although some vague thought of role and 'as if' situation is present, they are often too loosely developed to afford significant dramatic learning. It may be the case that mastering the particular skill of spontaneity and cleverness of dialogue dominates the individual's thinking and learning. The popular improvisation game, Is that your . . .? illustrates the point: one member of the group begins the improvisation by asking, for example, 'Is that your elephant on the footpath?' Another must spontaneously respond and develop the improvisation. Quick, clever and humorous dialogue is valued and players measure their skill development in these terms.

All the above activities share the function of preparing the individual and the group for drama. Whether or not this preparation is effective or not is questionable, but its most negative aspect is that progression into *drama* is often impossible. Even when the teacher wants to move on, the students seem hooked into a games and exercise syndrome and resist other ways of working. What began as preparation for the drama becomes the drama!

Warm-ups

Quite apart from the development of a wide range of skills, preparatory drama is often used as a beginning to the drama session. The traditional ten-minute 'warm up' combines simple exercises and short games as a means of limbering up, focussing energy, developing concentration and generally getting in the 'right' frame of mind for the drama that follows. More often than not there is no direct link between the preparation and the rest of the lesson. Students often choose which game they want to begin with and this might be balanced by a teacher-directed movement isolation exercise. Little impact is made on the quality of work in the rest of the lesson.

If the warm-up activities are to have a legitimate function, then the ensuing drama should be the criteria used for their selection. For example, a group of year 8 students were to do drama about assembly line workers in a meat factory (prompted by the kangaroo meat export scandal). They spent fifteen minutes on preparatory drama, but the teacher handled the warm up in such a way that it moved into a direct and complementary relationship with the drama. The students 'built' the imaginary factory floor, chose their individual tasks on the line and then spent time on movement work designed to focus energy and develop specific actions. To help stimulate and refine movement responses the teacher paid attention to the senses by developing, with the students, images appropriate to the tasks — 'headless frozen carcasses'; 'grey steel pulleys wrenching'; 'back breaking weight'; 'sharp blades slicing'; 'monotonous sorting of bones'. These images focussed energy, developed expressive skills and built belief in the drama. Time spent on unrelated warm-up activities would not have prepared these students nearly as effectively.

Fringe Drama

This classification of drama refers to expressive activity which has its own distinctive artistic form and language. Under this heading come puppetry, dance, mime, clowning, music and art. Although role relationships may be used in the activity, the expression and communication of meaning does not occur through the medium of acting in an 'as if' reality. Rather, the development of role assumes a more marginal, indirect relationship with the expression of meaning. If drama is used in the pursuit of these expressive forms, it is used as the means to another artistic end, a tool which stimulates experience and expression of a different order.

Artistic Process and Form

Now there may not seem to be anything particularly important about identifying some forms of drama activity as 'fringe' in nature. After all, drama is used as a tool to service learning in other areas of the curriculum, so why shouldn't it do so here where it appears to be much closer to its artistic home? The reason is simple and practical. More often than not, neither teacher nor student sufficiently understands the nature of the art processes and the learning encounters are hamstrung at an 'exploratory, playful' phase which becomes cumbersome and frustrating. The particular medium of expression fails to achieve artistic integrity and significance, and personal meaning is lost.

In itself this may be excused as just a few lessons which never seem 'to get off the ground' but unfortunately, many drama programmes include units of work or mime, puppetry, clowning and dance, for example, as a matter of course. What can easily happen is that much time is spent engaged in activities which have little relationship with drama or these art forms. In the classroom, students can be found 'acting out' situations in mime which are more akin to a game of charades than an experience in mime. Similarly, it happens with puppetry that a great deal of time is spent constructing the puppet and any emphasis on the expressive communicative form, and drama, is token. A small group 'play' may be acted out at the end of the puppetry class, with dramatic or artistic problem solving very low on the learning scale. At best in these pursuits, the individual is involved in free, hopefully creative play, at its worst, unfocussed energy results in expedient decision making which is artistically meaningless. The end product of such activity is often regarded without respect and sometimes with frustrated embarrassment.

Clearly, if the creative and educational experience is to be significant then, firstly, the nature of the particular artistic process and the form of its expression must be acknowledged as fundamental. And secondly, drama's relationship with that process must be clarified and made explicit in the experience.

Otherwise, the student is likely to leave as one leaves the smorgasbord feast — having partaken of an endless range of potential delicacies but with no recall of the flavours and subtleties of any particular one.

Focus on Drama

If these forms of fringe drama are recognised for their own nature and used by the drama teacher to heighten the quality of the dramatic experience, then they may assume a less cloudy place in the drama programme. Year 8 or 9 students, who are typically pre-occupied with humour and caricature in their work, gain satisfaction and skill development from using mime techniques to highlight the exaggeration. Similarly, individuals who lack confidence in using role may be encouraged into drama through a well-considered use of puppets or other art forms. In the videotape *Through the Looking Glass*, the year 9 students are led into the drama via the construction of life-size, cut-out characters. There is no doubt that the art experience works effectively to aid the dramatic processes and heighten the quality of learning. The art pieces in this drama helped to build character and commitment whilst constantly serving to remind the students that they were involved in a creative medium which they themselves were expected to manipulate and control in the pursuit of meaning. Perhaps it is significant that the drama teacher, in this instance, is also a teacher of art. It appeared that Emily Parker, unlike most drama teachers, was confident in her knowledge of the art process, its form and its relationship with the drama. In the same way, the drama teacher who has, for example, also studied dramatic literature, or dance, can be expected to have acquired the necessary skills and knowledge of these art forms to be able to used them soundly to stimulate the students' individual dramatic development.

Simulation Games

Although the wide range of simulation games available does not readily fit the earlier description of fringe drama, this form of activity also needs to be scrutinised to see how it relates to drama.

There is a considerable body of literature which explores the relationship between play, games and dramatic activity. Strong links exist between the psychological and social development of the child and such activity. John Deverall (1981) highlights and extends this relationship, pointing out that many teachers are attracted to the use of simulation games in the classroom because they 'provide the teacher with a comparatively controlled and predictable environment in which to work'. In this sense, there is no doubt that the game will.

> '. . . offer an easy solution to two very pressing classroom problems — motivation and management . . . particularly with those teachers who feel unsure of themselves and of their methods and materials.' (p. 39)

On the surface, simulation games appear to offer all the ingredients for good drama — content, role relationships, an 'as if' reality, and the 'rules of the game'. Closer analysis reveals, however, that these rules of the game are not cemented in the conventions of the dramatic event, but rather are the highly specific guidelines that control and dictate interactions within the game so that predetermined learning can occur. The rules must carry the capacity to engage the emotions of the participants and strongly motivate their involvement. Teachers must assume the role of referee, and intervene only when a stated rule has been transgressed and is likely to undermine the objectives of the game. Clearly the management of the class is straightforward — the usual uncertainties of the drama and constant decision making are removed.

Playing the game, however, has little to do with drama and the creation of meaning through role relationships, for role development is subverted by the notions of game and rules. Dramatic action does not occur as a result of 'characters' responding to one another or to the manipulation of artistic elements. Characters, or roles, can only be developed in response to the rules of the game.

The disconcerting by-product of this structure is that the personal and social realities of the group cannot therefore be transcended sufficiently to provide the protection and safety that is possible in drama. Individuals find themselves trapped in a raw emotional experience where the most important objective, for example, is likely to be the accumulation of tokens, of winning the game no matter what.

Ostensibly the simulation game explicitly teaches towards its learning focus, but in reality the game itself becomes the focus, with emotion and action tied to the rules of the games rather than its content or its roles. An educational point may be made but an artistic one will not!

Whatever activity is happening in the drama classroom, its relationship with drama needs to be understood. Increased awareness of the nature and purpose of particular activities must help teachers to clarify their curriculum decisions and develop confidence in structuring drama programmes of sure-footed, high quality experiences. Some activities might well be discarded forever, while others will be manipulated to

Figure 5: Classification of activity and its relationship with drama

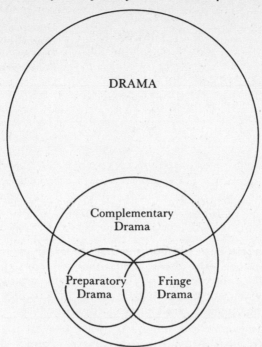

effectively serve the drama. Figure 5 illustrates the relationship between the various activities of the classroom as they have been classified in this chapter.

In Figure 5 the Drama circle assumes the dominant position and expresses the primary importance of role relationships and dramatic activity in the drama programme. This circle contains the four basic components of drama — dramatic content, dramatic situation, dramatic action and the conventions of drama. Linked directly to this action is complementary drama, the necessary adjunct to the drama event, although a considerable proportion of this activity falls outside the circle of drama and the interaction of the components. Any preparatory or fringe drama has been manipulated so that its relationship with drama is essentially complementary and in part, directly dramatic in structure. Some preparatory drama is fringe in nature and vice versa, such as puppetry, mime or dance. The type of relationship that is forged between these activities will depend upon the teacher and the explicit emphasis and function of the basic drama components. Whilst all action is either drama or complementary drama in essence, it is the dominance of drama.

Figure 6: Direction of curriculum decisions in drama

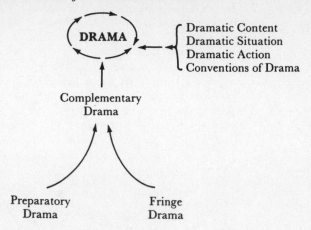

and its basic components that is vital. In planning drama, the teacher seeks to ensure that these relationships are achieved. Thus the constant pull of all action is toward the goal of experience and knowledge through drama. Figure 6 represents the direction of all curricula decisions.

Establishing Planning Principles

At the outset of this book we began a search for a common understanding of drama in education that would provide a clear basis for planning and teaching drama. It is now time to consider what basic principles can be established from our analysis of the activity of the classroom and the fundamentals of the drama in education process. The following principles also serve as a brief summary of what it means to be **doing drama**.

Principles for Planning and Teaching Drama

1 The student's knowledge and experience of life is central to drama.
2 Drama is content dependent.
3 Content arises out of all knowledge and experience of life.
4 Role relationships are essential to drama.
5 Role relationships are created through an oscillation of the student's subjective and objective realities.

6 Role relationships occur within an artificial reality.
7 The artificial reality of drama gives rise to artistic and symbolic meaning.
8 Doing drama enables students to learn about the human condition and the art form.
9 Drama programmes must acknowledge the dramatic development of students.
10 Drama structures must involve students in experiential, communicative and expressive action.
11 Drama structures must involve students in reflective action.
12 The teacher's role in drama is one of confident, responsive and varied intervention.
13 All activity in the drama classroom is manipulated to complement the drama.

5 Objectives and Assessment in Drama

To this point, we have established that in drama students learn about the art form and human development through a particular topic which is significant and meaningful. For this to occur, teachers must have a set of learning objectives designed to achieve these ends. It follows that control of learning objectives is tantamount to control of the drama curriculum. Further to this, a set of learning objectives for drama will enable teachers to plan classes and to indicate the range of activities in which the students will be involved.

> 'It is very useful in drama to *express* evaluative and assessment criteria in terms of specific learning objectives ... assessment criteria in relation to those activities are highlighted for students ... objectives provide a convenient way of opening up a programme to external scrutiny. Objectives provide a succinct overview of both the activities and learning potential of the drama programme. This can be particularly useful for parents, school administrators and members of the community ... objectives provide a "grid" to be laid on drama experiences. This grid forces the experience into patterns so that it can be easily understood. Comments can then be made about students' work ... The formulation of educational objectives in drama primarily aims at answering the following questions:
> What do you want to go on in the drama?
> What do you want the students to learn?
> ... objectives will therefore generally direct attention to the type of activities which will be set up in drama classes.'
> (McLeod, 1983)

What then, are the learning objectives in drama?

Learning Objectives

Expressive and Communicative Development

1 The drama must provide maximum opportunities for the students to: Explore through role a range of human ideas and experiences from many perspectives.

2 Develop the expressive skills of voice, movement and improvisation in order to explore and express human experience.
3 Develop the expressive skills of voice, movement and improvisation in order to communicate meaning to an audience.
4 Develop ability to receive, offer and initiate artistically sincere and logical character actions within the dramatic situation.
5 Develop appropriate dramatic images to explore and extend the drama.
6 Select and use appropriate elements of the art form in order to work towards meaning.
7 Use other expressive forms (e.g. puppetry, mask, dance, mime, lighting, music, set design) to enhance the emotional tone and meaning of the drama.

Analytical and Evaluative Development

1 The drama must provide opportunities for the students to reflect, analyse, evaluate and articulate, orally and/or in writing, an understanding of:
the ability to sustain and extend commitment to role within different dramatic structures;
the ability to manipulate elements of the art form through movement, voice and improvisation in order to express and communicate meaning;
Personal development in relation to specific drama objectives;
Self in relation to the ideas and experiences of others.
2 The drama must provide opportunities for the students to select relevant and appropriate data in order to:
extend the ideas, themes or concepts of the drama;
relate and use the data in the drama;
competently discuss and evaluate the data in relation to the drama.
3 The drama must provide opportunities for the students to describe, analyse and evaluate orally and/or in writing.
process involved in the creation of specific products (e. g. mask, costume, lighting block) related to the drama;
the extent to which the product fulfils its particular aim or function in the drama.

Elaboration of the Objectives

Expressive and Communicative Development

1 Perspective — dimension, new angles of viewing. Clearly all perspectives interrelate. Focus on a particular perspective will alter the content and structuring of the drama:
personal perspective, for example, policeman, father, child, King;
political perspective, for example, ideological approaches to the organisation of society;
time perspective, for example, past, present, future;
cultural perspective, for example, community, tribal, national.
2 Dramatic image — crystallisation of thoughts and feelings through role into a coherent, concrete form.

Analytical and Evaluative Development

1 Reflect — to recall the events and feelings of the drama.
2 Analyse — to divide and examine the various elements of the drama.
3 Evaluate — to assess the significance of the meaning created in the drama.
4 Articulate — to clearly express thoughts and feelings.
5 Commitment to role — 'the reconciliation between subjectivity and objectivity. The former precludes other viewpoints; the latter is characterised by detachment. Commitment is the ability to follow through the implications of a particular stance and make it a true and reasonable course of action.' (McLeod, 1980)

The Absence of General Objectives

Dramatic literature in the sixties and seventies usually listed a set of aims and objectives for drama. These were frequently expressed in general terms of 'encouraging initiative and sensitivity', 'developing leadership skills' and 'developing the ability to work co-operatively with other students'. Brian Way's *Development through Drama* and most subsequent literature stressed the personal development aspects of drama which, in part, led to the notion that drama was aligned with the pastoral curriculum of the school. Teachers regarded general aims such as 'developing personal concentration, use of senses, (developing) imagination ... social communication ... overcoming self-consciousness' (Way, pp. 156–9) as ends in themselves. If a child reacted imaginatively in an activity, then that child had achieved one of the objectives in drama. This approach has been reflected in almost all drama curricula since the sixties. It is possible that this approach arose from teachers interpreting Slade's work as 'advocating total freedom without constraint and then (teachers) wondered why they had discipline problems' (Hogan, 1983). It is clear that teachers were devising curricula based on personal development objectives rather than the specifics of the drama discipline. This emphasis on the personal development aspects of drama tended to distort our understanding of the nature of drama and has clouded the process of content selection. The absence of a drama syllabus in most school appears to support this emphasis. As Pat Cook states:

> '. . . extravagant claims of what could be achieved in these areas have remained unsubstantiated. This dominant trend . . . has also led to a good deal of vague and obscure thinking about what is integral to the drama process. Although it is quite proper that drama should be child-centred . . . the focus should be on the child's learning rather than his maturation . . .'
> (Cook, 1982)

Several colleges of advanced education and teacher training institutions established courses in 'Communications' to aid the personal development of their students. The activities in these courses were often misinterpreted as drama. Quite obviously, personal development goals are ones which are common to most teachers, not, as much dramatic literature would suggest, only to drama teachers.

Drama practitioners must recognise the need for objectives which belong specifically to the discipline of drama in order to plan meaningful and significant lessons for their students. For this reason the authors have deliberately omitted general objectives for drama.

The Social Health of the Group

Again, a teacher's desire for a good working relationship between students in the classroom is common to all subject areas. English teachers and Maths teachers, for example, would hope to establish a good working relationship just as the drama teacher does. In the past, in drama, this desire has been translated into games and play activities designed to promote social health before the 'real' drama can begin. As we have mentioned previously, in some circumstances these activities became the drama programme.

Certainly, a degree of social cohesiveness and some basic collective commitment to the drama is necessary for learning to occur. The majority of students are quite able to accept the conventions of drama and to focus energy on particular tasks. For the majority of classes, drama will enhance the social health of the group. It is not necessary, contrary to popular belief, to engage in activities designed to instil the 'healthy attitudes', of 'co-operation', 'sensitivity to peers', or 'collective commitment', for example. Just as, in English, when a small group of students discuss their interpretation of a poem they simultaneously develop communication and co-operation skills, so too in drama, students develop these attributes through the drama task.

However, in unusual circumstances, the nature of the group will mean that it will not be possible for the students to understand or apply the conventions of the drama. For example, students in corrective institutions, or in schools with a high non-English speaking population, or where there is extreme peer conflict. In these cases, it is probably more worthwhile to adopt a different range of activities before the students are expected to engage in drama. The 'different' activities may include excursions, simulation games designed for group interaction and co-operation and team-effort tasks such as running a pancake parlour for the school fete. It is the teacher's responsibility to determine which of these approaches is most appropriate for the teaching context.

Examples of High and Low Achievement within the Drama Objectives

Expressive and Communicative Development

To explore through role a range of human ideas and experiences from many perspectives:

High achievement. During a role play exploring worker and management relationships, a year 10 student was able to develop and sustain several different roles within the drama — e.g. General manager, young executive, new worker and union leader.

Low achievement. When playing the role of key worker in the factory, a student demonstrated appropriate role behaviour but was unable to sustain commitment to other roles of a family member, a television interviewer or a member of the Board of Directors.

To develop the expressive skills of voice, movement and improvisation in order to explore and express human experience:

High achievement. A student in year 12 was able to employ a wide range of vocal skills to clearly express subtleties of experience, when exploring the role of a priest.

Low achievement. A student always adopted loud, assertive vocal tones regardless of character or context.

To develop the expressive skills of voice, movement and improvisation, in order to communicate meaning to an audience:

High achievement. In a year 10 drama performance involving the selection of a human sacrifice for an ancient religious ritual, a student chosen as the sacrifice moved slowly to the altar in a manner which clearly communicated the subtle range of feelings from quiet courage and dignity, to vulnerability and fearful anticipation.

Low achievement. In the same performance, a small group of students were performing a ritualistic dance as part of the sacrificial ceremony. One of the dancers were merely following the movement steps of the dance with no ability to portray the sense of awe, significance and spirituality of the moment.

To develop the ability to receive, offer and initiate artistically sincere and logical character actions within the dramatic situation:

High achievement. In a year 7 improvisation a student playing the role of a mother arrives home through the front door looking depressed and tired. Another student playing the role of the teenage son expresses concern at his mother's state and says 'Sit down and I'll make you a cup of tea. Don't worry, I'll cancel basketball training and get the dinner tonight'.

Low achievement. A year 7 student playing the role of a mother walks through the door as if she were dripping wet and freezing cold. Another student playing the role of the father says, 'Hello, you old bag. Let's go to the beach for the day'. Obviously, this student is not responding sincerely or logically to the images created by the mother.

To develop appropriate dramatic images to explore and extend the drama:

High achievement. Year 8 are doing drama about a commemorative service extolling the heroic virtues of Australia's notorious bushranger, Ned Kelly. A student in role as Ned Kelly carefully plans an ambush of the mail coach with his fellow bushrangers. The student assertively condemns the judicial system of the time and rallies support of the gang for the planned ambush.

Low achievement. Another student in role as Ned Kelly portrays him as a bumbling, incoherent fool. This denied the possibility for other students to feel respect or admiration for the man. The dramatic image was therefore inappropriate and could not extend the drama.

To select and use appropriate elements of the art form in order to work towards meaning:

High achievement. In a year 10 drama exploring the effects of conscription on family relationships, a student playing a conscientious objector suddenly quells the family discussion by purposefully and reverently placing his grandfather's writings on the table. He gently opens the book and recounts his grandfather's fervent appeal for non-violent action in all circumstances.

This student used his grandfather's words as a symbol to encapsulate his family's unity and values. He was able to give a dramatic focus to the improvisation and highlight the significance of his stance.

Low achievement. In the same drama, another student interrupts a tense family discussion about the cowardice of conscientious objectors by bringing in a travelling salesman who is selling garden fertiliser. Obviously, this was an inappropriate use of the art form elements to work towards meaning.

To use other expressive forms to enhance the emotional tone and meaning of the drama:

High achievement. In a year 11 drama about child-bashing and abuse, a student creates a life-sized, caricatured parent figure. This puppet depersonalises the parent figure and thereby distances the audience from the sensitive nature of the issues involved and, through the fantastical behaviour of the puppet, highlights the grotesque and pathetic aspects of child abuse.

Low achievement. A student creates a caricatured small puppet wearing outlandishly enormous boxing gloves. As the parents attempt to use violence on the child, the puppet's gloved hands counter all aggressive blows. Clearly, the dominance of the child's puppet denies the drama its appropriate focus, which is the child's vulnerability in child abuse situations.

Analytical and Evaluative Development

To reflect, analyse, evaluate and articulate an understanding of the ability to sustain and extend role within different dramatic structures:

High achievement. In a Year 8 drama about setting up an exploration team in Antarctica, team members are reporting the malfuncation of a vital generator to the commander. Team member A quietly but urgently reports in detail on the malfunction in engine 2. In discussion after the drama, student A is able to identify and articulate that, by drawing on the past experiences of the character, he deepened his belief in the role and was able to find new directions for the drama.

The student explained that his character was always efficient and able to organise other team members, so he knew exactly what to do in this situation. Student A sustained commitment to role and extended that role by suggesting that his past experience would allow him to undertake repairs if given three other team members to assist.

Low achievement. Team member B slouches with hands in pockets, looking self-consciously at peers and is unable to respond to the commander's questions.

This student, in discussion, is unable to analyse either his use of role or that of other group members. He clearly has a low commitment to role and is certainly unable to sustain or extend the role.

To reflect, analyse, evaluate and articulate an understanding of the ability to manipulate elements of the art form through movement, voice and improvisation in order to express and communicate meaning:

High achievement. After an improvisation about children visiting a haunted house, student A articulates the effect of an unexpected loud screech just as the children crept slowly up the stairs. She felt that fear and excitement were generated at this point.

Low achievement. Conversely, student B merely comments upon how stupid Danny looked as Dracula and after further questioning was unable to extend this response.

To reflect, analyse, evaluate and articulate an understanding of personal development in relation to specific drama objectives:

High achievement. A year 9 student, after completing a feature programme about Australian heroes, articulates the differences in her ability to sustain role during performances as compared with workshops. She stated that her research on the months leading up to the Gough Whitlam/John Kerr controversy clearly aided her ability to sustain the role of Kerr during workshop exploration and in the performance.

Low achievement. Another year 9 student regards her ability to attend all lunchtime rehearsals on time as reflecting significant personal development. The student did not analyse her limited ability to adopt and sustain role during workshop exploration of the performance material. Although her punctuality may have suggested a commitment to the ideas or themes being explored, this development is not related to any of the drama objectives. Quite obviously, the teacher should commend the student's new-found punctuality, as this praise may be a prime factor in engaging the student more fully in the drama.

To reflect, analyse, evaluate and articulate an understanding of self in relation to the ideas and experiences of others: *High achievement.* A year 7 student, discussing her contribution to the planning stages of the 'haunted house' drama, comments that her idea of finding a long tunnel that led to a strange, new land was rejected by the rest of the group, who were more interested in finding Count Dracula in the house. However, she also stated that she was able to involve herself in the group's ideas and found that her role of the victim was helped by a fellow student, playing the role of a considerate caretaker.

Another student recalls her experience of a novel where a teenage runaway was forced to hide in an abandoned old farm house. The drama about the 'haunted house' highlighted the fear that the runaway felt whilst isolated in the farmhouse at night.

Low achievement. Another student whose ideas had been rejected by the group was unable to contribute ideas to the planning of the 'Count Dracula' drama and, during discussion, was unable to see why he was satirising the work of the group. The student's involvement in the role play was limited to his mimicking of Count Dracula's mouth movements.

To select relevant and appropriate data in order to extend the ideas, themes or concepts of the drama:
High achievement. In a year 10 drama exploring the theme of the future, a student brings to class an extract from a current science journal which suggests that a human's life expectancy will increase to 137 years by the year 2000.
Low achievement. Another student brings to class a picture of the Muppets clothed in futuristic space outfits.

To select relevant and appropriate data in order to relate it to and use it in the drama:
High achievement. In discussion, the student with the science journal article clearly relates the data to the possible socio-economic implications of this longevity. The student suggests the drama could explore the concept of society's acceptance of a large, working, geriatric population.
Low achievement. The student with the Muppets picture suggests that in the future we will look different, and this is the only way in which the student can relate the data to the drama. Furthermore, the student suggests that in workshop exploration of the theme, the class should be dressed as closely as possible to the picture.

To select relevant and appropriate data in order to competently discuss and evaluate the data in relation to the drama:

High achievement. A student clearly expresses the notion that the costuming adopted during workshop exploration of the 'future' theme actually impeded role development and destroyed serious extension of the theme.

Low achievement. Another student, commenting on the use of costuming, states that the drama looked colourful and impressive and made the audience respond with laughter. The student further suggests that in performance, if a larger audience responded similarly, then the drama would have been highly successful.

To describe, analyse and evaluate processes involved in the creation of specific products related to the drama:

High achievement. A senior student preparing masks for a production of *The Royal Hunt of the Sun* isolates the research of Inca art as being the most valuable process in the creation of the masks, and secondarily, experimentation with various mask-making materials.

Low achievements. Another student simply described the construction of the bird masks. No analysis of the need to portray particular ominous or other artistic qualities in the masks was mentioned.

To describe, analyse and evaluate the extent to which the product fulfils its particular aim or function in the drama:

High achievement. A student was able to suggest that the geometric shapes of Inca art, when combined with the stark colours in the mask, clearly captured the mysterious and ominous qualities required to highlight the differences between the Spanish and Inca cultures.

Low achievement. When asked to evaluate the effectiveness of the bird masks during rehearsal, the student was unable to identify any relationship between the masks, the themes of the play or the theatrical images created.

Achieving Art Form and Human Development Learning

We must, at this point, reiterate that art form learning and human development learning are present at all year levels, and that these learning areas can have an explicit or implicit emphasis depending upon the specific objectives of the lesson. Every lesson should contain an explicit focus on either art form or human development learning or an explicit focus on

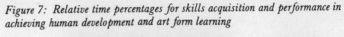

Figure 7: Relative time percentages for skills acquisition and performance in achieving human development and art form learning

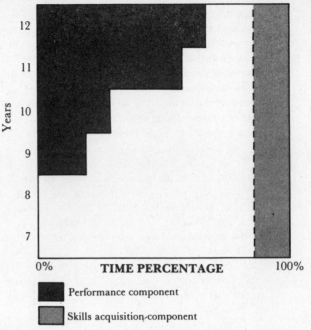

both. For example, a Year 9 drama class exploring the working conditions of the early settlers in Australia may have either a human development focus or an art form focus. If the emphasis was on human development, then particular attention would be directed to the feeling response of the students. Questions like the following may be asked:

'How did you feel when your horses were stolen?', 'In what way do you think the problems you encountered were common among the early settlers?', or 'At what point did you decide to move inland to the mountains?' Similarly, the drama tasks should aim to encourage a commitment to role exploration of the issues of the topic.

If the emphasis was on art form learning, then particular attention would be directed to the student's control and understanding of art form skills. Questions like the following may be asked: 'What was the effect created just after the gunshot was heard?', 'Why did you approach the door as slowly and carefully as you did?', or 'Why was the soldier standing on a higher level than the convicts?' Similarly, the drama tasks should aim to encourage a conscious manipulation of the elements of the art form in the exploration of a topic.

Furthermore, the students should be made aware of the explicit learning focus, both at the beginning of the lesson, during the activity and in final discussion. What has tended to happen is that the lesson ends before any reflection on its focus can take place. Often teachers fear questioning as they are unsure of what they want to find out or what learning they wish to reinforce. If they have a set of precise objectives, then they can prepare specific questions to crystallise the learning.

Therefore, the performance component and skills acquisition component are the *means* of achieving human development and art form learning.

Performance Component

The purpose of a performance component in Years, 9, 10, 11 and 12 is to achieve learning. Performance in drama must be designed to achieve specific drama objectives, unlike a school production which clearly lies in the domain of the pastoral curriculum. Whilst working on a performance project students in drama are applying both existing and new art from skills in order to communicate meaning to an audience. Often it is appropriate at the Year 9 and 10 levels to work on an original production on a topic or theme suitable to the students' stage of development. Then, at Year 11 and 12, scripted works may form the basis of the performance component. One further point worthy of mention is that the choice of theme or scripted work is of paramount importance. The material should be rich enough to provide maximum opportunity for role development and character portrayal tied to the specific objectives of the programme. A more detailed explication of themes and scripts will be presented later in this book.

Skills Acquisition Component

You will notice that, unlike the performance component, the time allocated to skills acquisition is common across all year levels. The reason for this is that at every year level the teaching of skills will be tied to the dramatic context. However, the teaching of art form skills in isolation is an appropriate activity for all year levels. For example, a lesson designed to teach a Year 8 class slow floating movements may be an appropriate first step before embarking on a unit of work on astronauts building a new society on the moon. Of course, there may be exceptions to this structure. For example, a school who has entered a group of Year 10 students in a statewide drama competition may spend a great deal of time on the teaching of voice projection. It is important to recognise, however, that unless this voice projection work is related to role development in the performance, then the students are not doing drama; that is, the meaning is isolated from the action.

The gradual building of basic skills has a spiral effect: students may then use these skills to explore increasingly complex material which, in turn, refines skill development, and brings about human development and further art form learning.

Assessment in Drama

Having expressed drama learning in terms of specific objectives, it is now possible to assess student achievement in drama more precisely.

Assessment is generally regarded as an estimate of the quality of a student's work; a summative process involving measurement and gradation. Evaluation, on the other hand, tends to be a holistic appraisal of a year's drama programme. Evaluation includes teacher reflection on lesson strategies, teacher role, developmental frameworks and any subsequent adjustments. Assessment, therefore, can be seen as a subset of evaluation, and this chapter will confine itself to a discussion of how to assess student performance in drama.

Assessment and reporting in drama have proved to be problematic and diverse. Reporting procedures have varied markedly between schools. Again, this difficulty in establishing common assessment criteria and procedures can be directly attributed to the lack of a sound theoretical base for dramatic work. Many teachers confined report rewards to the students' attitude and effort. The passive, co-operative student often achieved a high letter grade whilst the 'loudmouth' Year 8 student was severely admonished. We have probably all written reports such as:

> 'Mary is a pleasant, well-mannered student who has worked well in drama this year. She is a delight to teach. She has made rapid progress in this subject, and her co-operative attitude has allowed her to work productively with other students.'

and:

> 'Joe is a disruptive, inattentive student. He often distracts other students from their work. He constantly interrupts others and teases the girls in the class. Subsequently he has not achieved a satisfactory standard in this subject. He needs to apply himself fully in drama in the future if he is to progress.'

One wonders how these reports can inform students or parents of exactly what the student has achieved. Surely the value of a superficial personality judgement is questionable. However, lacking any clear objectives for drama, is it any wonder that teachers searched vainly for an approach to assessment and reporting? Remarks made by teachers in reporting on students fell into the categories of:

— participation in the activities;
— co-operation with fellow students;
— degree of self-confidence.

The following situation was observed at a recent parent/teacher night:

> 'The Maths teacher was bemoaning the fact that Mrs X was very upset that her son had failed Maths. The drama teacher retorted, 'It's a pity that Mrs X wasn't upset about her son's drama report. Let's face it, if a child fails Maths, the child has merely failed Maths; if the child fails drama, the child has failed as a human being.'

This observation clearly illustrates the drama teacher's preoccupation with the development of personality. An adjunct to this pre-occupation was the teacher's unwillingness to rank student abilities. Letter grades or any achievement marks were shied away from, even at the senior levels. It was the students' effort and attitude which became paramount in assessment and reporting. If a teacher did establish clear assessment criteria, these were usually couched in terms of the social development of the child.

Having established a set of learning objectives for drama, we can provide lucid reports of a student's development in drama and the degree to which the objectives have been achieved. All teachers have a professional responsibility to provide credible, meaningful reports for students, parents and the community. This responsibility is even nore obvious nowadays when the demands for professional accountability have increased, and when schools are under close scrutiny.

What is the most appropriate form of reporting for drama? There are, of course, many advocates of non-competitive assessment and non-grading of students. It is a truism that most western societies provide reward for ability and achievement; not to distinguish between students' varied abilities would be to go against the educational tide of the eighties and perhaps deny students the impetus to realise their full educational potential. As was described earlier in this chapter, there are clear distinctions between high and low achievement in drama, and students should be made aware of the degree to which they have met the objectives of a drama course. To some it may seem that in providing a descriptive assessment of the students' work and a letter grade, we may be attempting to have our cake and eat it too, yet this combination works particularly well for drama. The letter grade allows for a succinct summary of a student's achievement in relation to his or her peers. The descriptive assessment conveys the detailed portrayal of the student's work and development, in relation to the learning objectives, and the student's individual progress. For example, a student in drama may have progressed throughout the year from an 'E' standard of work to a 'C' standard. This degree of improvement can be described clearly in the report. The letter grade alone does not give an indication of the amount of progress made throughout a course.

Before we go on to providing sample reports for drama, we first need to establish some general principles for the writing of descriptive assessments:

1 The criteria for assessment should be explicit. These criteria are the learning objectives for drama, therefore comments should refer directly to the objectives.
2 The report should describe what the student has learned, with direct reference to actual activities so that the comments are clear and reasonable.
3 Descriptive reports should allow the student's development and improvement throughout one year or many years to be recorded. It can be an ongoing record of the process of learning.
4 The report is an account of a student's particular stage of development in drama. These achievements, including strengths and weaknesses, should be cited.

We have already established in this chapter that general social objectives are not the specific responsibility of the drama classroom; moreover, to describe aspects of a student's personality which are not directly relevant to classroom achievement is not the function of a report. If a student appears to be ill-mannered, this may have little to do with his/her ability to take on a role, for example. Good manners, whilst desirable, are not one of the specific learning objectives for drama, and unless they are a stated objective, it is unfair to refer to them in a report. This type of social learning is every teacher's responsibility.

All students should be given a copy of the learning objectives at the beginning of a drama course. Clearly, not all objectives apply to Year 7; those that do should be written in a language appropriate to Year 7, distributed and explained.

Once this is done, then the students know how they will be assessed and what will be expected of them.

In writing reports, teachers need to remember the 'dramatic age' of the student. In Year 8, for example, it is unrealistic to expect that the students will display 'role truth'. If, in the report, the teacher describes the student's role work as unsatisfactory because it is stereotyped, then this description totally ignores the student's stage of development, and makes unfair expectations of the student's achievements.

Let us now look at several sample reports:

Year Seven
Student's name: Mary Smith
Letter grade: A
Mary's achievement in drama has been excellent. She explored a range of characters and situations with lively insight. She made unusually perceptive connections between the drama and real life. This was particularly so in our work on factory conditions during the Industrial Revolution, and Outer Space. She collected newspaper clippings on U.F.O. sightings and used these to imaginatively extend the story line of the Space drama.

Year Eight
Student's name: John Murphy
Letter grade: D
John's achievement has been satisfactory. He played a variety of characters in drama, although he usually manipulated the role so that the same loud and aggressive characteristics were dominant.

At times these roles have been appropriate but in our work on spies, for example, his over-reliance on this type of character hindered the work of other students and the general progression of the drama.

It is important that John focusses on using different character behaviour so that he can gain a broader understanding of drama and its relationship with real life.

Year Nine
Student's name: Anne Jones
Letter grade: B
Anne has shown a very high level of achievement in drama. She made excellent progress in experiencing and portraying many different characters, both in classroom exploration and performance work. In the Feature Programme performance her voice and improvisation skills demonstrated intense

concentration of energy and thought. This resulted in subtle and truthful drama.

Anne works supportively with small groups in solving dramatic problems; she showed imaginative initiative in exploring several poetry pieces. During discussions Anne has demonstrated a very good understanding of how art form elements work in drama.

Year Ten
Student's name: Ben Ascot
Letter grade: C
Ben has shown a good level of achievement in drama. He worked hard to develop his movement skills and is to be commended for the way he used these in the ritual dance performance. He created clear and meaningful images for the audience.

In exploring situations in improvisation, he did find it difficult, however, to respond appropriately to other characters, and this limited his opportunity to explore human experiences. On the other hand, Ben clearly analysed and articulated his learning in some areas of the drama. Sound connections were made between the role behaviour of tribal leaders and contemporary authority figures.

Year Eleven
Student's name: Sally Windsor
Letter grade: E
Sally's achievement in drama has been unsatisfactory. Rarely was she able to develop characters sufficiently to explore situations and content from different viewpoints. Despite considerable rehearsal time, for example, she was still unable to develop the character of the Female Factory's Matron fully enought to carry the meaning of the scene during performance. This situation often repeated itself in classroom group drama.

Sally did not complete the required research or reading and was therefore not able to make meaningful contributions to the planning or evaluation of the drama.

Year Twelve
Student's name: Tom Robinson
Letter grade: A
Tom has shown an excellent level of achievement in Year Twelve drama. He was able to employ a wide range of vocal and movement skills to clearly express and communicate role subtleties and readily explored and sustained a range of different characters. In our production of *Royal Hunt of the Sun*, for

example, he was able to portray three contrasting roles clearly, which demonstrated highly refined improvisation and characterisation skills.

His set design clearly reflected the emotional tone and meaning of the play and he was able to clearly evaluate the extent to which this product fulfilled its function in the drama.

His written submissions clearly described his understanding of how several elements of the art form were manipulated to add impact to the ideas of the script in performance. In character work he responds with honesty and subtlety to the dramatic images of others, thereby extending his commitment to role and his ability to learn through the drama.

PART TWO:

Controlling the Drama.

6 The Teacher as Leader

Introduction: The Role of the Teacher

When it comes to putting drama principles into practice, the would-be teacher seems to be plagued by a series of doubts quite unlike those associated with the teaching of other subjects. Relationships with students and classroom management techniques are suddenly thrown into a new light and seen as far more crucial to drama than other subjects. How on earth does one discipline a student, for example, and then expect that student to spontaneously participate in a make-believe world? How can a teacher encourage risk taking in this creative process if fear of discipline for free, playful activity is present? How can role be used so that the students don't 'get out of control'? And if the class cannot co-exist co-operatively and have respect for each other's contributions then what hope for doing drama anyway?

For many teachers these questions remain unanswered and provide a constant source of irritation. Vague resolutions manifest themselves in one of two general approaches to teaching drama. The first resolution is available through a tightly structured, controlled, exercise and theatre-based programme (what Gavin Bolton [1980] classifies as 'type A' and 'type C' drama). Here the teacher can set up a multitude of tasks whereby a range of skills can be taught and then applied — to script work, for example. Unfortunately, with this approach it is unlikely that the student's knowledge and experience will be central to the drama.

Tasks and scripts are often such that they have no personal, creative relevance for the students.

A second very popular way of resolving the issue has been to adopt a passive, facilitator approach to running the drama class. All the teacher has to do is present the class with a topic for their play, cast a pastoral eye over the groups and organise the order of presentation and the concluding discussion. The disadvantage of this approach to drama lies in the *ad hoc* and superficial nature of the learning. It may be fun and easy, but the complexity and challenge of drama is lost. The concepts of simplicity and ease associated with facilitation allow the teacher to rest too easily in a passive leadership role. To expect the students to have the skills and knowledge to progress unaided in drama is as unproductive as to think that the teacher must be responsible for the lot. Obviously in drama, as in all teaching, the profitable balance lies somewhere between the two.

Finding a Focus for the Role of the Teacher

In the past, the drama teacher's role has been obscure and mysterious. In part this has resulted from the emphasis of drama in education on spontaneous creative play as the central factor in the drama process. This misses the point. Spontaneity, creativity and playfulness are some of the many important elements that are used in the individual's dramatic action but, as John McLeod (1980) has articulately discussed, so too are the elements of imagination, identification, empathy and commitment. If the emphasis is placed where it more accurately belongs, with the basic components of drama, then the teacher's role is clear. Intervention will constantly be needed to ensure that the student's energy is focused within these components, and on the pursuit of dramatic meaning. A doting aunt approach which indulgently facilitates and praises all kinds of activity in the belief that spontaneous creative play is too personal and precious to interfere with, has much to answer for. A good drama teacher ought to be more like a good coach, and since we are in the business of drama, then the work of such people as Stanislavsky, Brecht and Brook offer more fruitful models for our behaviour.

Fundamentally, the nature of teacher intervention in drama arises directly out of the components of drama and the reality of classroom management. The teacher's role is varied and distinct. It involves decision making from four specific platforms:

1 The teacher as leader
2 The teacher as playwright
3 The teacher as director
4 The teacher as actor.

The Teacher as Leader

It is understandable that the student teacher finds the transition from group member to 'leader' of the group one of the most difficult adjustments that has to be made. Extension of self into this social role of responsibility can create more apprehension than the thought of playing Antigone or Hamlet to a packed house. Coming to terms with the complexities of these characters appears less daunting than leading a group of twenty or thirty students in some exploratory piece of drama. Likewise, the experienced teacher taking up a drama allotment for the first time often finds that the confident leadership displayed in other classrooms is now replaced by misgivings and timidity. For a variety of reasons a range of behaviour is tolerated which works against achieving purposeful direction in the drama and satisfying development in the students.

The first step towards overcoming such problems is to realise that the teacher's criteria for establishing what is acceptable behaviour does not change simply because the subject is called Drama. Nor should the students in drama feel unsure of the leadership of the class and what actions are to be tolerated. Security and confidence about this is essential for both teacher and student if the appropriate environment for dramatic experience, communication and expression is to be created.

Group dynamics and the social and personal realities of the class will have a direct bearing on the kind of rules that need to be established to achieve safety and security for group members. The teacher's own values, teaching strengths and tolerance limits will be part of that reality. What is important, however, is that whatever rules are made, members of the group accept them as being purposeful and fair. It helps, therefore, if students are invited to make their own rules, with the teacher offering suggestions based on experiences that may be relevant but unavailable to the students. One such experience concerned a year 8 boy falling from his seat on a high rostra block. He ended up with several stitches in his ankle, not to mention an extremely painful foot for a few weeks. This teacher was severely reprimanded for having allowed the student to feel that this was an acceptable position to be in for the commencement of a class.

When making rules, teachers need to be aware of the potential trouble spots in the classroom and within the group. These should be the guidelines for decision making.

Making the Rules

Drama space. At a simple legal level the teacher is responsible for seeing that reasonable and due care is taken to ensure the safety of students. It is important, then, that students fully understand their relationship with the physical resources and environment of the drama space. Some areas may be taboo territory for certain age groups unless attended by the teacher. Clear signs with instructions for use are helpful around sound and lighting equipment, for example.

Personal space. The freedom of open space and no desks can be rather a burden for some highly boisterous groups of students. Establishing an understanding about physical contact and rough-housing is necessary if energy is to be controlled and focused in the drama. Respect for the actor's personal space is an awareness that has to be developed in improvisation and this can provide a parallel model of behaviour for the social interactions of the group. Encouraging self-discipline in these areas reinforces this vital drama skill and simultaneously provides a framework for the development of social skills.

Difficult students. It has been popular in drama to allow students to make their own decisions about whether or not they should participate in the drama. Unless the teacher wants to be plagued by egocentric and whimsical excuses as to why individuals don't feel like being involved on a particular day or in a specific activity, an understanding that everyone's participation is required needs to be stated at the outset. This is expected in other subject areas and drama should be no different. Such an understanding helps the reluctant or socially isolated child to rise above subjective feelings rather than indulge them. The onus is on the teacher and the group to find ways of encouraging this involvement, despite the fact that this is often extremely difficulty and, on rare occasions, impossible. Obviously the simplest of tasks and roles, with minimal demand for group interaction will be tried at first. Assisting 'teacher-in-role' can be a positive way of providing strong support, encouragement, direction or control for a problematic student. Creating a dependence on the teacher, however, can be destructive, so the strategies adopted need to take the goal of peer interaction and co-operation into account. Some students are being helped by Special Services personnel in the school and consultation with these specially qualified people can help to determine appropriate leadership strategies for the group. In especially difficult situations the help of these specialists provides the teacher with carefully considered judgements about particular students. This enables the teacher to proceed with much needed confidence in the management of the group.

Ultimately, if a student is unable to participate in the drama without destroying the work of particular individuals, or of the group as a whole, the teacher must protect the working environment in just the same way as would happen in other classrooms. The individual must be made aware of the destructiveness of particular actions and the need for positive co-operation to build the drama. Responsibility for accepting the consequences of negative actions must rest with the student. Ensuring that the consequences are met rests with the leader. Unpalatable as it may be for teacher and students, there are times when an individual has to be removed from the drama. A spell on the sidelines watching others allows the drama to proceed and reinforces the idea that limits of behaviour operate here as elsewhere. Moreover, the student/s learn that one, or a few, cannot hold the entire group's work to ransom. Overlooking transparently destructive actions invites a rippling effect that makes for troubled waters in the leadership of the class. The students understand this and look for fair and confident leadership that encourages self-discipline, self-motivation and the development of a positive working environment.

Group Co-operation

Drama asks individuals to put themselves on the line as no other subject quite does. As the self is both the medium and the object of expression there really is no refuge from the eyes and ears of others. And if personal relationships are uncertain or hostile, drama can become all the more threatening. As Ken Robinson (1980) points out:

> 'The actions of a group in a drama session, in role or out of it, are not just a response to what the teacher asks them to do. They are also responses to the expectations they have of each other. We do not simply drop our normal social roles just because we are asked to act out another one. On the contrary, we now have two sets of roles to handle.' (p. 165)

Being laughed at or ridiculed for particular actions in drama is hardly conductive to providing personal and creative safety for exploration and development. If everyone knows and is encouraged to play 'the rules of the game', (Courtney 1980), trust, support and security will develop in the group. This built-in protection helps to foster confidence and creative risk taking. The quality of the drama soars.

Richard Courtney (1980) presents us with the following fundamental 'rules of the game', as the major device in controlling drama and providing a feeling of 'safety' for students.

'(a) What is true in improvisation is accepted — whether it contradicts life or not;

(b) What is acted honestly is accepted honestly;

(c) Apart from necessary preparation, the student in role discovers what happens next in the situation while he or she is improvising;

(d) All energies of a group are focused on the specific task;

(e) Drama activities are meaningful and significant, and both teacher and class have a commitment to them.'

These rules are directly tied to the nature of the dramatic event; without firm leadership in implementing them, the quality of drama flounders. Lack of respect for the subject is then more likely to be fixed to the poor quality of the learning experience than some prejudice about the eccentricity of the arts. It is worth remembering, too, that as the individual matures, spontaneous, open-ended play for its own sake gives way to play bounded by rules. Part of the joy of playing becomes the challenge of developing skills directly related to the constraints applied to the game by particular rules. Implicit in drama, as in any artistic event, are fundamental rules associated with expression and communication through that medium. Teacher and students must agree to work together in defining rules and goals with respect, trust, much good humour and a generosity of spirit. This cannot be achieved in a few quick games sessions; it is a continuing social learning process which requires patience, encouragement, support and reinforcement.

Paradoxically, one of the strengths and weaknesses of the dramatic event is its dependence on group work. It is not unusual for teachers to argue the case for drama on the basis of the positive personal development to be gained through the social interactions of small groups as they plan, act out and discuss the drama. In sharing ideas, expressing thoughts, clarifying opinions and negotiating in problem solving, the student is obliged to engage in informal learning of a quite challenging kind. But whilst this aspect of drama is important and positive, it is also a weakness which can threaten the dramatic development of the students, for two reasons.

Firstly, individuals can quickly sort out which group allows them most easily to adopt the behaviour they feel most comfortable with. Confident talkers assume the leadership roles while the passive onlookers rest easy in their subservience to the ones with the ideas. Roles are cast in the drama according to peer pressures rather than dramatic considerations. Extension and development of the individual is retarded. Secondly, in sharing ideas and negotiating the content of the drama, personal feelings and thoughts are modified through compromise. The ideas and the drama are in danger of becoming at once everyone's and no-one's. Subjective experiences needed for the individual's stimulus for role taking and dramatic expression can be lost to the collective, objective ideas of the group. As a result, the drama loses its experiential and expressive sharpness and the meaning communicated in the action becomes paler and more insipid than is desired — something like partaking of an artificially matured cheddar or champagne, the experience of it leaves one thinking wistfully of the fullness of the real thing.

By being aware of the weakness inherent in this kind of group organisation of the drama, the teacher can adopt structures and strategies which take account of the above factors and promote positive rather than negative outcomes. Sometimes groups are willing to accept that one of the rules of drama is that individuals work in different groups each week, but where it is obvious that this is simply 'not on', the teacher can adopt planning rules which attempt to circumvent the weaknesses. For example:

(a) Planning and showing work in small groups is avoided as the predominant way of structuring drama.

(b) Where groups are used, they are devised through random selection, such as numbers games, or allocation of coloured discs/cards which then signify the tasks or role for the drama.

(c) Whole group improvises the drama together with small group structures contrived within the action so that 'characters' with similar interests or motivation interact to solve problems, discuss issues or compile data necessary for the drama.

(d) Stimulus material is provided which gives a concrete focus for the group's ideas and negotiation of the drama. Such material may include some details about characters, action or facts about an incident. Newspaper articles, excerpts from history or literature can be used.

This approach aims to remove the 'pressure for ideas' from the confident, imaginative or talkative few; the more passive feel less powerless in creating the drama. At another level each individual must interpret his/her personal experience in the wider context of the stimulus material, not just in the light of the peer group.

(e) Improvising, working spontaneously from bare but significant details, is emphasised in planning.

(f) Structures are used which give maximum opportunity for individuals to find appropriate and clear dramatic expression for their own ideas and feelings. This will mean that students often work on their own, in pairs or with the whole group in spontaneous, improvised drama. At times a small group will work spontaneously on dramatic problems while the rest of the group watches and contributes, through suggestion, to solving the problem, or exploring specific meaning.

Organisation of the group is essential to controlling the drama and maximising the individual's development. Leadership must be confident and linked assuredly to the nature of the dramatic event. To be squeamish about this authoritative stance ultimately undermines the learning process.

The Serious Business of Fun in Drama

Hand in hand with this leadership role and the teacher's knowledge of the dramatic event goes the ability to stimulate and focus the interest and energy of the group. Clearly the teacher must find appropriate ways to encourage, support, coax and guide towards development in drama. Humour and a sense of fun are important aids in this respect. When the group and the teacher can laugh and smile with each other through the good and bad moments in drama, personal efforts are more likely to be encouraged. The creative process (and this includes all learning, not just drama) is at once demanding, frustrating, joyous and exhilarating. As Brecht has taught us, fun and pleasure in the theatrical event are important ingredients for its success, yet this does not exclude the quite specific and significant learning associated with that event. The teaching function of Brechtian theatre used amusement and pleasure as one of its vital tools. We can do the same. By understanding both the complexity and simplicity of this, the drama teacher can make enormous headway in leading the group towards its learning goals. The worn out cry of 'Drama should be fun' needs considerable rethinking. If we look to Shakespeare and Brecht for some guidance, we are already stepping away from the self-indulgence of pursuing activities which generate momentary pleasure but have no lasting significance. Babysitters may productively adopt such a strategy, but as educators in drama we are bound to action of a different order.

Making Drama Happen

As was stated in chapter 3, participants in drama must make a conscious decision to behave in a way that allows the drama to happen. There must be an agreement to pretence, to build a make-believe reality within the reality of the classroom and the mundane experiences of the school day. The fragility of classroom drama is linked to the difficulty that many students have in straddling these realities. At base it is an act of individual will. Each participant must agree to let the drama work upon him/her, and at the same time undertake to make the drama work upon him/her. The attitude of 'I will let the drama work upon me' abdicates responsibility for the input of personal creative energy needed to bring about learning and development in drama. If the teacher, for example, playwrights and directs the drama with the view that he/she alone must make the drama happen to the students, it is quite likely that little will happen. The teacher's constant instructions, directions and explanations prevent the students actively contributing to the satisfactory building of role and belief in the drama. Hurried and impulsive actions are likely to result in superficial drama which loses its 'similar to life' quality and its artistic sincerity. The 'I am letting it happen' dominates.

Leadership strategies which give consideration to the 'I am making it happen' aspect of drama will reap rewards in terms of student involvement and development. Time must be allowed for students to think, experience, make decisions, shape, order and express in drama. If the teacher understands the strengths and weaknesses of individual students in making the drama happen, confident intervention can occur to circumvent the problem and save the drama.

An example of this leadership occurred with a year 8 class when a group of boys were acting out an improvised play that involved the 'headmaster' dealing with three 'recalcitrant students'. The drama was progressing well until the 'headmaster' commanded one of the students to hold out his hand for three strokes of the strap. The boy defied the conventions of the drama and refused to accept the dramatic actions of his friend. 'Ah, no ya don't', came the muffled reply through stifled giggles. The 'headmaster' struggled to sustain commitment to the drama and again issued the command. Same responses from friend, only larger! Firmly and confidently the teacher intervened from her position across the room. 'Let him strap you', was all that was needed to remind the boy of his responsibility to the drama. In this instance the play continued, its meaning sufficiently intact to be communicated to the audience. The conventions of the drama had been reinforced, everyone was implicitly reminded of the 'I am letting it happen — I am making it happen' rules. And instead of turning the lapse of concentration into a disciplinary issue, the teacher had simply used the role of leader to upgrade the quality of the work.

All the time we are teaching in drama, we must be teaching about drama. Sometimes the teaching will happen implicitly, as in the above example, but just as often conventions and rules may need to be openly and clearly restated and reinforced. Why there should be mystery and preciousness about the dramatic process is difficult to fathom. Teachers and students need to understand that it doesn't just happen — it is made to happen!

7 The Teacher as Playwright

Theatre recreates life with a robustness, definiteness of form, and coherency of order far greater than we experience in everyday life. Participants in a theatrical event have the opportunity to see their mundane, chaotic and repetitive experiences in a crisp, clear light. The play's capacity to bring about this heightened awareness is tied to the playwright's ability as an artist and observer of life. Both explicitly and implicitly, play scripts offer knowledge about life and about the artistic elements used in the making of the script.

In the drama classroom, the teacher as playwright accepts responsibility for ensuring that the drama lesson — 'the script' — is capable of supporting this same learning about the human condition and the art form. In striving to achieve this, the teacher is conscious of the need:

(a) for **dramatic situations** and **dramatic actions** to be in a form which exposes the meanings inherent in the content;

(b) to make explicit the function of the art form in contriving dramatic tension and heightening meaning;

(c) for the students as actors to become increasingly confident in playwrighting in order to constantly move the drama towards meaning.

Content

Scripted Drama

Obviously the easiest way of approaching the drama lesson is to provide the students with a published script and let them get on with the business of 'putting on' their interpretation of it. In this way no demands are made on the teacher's playwrighting or lesson-structuring skills, content is already fixed, and the running of the class will, for the most part, only call upon the teacher to organise and control the group. As a way of saving teaching energy and ensuring survival, this approach is not unattractive. The demand for commercial drama kits, books of scripted plays, of drama games and lesson ideas, highlights the difficulties teachers have in coming to grips with this part of drama teaching. The very real weakness in going about things in this way, however, lies in the inappropriateness and irrelevance of much of the material available. Play scripts are usually too long or of poor quality in terms of the issues explored and/or artistic challenges offered. It is not uncommon to see young students putting most of their energies into English or American accents, for example, because the scripts they are dealing with are so obviously alien to their experiences. In most cases it would serve the students' development much better if the teacher were to extract the issues or themes from the script and have the class workshop them.

As a way of finding a new perspective on the students' ideas, the script, or part of it, may be useful and any preoccupation with accents is then irrelevant.

It is also important to realise that by offering scripted plays too early to students, their capacity for spontaneous expression and decision-making within drama runs the risk of being retarded. Language flow in improvised drama can be inhibited and self-conscious, because words provided by a script seem more 'dramatic' and 'real' than the students' own. A more open-ended lesson script offers greater opportunities for much wider learning and skill development. When students are ready to approach the fully scripted play they will need to have adequately developed the skills of analysis and interpretation so that in giving dramatic life to the words, the richness of the subtext is available and used to inform their expressive behaviour.

Non-scripted Drama

Experimental theatre of the sixties and early seventies promoted self-expression and the experience of the moment as basic to the dramatic process. In such an artistic climate the value of preconceived drama in the form of scripts was minimal. Movements in education reflected the same preoccupation with the supremacy of self and drama teaching was certainly no exception.

For some teachers these issues have still not yet have resolved; any planning or scripting of the drama lesson is seen as antithetical to the creative drama process. The ideal lesson evolves from the teacher's 'What shall we make a play about today?' The writers' reservations about such an approach are threefold. In the first instance emphasis on personal and social development through peer interaction and spontaneous self-expression devalues the drama experience. Secondly the 'play' usually remains at a plot level where the superficiality and sensationalism of the action dominate the work. And thirdly, skills in manipulating and guiding the direction and experience of the drama need to be extremely well developed if confusion is to be avoided. The teacher's knowledge also needs to be broad and rich and his/her ability to make spontaneous abstractions and concrete connections needs to be sophisticated — quite a tall order in the course of a busy teaching day. Playwrighting the drama in this way requires a great deal of energy and precision of thought that cannot let up for the duration of the lesson — fifty to 100 minutes, and perhaps another 200 minutes of drama left in the day ...? A much sounder alternative is to write the script before the lesson and then be prepared to leave the responsibility for its execution to the teacher/director. Margaret Croydon's comments (1974) on the experimentalist theatre movement offer food for thought about some of our approaches to drama in the classroom.

> 'A serious problem ... was the experimentalists reliance on self-expression as a predominant aesthetic — the old romantic tenet. Self-expression became the answer to all arguments and served to hide a dearth of shallow ideas and unworkable theatrics ... self-expression cultivated an intense and limited subjectivism and bred, in the name of an ill-defined individualism, a new anti-intellectualism.' (p. 289)

The Lesson Script

Content — Drama is contrived from our knowledge and experience of life. Events from the most mundane to the highly extraordinary provide raw material for the playwright. This is the content of drama and, with such an abundance of raw material, designing lessons ought to be easy, but it isn't. Selection of content is simple: tables, watching television, doing the shopping, icecreams might be regarded as content. Finding the significance of content, however, and knowing what relationship it holds for individuals and groups, is of greater importance. If the drama is to have worth, then the teacher/playwright needs a very clear understanding of the implications of the specific content selected. We must be able to make a wide variety of connections at both abstract and concrete levels which will help create a richness of experience within the lesson script. To do this, the drama teacher must be prepared to observe, to read, to research, to collect resources and, perhaps above all, to contemplate and to make connections. All in all, a kind of continuous super brainstorming.

By paying tribute to the place of content in our teaching we are not only demonstrating an understanding of the nature of drama but also acknowledging our role as educators. It is simply not possible, for example, to learn significantly about the complexities of status by playing theatre games such as the popular 'status hat game', where those in positions of authority go about their business wearing hats which those beneath them attempt to surreptitiously remove and wear in order to change their status. Nor can you expect the students to learn about the complexities of isolation by blindfolding them and subjecting their senses to a variety of stimuli. What is evident here is a misunderstanding of the nature of learning in these activities and a somewhat idiosyncratic focus on the subject of drama. The place of content in the making of drama has been ignored.

One very easy way of providing content which challenges and extends the experiences of the group is to use literature of all kinds. It may be used simply to stimulate the teacher's thinking and planning, or it may become a concrete part of the lesson itself. Issues, themes, and metaphors can be abstracted and the drama scripted so that learning occurs around what the content has opened up. Thus a Roald Dahl short story is not 'acted out', but provides the starting point for an exploration of 'the bizarre'; a Bruce Dawe poem pins the drama to a sequence of improvisations designed to experience and express aspects of pride and self-esteem..

Whatever content and related issues are selected for the drama, it means that the decision to pursue that particular path necessarily removes the possibility of other specific learning. The playwright's choice of material and his attitude towards it results in a particular play with a specific capacity to illuminate some aspect of life's experiences. Within a specific drama lesson only a limited exploration of a particular theme will be possible. To allow for sound learning new perspectives on the issues involved will need to be planned for and pursued in subsequent lessons. If, for example, we return to the concept of family, and playwrights through the ages have found it compelling content for their drama, there are many perspectives and issues which could be scripted into a sequence of lessons. A 'one-off' approach will deprive the content of its teaching potential. The manner in which the content is scripted and the extent to which issues are explored will of course be determined by the particular group for whom the drama is designed. Insights gained into the human condition will vary according to the perspectives which are offered by the lesson script. Possible perspectives for consideration might be:

Personal

Parents — mother   father   single parent (ages can become significant added perspectives, as can social and economic status).

Children — sex   age   occupation (student, worker)

Relatives — Grandparents

Other people who have contact with members of the family from a more distant perspective — Teacher   Employer   Neighbour.

Time

Past — By moving into the past, experiences from the present are given added meaning through contrast and comparison. The specific perspective is selected for its ability to illuminate the themes of drama. Possible choices:

Families in Victorian England;

Australian pioneering families;

Families in the Second World War.

Future — By moving into the distant and imaginative unknown, ideas about the present can be made more vivid.

Social/cultural/political

Any of these perspectives may influence the details of content selection and provide fresh ways of making sense of the concept of family.

Attitude

Humourous — satire, farce, melodrama

Serious — light drama, tragedy

Style

Having selected content the manner in which it is to be experienced in the lesson is decided. Between the extremes of serious experimental drama and light-hearted, caricatured comedy and satire there are a variety of approaches to the dramatic experience that can be taken. The social and intellectual nature of the group and the dramatic development of the students will help to suggest the most appropriate form for the drama. Although three broad styles are discussed here, obviously there are variations and extensions possible in each.

It is also feasible that within the course of one drama session, elements from each dramatic style might be used to most effectively serve the teaching objectives.

Naturalistic

Whether it is in spontaneous, improvised drama without an audience or polished improvisation to be performed to the group, the manner of acting is natural and emphasises the experience of the role and situation. Actors are asked to assume a 'fourth wall' approach to their drama space and behave 'as if' it were really happening. Natural use of voice and gesture are called for; pretentiousness, stereotyping and caricature are avoided. Realism and illusion are sought. The drama is ideally suited to the pursuit of knowledge about personal, social and political concerns.

The audience is expected to identify with the characters. The audience's attitude should be one of privileged watchers of a private affair. Plot and humour are important only in so far as they advance the situations and problems being confronted in the drama. Reflection and discussion within, or following the drama, will be concerned with the emotional, psychological motivation for certain actions and ultimately what the drama highlighted about the issues being explored.

Depending on the age and dramatic development of the students, acting may occur in the round, in a thrust or tongue formation, or in a more formal boxed arrangement. Costume and lighting is used only if essential to creating and maintaining a natural atmosphere. When working with young students, the addition of adult costuming does more to break the illusion of realism than promote it. The same can be said for the gimmickry of coloured lights or lighting changes. Participants are at once reminded of the unnatural, theatrical form of the event. Meyerhold's innovations in naturalistic theatre offer the teacher a flexible and appropriate variation of Stanislavsky's realism. All lights were turned on, mobile cubes and rostra were used for actors and audience and a number of short scenes staged rapidly like montages. And although he based his theatre on dramatic literature, he changed it ruthlessly to suit his actors and his audience. Later still one of his pupils was to introduce the spontaneous, improvised drama that suits so well the exploration and discovery associated with classroom drama.

Epic

The plays and theatre of Brecht offer the teacher a valuable alternative model for structuring drama. Here the emphasis is placed on thought processes rather than emotions, on entertainment and on getting the message across in a casual atmosphere of fun. The drama is expository, didactic and narrative, openly using its scenes and images to air social and political problems through the telling of stories. The notion of change and revolution is implicit in epic drama.

Special effects are used to break down any notion of illusion, or intention of identification and empathy with characters. Actors are asked to use their ability to demonstrate rather than feel and express. Everything emotional must be externalised and developed into gesture. Whilst the drama has an artistic sincerity the 'as if' quality changes gear to become 'an appearance of' or 'a commentary upon'.

Actors working in this epic mode are free to talk directly to the audience, to give instructions or communicate facts necessary to the meaning of the play. A variety of media is used in the demonstration of ideas: music, films, placards, song. If costume, make-up and light are used, they must exaggerate the drama, counter any illusion of reality and highlight its teaching point.

This particular style of drama is aptly suited to the young adolescent who finds emotional identification and expression an extremely threatening and self-conscious experience. Because the showing and the meaning is emphasised rather than the feeling, there is a much greater sense of security and self-protection available.

Reflection and discussion in relation to the drama will now focus on the medium of communication and the clarity of the message received. Clearly in this approach to the drama experience, an audience is necessary.

Anti-theatre

Many senior students are struggling to decipher a world that seems frightening, complex, exciting and, hostile. Their experiences are filled with images of beauty and horror, scenes that are bizarre, unreal and nonsensical. Life takes on a sense of urgency, an emotional and intellectual intensity that at times threatens to engulf. Coming to terms with the reality of such an unjust and hypocritical existence suggests the wisdom of a non-rational way of perceiving the world. Perhaps for these reasons alone, there is an attraction for the images of dadaists, surrealists and absurdists. Here images speak forcefully of the primitive and deep unknown; they capture the emptiness and despair of the current generation who understand what it is to feel powerless and alienated from their lives. Within the drama there is a need to express grotesquely and loudly through distortion, nonsense language and bizarre characters. In exploring content in this anti-theatre style, metaphor, symbol, disconnected rhythmic thought and a language of sound, silence and movement offer exploratory, expressive challenges. The function of art, drama and theatre is called into focus and a wide variety of *avant-garde* dramatic styles and theatrical techniques are used in experimentation. Accompanying this journey into anti-theatre there will need to be an understanding of its relationship with the classical and contemporary theatre. A critical appreciation of a range of drama experiences and theatre movements provides a sound counterpoint for the student's development. The work of Peter Brook and his contribution to experimentation in theatre can offer a stimulating focus.

In the interests of drama and theatre, our senior students' love for drama needs to be nurtured through a variety of soundly guided experiences, into a lasting passion for the subject. We are surely not in the business of working with students for five or six years simply to have them regard the experience as a pleasant way to develop self-confidence. Dispensable drama deserves a dispensable place in the school curriculum.

Unity

In the play script and theatre, indeed all art, there needs to be a sense of each part essentially contributing to a whole. Characters, situations, images and scenes need to be interdependent and to build a satisfying overall impression. If this doesn't occur, participants in the event are likely to lose concentration, become bored, confused and dissatisfied. A lesson script presents the same possibilities. Unless its parts can be experienced as essentials building towards a moment of insight and purpose, the students' concentration, commitment and learning will be fragmented. Time will have passed but little more will have happened. Regular experiences of this kind soon lead one to assume that nothing much of significance happens in drama.

One way of achieving unity in the lesson script is to build activities around a central focus.

Focus on Character
When a particular character has been selected, activities are designed which reveal the complex web of desires and

interactions which have 'made the man'. A personal, social emphasis might be aimed for, in which the character's attitudes and values, and what has contributed to them, are explored. If literary stimulus is used (a poem, newspaper or magazine article, for example), interpretation of words and phrases can be used as the basis for the drama experiences. In this way the purely subjective or stereotyped responses of the group can be challenged and ideas extended. Bruce Dawe's 'The Family Man', 'At Shagger's Funeral' and 'Flashing of Badges', or Judith Wright's 'The Metho Drinker' are readily accessible resources which offer excellent stimulus for such work. Political, historical or mythical figures, such as John Kerr, Ned Kelly or Joan of Arc, present interesting and challenging material for the focus of the drama. By supporting the lesson with well-chosen stimulus material and/or carefully guided research, the quality of experience within the drama can be heightened.

Focus on Event
(The Drama Plot)

Applying for the dole; An act of treason; Visiting a political prisoner; Murder; Suicide; Cheating in an exam; An act of fraud; Declaration of war; Leaving home; the possibilities are endless. The drama is structured so that the event is explored for its causes and its effect. Each situation in the drama must be able to provide a logical connection with the central moment.

Focus on Place

Prison; School; Home; An aeroplane; Hotel; Social Welfare Agency; High rise flats. What goes on between the characters within the particular place might be extremely varied and bear a relationship with others only by virtue of the location. By the same token a diversity of interests and personalities might be drawn together in the particular place by a common desire or specific dilemma.

Focus on Time

Within the course of drama, time can be used as a tool for heightening dramatic tension and intensifying the learning. Events that would take place over a considerable period of time in real life are compressed and experienced within a short space of time. For example, students could plan and conduct a revolution, a bank robbery, an escape from prison or develop strategies for the survival of earth.

On the other hand, by focusing on a particular moment in time, the same heightening of tension can occur. Thus two opposing armies in their separate trenches await the battle signal which beckons their confrontation with death. A group of refugees wait for news which will take them to freedom, or condemn them to perish.

Time is also used to suggest mood and atmosphere. A particular scene (e. g. leaving home) which takes place at midnight in winter — sunset in summer — at dawn — at breakfast, will have its meaning modified. A cheery departure at midnight in winter reveals an important subtext to the action which the same departure at sunset in summer will not be capable of.

Time will not be used as a separate central focus so much as it will be used to heighten the tension and meaning of the drama that occurs around character, event and place.

Impact

A major consideration in structuring drama is the extent to which its various parts will carry particular meaning and, of course, hold the interest of those involved in the experience.

This is so in theatre and it holds equally true for the classroom. For example, in a short, improvised piece of drama in which members of a family are discussing what to do with a problematic aged relative, the predominance of casual, colloquial speech may seriously weaken important meaning within the action. And should a number of groups be asked to prepare and show the same scene, interest in the drama is likely to wane. If the lesson script prescribes alternative ways of approaching the content, however, the impact of the drama can be increased through a heightened dramatic tension. Some specific tools for achieving this are worth describing.

Variety of Experience

Careful juxtaposition of contrasting perspectives, as well as the nature of the activity, are simple devices for manipulating the dynamics and focus of the drama. If we return to the improvisation in which the characters are discussing the aged relative problem, the lesson script could well ask that exploration of the issue occur in the following ways.

Activity 1. Individuals are asked to sculpt their bodies into a shape which depicts 'youth and vitality'. This is followed by finding a movement sculpture which depicts 'very old age'.

Activity 2. A portrait/photograph of an aged person is used to stimulate an imaginative building of a character profile. Participants speak in first person — I remember him/her telling me about the hardship that followed the bushfires of Black Friday', etc.

Activity 3. Small groups are asked to prepare an improvisation.

(a)   Group 1 — a scene which exposes the dilemma facing the family with whom the relative is living.
      Characters: Individual family members
                   Aged relative.

(b)   Group 2 — a scene which shows the family discussing the problem with the relative.

(c)   Group 3 — a scene which shows the family discussing the problem without the relative present.

(d) Group 4 — a scene which satirises the issue.

Activity 4. Small groups simultaneously and spontaneously play through the following scene: Family members make a visit to the aged relative, who is now in a nursing home.

Activity 5. After watching the work of the groups, pairs are asked to find three gestures, and three words or sounds, which can be repeated in a sequence to express the concepts highlighted by the drama.

Obviously there are a multitude of approaches which can be taken in any particular drama. What is important is that each activity adds an important step which broadens and deepens the experiences of the action. A common weakness of drama lessons is the sameness of the activities prescribed for the group, so that after the initial experience (perhaps the showing of the same improvised scene), a sense of dullness and *déjà vu* sets in. All that occurs is a range of minor variations on the same ideas. For the drama to have vitality and depth of meaning, contrasting experiences need to be called for. For the most part this is possible even in a forty or fifty minute session. Gavin Bolton's (1981) 'type D drama' notion of weaving a variety of experiences (exercise, dramatic play and theatre) into the drama, highlights this need for variation in maximising student learning.

Whatever activities are used in the lesson, unity must still be preserved. We are not discussing a range of disconnected events, but rather a variety of linked approaches which add impact to the drama and its central learning issues.

Language Theatrics

(a) Restricted language — this involves a compression of thought, emotion, gesture and speech. The scene is reduced to a limited number of ideas and images, thus sharpening its action and emotional/dramatic intensity. Only short sentences or single words are used. Movement is reduced to a series of single gestures. Variations can occur, such as characters being asked to use short sentences of the same length which, with the help óf pauses, gives a rhythmic quality to the dialogue. Repetition of key words or short phrases throughout the scene can also add impact to the experience of the drama.

(b) Elaborated language — a particular character is given the opportunity within the drama to present a speech which expresses his/her private thoughts and feelings. This may be spoken to other characters, become a soliloquy or, if appropriate, be directly addressed to the audience.

A narrator may be called upon to present added information or simply pass attitudinal comments upon the action. This may occur as a prologue or epilogue to the scene.

The use of a small number of participants as a chorus (even two will do) is also an interesting way of increasing the impact of the drama. (It is also an excellent way of involving the shyer student who doesn't feel comfortable 'acting'.)

In the above instances, of course, preparation time will be needed to ensure adequate confidence in dialogue, otherwise the impact will be lost. These devices are also appropriate for linking together a number of scenes which explore the same idea, but which do not have a logical and clear connection between them.

Dilemma

Once content, situation and characters have been defined, the action and meaning of the drama can be intensified by the introduction of a particular problem, or indeed a series of problems throughout. Let's say the drama is about a journey to planet Z and, with much excitement and apprehension about journeying into the unknown, the action proceeds at a fairly straightforward, simple plot level. Very soon the spaceship is on the planet. By introducing certain dilemmas, the progression of the drama can be slowed down and the impact of action heightened. Thoughts and deeds now have to be carefully considered because their implications have become more vivid and their consequences more binding. So, news is communicated to the space travellers that one of their group has been taken hostage by the aliens and will be returned only in exchange for top secret information about their country's satellite stations. If desired, the personal details of characters can also be contrasted so that the dilemma is even more complicated. Thus, the hostage does not possess the information but certain other group members do. Having reached this particular fork in the drama, a definite path must be chosen. Whatever decision is finally taken, the awful consequences cannot be avoided — sacrifice a team member, or become traitors to their country! The meaning of the drama is bound up with the dramatic tension that arises out of the attempt to cope with the dilemma. It is in this sense that conflict evolves subtly but strongly within the drama; it is the result of contrasting attitudes and desires, rather than the direct clash of opposites.

By scripting contrasting personal details and dilemmas for characters, and posing problems which the whole group must deal with, the plot of drama moves from a simple to complex level. A series of sub-plots develop as the drama intensifies and 'the plot thickens'. Depending upon the aims of the drama, it may be that the action concludes before the decisions are made. If however, understanding about the difficulty of living with consequences is important, then ways must be found to achieve the decision. The direction of the drama is then altered. It may be that a change of event, place and time is needed — all space travellers may now find themselves political prisoners on trial for treason in their home country.

Surprise, Suspense and Irony

In the space example above, the element of surprise was used by introducing the idea of a hostage. Further surprise could have been used if, upon the smug meeting of the aliens' demands with false information, it was stated that the planet's research to date clearly showed that trickery was at work. A new aspect of the action has now to be dealt with ...

Surprise in drama, however, should be used with caution. Unexpected events can easily startle participants if the surprise is accompanied by outrageousness and unbelievability. Highly emotional events such as deaths can lead to loss of commitment to the drama, especially if one of the group is asked to appear as the dead victim.

It is worth being aware also that the sudden introduction of a bizarre or comic event can just as readily threaten the drama — a drunken alien, for example, who lurches into the space ship to offer the keys to the hostage's freedom, is more likely to produce hilarity outside the drama than internal impact.

It might serve us well to take a lesson from Greek drama and have the surprising event reported to the players instead.

In the space drama, for example, all action to do with the aliens can simply be communicated by using the strategy of 'teacher in role'. Careful use of language and role by the teacher can provide all the innuendo or detail that is needed to create the appropriate impact. Finally, the over-riding consideration is to ensure that the surprise is relevant and, above all, able to be perceived and accepted as an integral part of the drama. Otherwise tension of a non-dramatic nature will result.

Suspense is closely related to the manipulation of time in the drama. Waiting for an anticipated event can provide far greater dramatic tension than participation in the actual event often affords. We are all too familiar with this concept from experiences in our everyday living. 'If only we could get on with it', 'Is it ever really going to happen?' contain a wealth of personal energy, thought and emotion. Soldiers waiting for the battle signal are trapped in a time limbo which paradoxically increases the experiences of the living moment. In the space drama, suspense can be achieved by holding the group captive whilst the aliens consider what is to be done with them. Interest and fear combine to achieve the impact.

Irony is the element of certain people being 'in the dark' about events or actions going on around them. If some characters within a spontaneously acted play have information that others are not party to, then irony will be added to what is done and said in the drama. The dramatic effect is immediate; the moment is heightened in intensity; new meanings are revealed. If we turn to the space drama once again this can be illustrated. Certain members of the space group are aware that the so called 'hostage' is already dead; they killed him because he had discovered their complicity with the aliens. Or alternatively, having decided as a group to give the desired information to the aliens in exchange for the hostage, they find too late that their fellow traveller had escaped and was safe in the space ship.

In planned and polished drama, a chorus or narrator can use irony simply and effectively, by giving the audience facts that are unknown to the players. Either comic or tragic impact can be achieved in this way.

Will any of us, in contemplating the use of irony, not think automatically of Sophocles' gripping and masterful use of irony in *Oedipus Rex*? A powerful dramatic device indeed.

Symbol

As was briefly mentioned in chapter 2, any object which is capable of suggesting meanings far greater than its material self can be used to add force to the thoughts and emotions of the drama. Ibsen's plays abound with symbols used to powerful effect; the manuscript in Hedda Gabler which is referred to as Lovborg and Thea's 'child' is just one illustration. The way in which certain objects function as symbols will depend upon the context of the drama. A smashed photograph, a sealed envelope, a loaf of bread, a recorded voice . . . may all carry a wealth of meaning in particular dramatic situations. When the object or sound is seen or heard, the participants in the drama are caught up in the suggestion of life forces which are deeply stirring, perhaps feared and not wholly understood. The meanings continue to reverberate throughout the action. Scripting symbols into the beginning of lessons can often be a powerful way of gaining motivation and commitment. The object instantly calls up meanings upon which the action can build.

In this chapter we have been concerned with articulating ways in which the drama teacher can effectively playwright the drama so that learning about the art form and the human condition is maximised. The writers believe it essential that teachers understand the devices that can be used and the effect that they may produce so that the drama experience can be strengthened in its vitality and learning potential.

Of course we must realistically acknowledge that by scripting lessons from such a perspective we have merely increased our likelihood of improving the form and quality of the drama. But the proof of the pudding is in the eating and the script must move with the teacher to the classroom, the students and the specific moments of the drama. There the emphasis must be on flexibility, adaptation and collaboration in order to achieve the lesson aims. The playwrighting function of the teacher does not end with the beginning of the drama. On the contrary it works hand in hand with the added responsibility of direction.

As players in the drama, the students experience the effect of the different approaches and gain implicit knowledge of their application. It cannot be assumed, however, that this will occur by a process of osmosis which results in the student being able to use the techniques in drama. Reflection on their drama experience to identify reasons why learning was heightened or weakened must be made explicit through discussion and further practice and experience. After all, in the long term we are ultimately aiming to have the students capable of controlling their own artistic experience. If they are not provided with the tools and the insight to do so, their years of drama and their command of the art form will have given much less than it inherently promises.

8   The Teacher as Director

As far as drama in education is concerned, it has been unthinkable to contemplate the notion of teacher as director. The idea has been associated with a heartless disregard for the creative, educational processes of the subject. Direction has been interpreted as a series of meddlesome, destructive acts that result in the students' mechanical, puppet-like responses to the drama. Individual and creative development under such conditions is necessarily inhibited.

Well it would be foolhardy to deny these latter charges. Bad direction will certainly produce bad results, so will bad teaching. The problem with this attitude towards direction and drama, however, is that it operates from false assumptions. Direction in drama and theatre has never aimed to deny the actor's creative process and thereby produce a puppet-like being; in fact it aims to do exactly the opposite. If directors have failed in this regard then they have failed to understand their role in drama and the means by which creative ends are achieved. The teacher as director and students as actors must work creatively together to establish appropriate role relationships with the characters of the play. The teacher must be the prime strategist in ensuring that character interactions can express the drama's symbolic meaning.

In this chapter we will spend time defining the creative, constructive intervention that constitutes good directing, and therefore good teaching, in drama.

The Aims of the Director

Broadly speaking, the director takes the work of the playwright (the lesson script) and a group of actors (the students), and goes through a series of processes in order to build creative, meaningful drama. Whilst the actor/student is absolutely central to this dramatic process, focus is always on the group's exploration, expression and communication of meaning. Any attention to skill development and personal expertise is relevant only in so far as it represents the means to this end. Bad teaching in drama has often been the result of a misplaced focus on characterisation and improvisation as ends in themselves. Their function in the making of the dramatic event becomes decidedly blurred.

To understand how the teacher as director functions to achieve good drama, we need to look at the assumptions which underlie good direction and the specific details of direction processes.

Attitude towards Direction

The Nature of the Process

First and foremost, the director needs to acknowledge that drama is a creative, collaborative process. Playwright, director and actor each bring their own experiences, knowledge and creativeness to the drama event. Creative interactions during the making of the drama may suggest that the script has to be modified to ensure adequate exploration of its meanings. Changing character details and/or finding new dramatic situations may be appropriate in the student's pursuit of meaning. Certainly the student is not viewed as some object for manipulation in the director's interpretation of the lesson script. Rather the teacher/director must value and seek to liberate and extend the individual's experience and creativeness. As educators, we can not assume that this will occur naturally; as drama teachers we are bound to find strategies which will unlock these processes in the individual and speed up the artistic and human development inherent in the subject of drama. In conclusion we offer some general guidelines for teachers/directors.

1 At all times the focus of the class is on exploration of lesson content and its meanings. Positive or negative comments from teacher or students must be firmly tied to this focus. The reasons for questions or instructions are explained so that students see a reason for what is done and, at the same time, they learn about the processes of their medium.

2 Keeping the development of the group in mind, don't accept obviously half-hearted, sloppy efforts within the drama. Be prepared to stop the action, if necessary, and begin again. Honesty of actions and responses is vital.

3 Use side-coaching to encourage commitment and support exploration within the drama.

4 Discourage notions of students acting to please teacher or entertain friends. Stop and refocus on the content of the drama. Question the students' actions for character motivation.

5 Commentaries and discussions are a necessary part of the drama process. Don't allow offensive or defensive behaviour to become part of the reflective process. Find the cause and handle accordingly. (A quick discussion of the issue after class may be less embarrassing and more effective than a public airing of unhelpful behaviour.) Be prepared to classify some comments as irrelevant or unproductive.

6 Watch for the effects of your instructions, questions and handling of particular students. Direction is a two-way communication between you and the student. Look to your own actions first for the possible cause of any weaknesses in the drama. Seek open, direct feedback from students — not just from the vocal few!

Individual Experience and the Dramatic Event

Knowledge and experience of life's events provide the raw material for the director, as well as for the actor. It is imperative that the director be just as ardent an observer and gatherer of knowledge as the playwright. Finding the richness of meaning within the script and knowing how to make connection with the experiences of actors is fundamental. And just as the director in theatre has to research background material for the play, so too does the drama teacher. In order to broaden the knowledge brought to the drama by the actors, research and observational tasks may have to be designed for them as well.

In some approaches to drama teaching, this broadening of knowledge is seen as important, but the drama experience is used merely as a tool for promoting interest in research after the event. What we are advocating here is the need for the drama to be experienced when the participants have learned enough to add greater significance to the experience. Where this is a fairly simple task, of course, the teacher as playwright must be prepared to take responsibility for the provision of the material as a stimulus and integral part of the drama. However, the order of the activities is crucial — the drama event is the artistic medium where synthesis of knowledge, experience and meaning is activated. In other words, not only does the gate need to be closed before the artistic horse has bolted, but the horse's cart should be loaded before the journey! Care is then needed to ensure that the cart is not overloaded and the horse not too overburdened to begin!

Understanding the nature of this balance between broadening experience and using it productively in drama is inextricably linked to the group of students with whom we are working, and the complexity of creative learning within drama. But by broadening the students' experiences in this way, the teacher as director is beginning the process of liberation and extension that moves the individual beyond prejudiced and stereotyped views of the world — a necessary prerequisite if the drama experience is to be a deeply satisfying one.

Some Useful Principles for Action

1 Where written stimulus is used as a part of the lesson, allow time for its meaning and impact to be absorbed. One reading of a poem, letter, magazine article, case study, etc., may not be sufficient.

2 Teacher as director (who has seen the material and is therefore familiar with it) reads the material first so that its meaning can be exposed.

3 Difficult vocabulary needs to be explained, questions asked for clarification. Material is re-read for crystallisation of images and meaning. (A student may now read if the meaning will be communicated clearly.)

4 Keep purpose of reading clearly in mind. Broadening of knowledge, heightening awarenesses, making connections between personal experiences and the ideas offered by the material, in preparation for the drama.

5 Complete the activity as efficiently as possible — the drama which is to follow is the ultimate learning focus. Don't get sidetracked into interesting discussions and personal anecdotes which disperse energy and remove the focus of the lesson.

6 During the making of the drama be alert to the meanings to be explored and, when unproductive divergence occurs, refocus the group by returning to specific details of the resource used.

When more extensive research is desired —

7 Enlist the aid of library personnel and prepare a box of material which can be taken to the drama space for easy access and quick focus. (This makes for easy leadership of the class.)

8 Ask small groups to research a particular aspect of a topic and have the information presented to the group as a whole.

Topic: Ned Kelly: Myth or Hero?
Areas for research: Background on Ned's family.
Settlers conditions in North-East Victoria.
Property laws and police attitudes.
Alleged crimes of Kelly gang.
At Glenrowan.
The trial.
After the hanging.

Focus of the research needs to be on people, what they did and why they did it.

9 Don't throw away details of research. Where appropriate keep manila folders and fill with details of topic, resources and the results of students' material search. In this way an ever-expanding body of knowledge is ready to be drawn upon by teacher and students.

10 If research is asked for, make sure that the results of it are used in the drama in a concrete and meaningful way. (That doesn't mean engaging in re-enactment theatre!) Obviously students will find it a meaningless task if connections are vague and tenuous. Reflection on the drama experience should direct attention to the similarities and differences between the drama and the knowledge gained through resources.

The Social Self and Role Taking

In chapter 2 we commented briefly on the changing capacity of young students to adopt and play out imaginary situations. The situation is little different with adults. Whilst we all have the capacity to adopt different social roles in the course of our everyday interactions (Goffman, 1971), and to present different faces within those roles, the extent to which any of us do this successfully varies enormously. So too does our ability to engage in imaginative projection and mental role playing. 'If I were this kind of person, in this particular situation, I would . . .' Flights of fantasy and daydreaming are occupations that from childhood are usually firmly discouraged as frivolous and empty headed, if not downright destructive. Taking another step then and acting out or hamming up a situation to which we have been party in some way (Brecht's Street Scene concept of role behaviour), can be quite foreign and certainly threatening. It's more likely that one simply speaks about such things, more or less emotionally, depending upon the context. Some will colour the situation 'tragic'; others will find humour in it. Exposure of self in the communication is usually minimised.

The situation is no different with our students. It cannot be assumed that they all find the taking of role natural, easy and pleasurable, or that they have a broad and flexible ability to manifest role in serious naturalistic drama, or exaggerated gesture and comedy. One of the drama teacher's most burdensome handicaps is the belief that a group of students ought to be capable of quickly assuming role and entering the imaginative world of the play on the teacher's instructions. Disappointment, frustration, loss of patience and anger are destined to go hand in hand with such a view. The ideas of Slade, Brecht and Goffman give us valuable insights into role taking, but insights which need to be tempered with a common-sense approach to what is occurring before our eyes.

George C. Scott once commented that acting was schizoid because it required that the actor be himself, somebody else (the character) and, at the same time, a member of the audience looking on at what the other two were doing. That concept of the actor's 'self', however, is not so easily isolated, especially in the reality of classroom group dynamics.

Individuals have their inner self to contend with, as well as the self they wish to project to their particular peer group. After that comes the dramatic role, with its participant/spectator duality — I am me, I am me playing the role of another.

So what has this got to do with drama? From the teacher/director's point of view it can have a great deal to say about the honesty of role taking and the sincerity with which roles are used to explore the dramatic content. Students who feel isolated and insecure within the group may build roles which call for a passive and/or peripheral contribution to the action. Dead bodies and statues offer the ultimate escape and self-protection, but policemen, maids, delivery boys and a host of other characters can be manipulated so that their roles and interactions with others remain very much these of a passive bystander.

On the other hand, if individuals feel insecure with their peers they may create relatively self-confident, humorous, dominant or bizarre roles in the hope of gaining the group's positive support for such interesting action.

As the teacher/director aims to keep the focus always on the content and meaning of the drama, sensitive and constructive intervention is needed so that this 'real social' use of the drama can be minimised or removed. Development of the individual and the progress of the group in drama is dependent on this. During the course of the drama, some quick thinking on the teacher's part can change the direction and emphasis.

(i) A statue is suddenly endowed with a life which allows communication with other inanimate objects — the imaginary lamp post or the wishing well. The result is a new perspective on the actions and motives of characters.

(ii) Alternatively, the concept of Brechtian narration is employed and the statue now finds itself directly addressing an audience, or other players in the drama.

(iii) Where a dominant or humourous role has been created, a turn of events or a change in the dramatic situation might reduce or remove the power of the character. The aim of the change is to engage the individual in honest exploration of the character in changed circumstances — the deposed king, an ousted group leader, the clown without an audience. It goes without saying that appropriate teacher encouragement and support accompanies such changes. And, strangely enough, by finding these alternative roles for individuals seems to make peer group approval more forthcoming and genuine. Students are quick to recognise the integrity of each other's work and the satisfaction that comes from honest commitment to the drama. Such achievements are worthy of the increased pride that they feel in their work and learning in drama.

Audience and its Effect on Role Taking

Most of us have at some time experienced the self-consciousness that results from our suddenly being the centre of attention, or having to deliver a prepared speech to an audience. Feelings of trepidation and self-doubt have a way of surfacing. Until the moment arrives it is difficult to give proper attention to other things happening about us. Even the most competent and experienced of actors are beseiged by such anxieties. It seems that when the individual is on show and the success of the moment depends on one's 'performance', these natural anxieties have a way of complicating issues.

In theatre the responses of an audience can significantly alter what happens in the event. Actors feel the responses of the audience and adjust the pacing of their lines, for example, so that greater suspense is achieved or humour highlighted. Some actors inappropriately begin to play to the audience, seeking the thrill of gaining personal attention at the expense of the scene and the play as a whole.

In classroom drama, as we know, the pressure of an audience can result in considerable distortion of dramatic meaning. The teacher as director must be very sensitive and open-minded about using an audience in drama if role creation and symbolic meaning is to be protected. Let's look firstly at just what effect an audience has on expression and communication.

If a friend is one's audience the high degree of responsiveness and support encourages one to indulge in elaborate self-expression. There is no need to be anxious about shaping and ordering statements and signals so that the best possible form is found to express them. There is little real fear, either, that the audience will be unresponsive or critical.

In drama and theatre, the presence of an audience changes the manner of the communication in the following ways.

1 The communicator must now order ideas and present them clearly in dramatic images which can be understood by others. There is, therefore, a concern with form and the external appearance of the drama.

2 It promotes communication at both the 'real social' and the 'dramatic symbolic' level. The drama is shaped because of a direct awareness of the audience as separate individuals and because the communicator wishes to make a personal statement for his/her own benefit.

3 Members of the audience are fully aware of their role as observers. The critical appreciative function of spectator constrains the dynamics of the interaction.

To pursue this more fully we will look at dramatic symbolic role taking and its relationship with audience. John Seely's (1976) imitative role models, 'exploratory', illustrative' and 'expressive', serve as a basis for this examination.

Young children readily engage in the exploratory model of role taking in the course of natural play. It is a private, imitative and imaginative event in which the child explores a range of situations in a totally absorbed and sincere manner. Realism of action is, however, not necessary to its progression or its personal meaning. To adult onlookers external details may seem blurred and inaccurate. Such an interpretation is irrelevant; the importance of the dramatic play lies in its absorption and honesty of commitment. If the players become aware of an audience, dramatic actions are likely to become self-conscious and precocious — commitment to the role is broken. The following example from *Drama and Theatre — A Shared Role in Learning* clearly illustrates the contrast between spontaneous, absorbed dramatic play and that which is affected by an awareness of audience and performance. It also highlights the need for the teacher to understand what the focus of drama is and where the emphasis of action should be.

Some year 5 children were continuing working on a play they had been making about 'being marooned on a dangerous island'. It was the third session on the play and the children had been involved in a number of dramatic activities which focussed on immediate survival and eventual escape. Such horrors as the man-eating plant, which had prevented access to water, and the huge lava monster had to be mastered, if they were to live. After a concerted effort by the class, the man-eating plant (a student teacher in role) lay defeated on the ground. Burning torches had finally killed the deadly leaves! The surge of excitement at their conquest had just subsided when a girl (whose participation in the drama had fluctuated noticeably) moved to the wall of the classroom and, sweeping her right hand to her forehead in a large theatrical gesture, exclaimed loudly, 'Oh, won't someone please, please save me!' The girl was determined to reinforce in her mind, as well as the group's, that what her teacher had said last year about her being 'good' in drama was indeed true.

This exploratory model for dramatic action has been promoted as the ideal basis for drama in education programmes at both primary and secondary level. Teachers have attempted to use exploratory role as a means of broadening students' experiences of the real world. The role of teacher in this process has been somewhat confused by the difficulty of gaining the desired absorption, sincerity and unawareness of audience. On the one hand intervention has been deemed inappropriate to the process; on the other hand, a great deal of effort has been expended in creating an environment necessary for this natural and unselfconscious commitment to play — the blackened space, subdued lighting, etc.

The most common way of approaching the problem however, has been to create whole group drama where everyone is involved simultaneously in the action. This removes the problematic audience, but makes demands on the teacher that we are not always able to meet effectively. Despite this reality, teachers have remained bedevilled by an inflated regard for this type of dramatic role playing, especially in the secondary school. A manifestation of this is found in the endless programmes of relaxation exercises, 'mind trips' and concentration activities that fill out drama lessons. The hope is that with sufficient practice, these desired qualities of absorption and sincerity will be forthcoming. The teacher as director needs to temper the attraction of these child play ideals by paying attention to students' changing use of role and by acknowledging what drama and theatre styles highlight about role taking and the creation of meaning.

The illustrative model of role taking is characterised by students' desire to communicate through the drama. This is made difficult, however, because of adolescent identity confusion and personal vulnerability. Students are keen to use the drama as a means of imitating other people's behaviour to test out or prove points of view. Selfconsciousness is nevertheless a burden which requires sensitive handling by the teacher. Roles cannot always be sustained easily; awareness of observers or particular peers can result in fragmentation of roles and dramatic situations. Exaggerated roles and caricatures manifest themselves in the drama; garbagemen, an old wino, Dracula, school principal, gang leader. Through exaggeration of the story line, the students attempt to entertain the audience. Students hide behind these caricatures and find security in presenting outrageous events in their plays. The student/actor derives a great deal of satisfaction from this performance. The rest of the class is easily involved in the fantasy and enjoys sharing the action. The following example is typical of what occurs in drama at this stage:

The class is exploring the notion of authority and in this improvisation, **A** is playing the role of the principal, while **B** assumes the role of a student who has been caught smoking. During the scene, **A** exaggerates the role of the principal into a tyrannical despot, using snatches of a German accent to complement his loud, authoritative voice. The caricature is further encouraged by the audience's laughter and **B**, struggling to protect his self identity, undermines his partner's character by attacking his authority, telling him how stupid he is and asserting, 'I'll smoke any time I want to!'. Laughter and cheers from the audience are now for **B**.

There is no doubt that the caricatures have entertained, heightened interest and evoked sympathy from observers. There is a general identification with the characters as portrayed; the audience know what is being said about this figure of authority and share the fantasy of **B**'s actions in this situation. Everyone has a laugh, enjoying the moment for its outrageous cathartic nature. The humour is firmly pinned to the group's understanding of what really occurs in such situations. They know the helpless humiliation of submission to authority. Humour, stereotype and caricature express this safely.

Given this stage of development, the following situation is also bound to occur. In a new pair now, **A** takes the role of the principal seriously and, during the improvisation, questions the student about the incident with a concerned, counselling approach. **B**, however, needs the protection of exaggeration and so plays the 'dumb student', giving one-word responses in a 'spazzo' fashion. The audience laughs tentatively at this but the improvisation breaks down.

The teacher's task is not easy. Social role and dramatic role are intertwining and jostling for supremacy. Ways of varying the drama so that new content and different perspectives can be explored are constantly being searched for. Patience and persistence is needed as students are gently encouraged into a greater sense of security within the group and the drama. Firm, supportive control of the critical responses and comments of the peer audience will be needed. The meaning of the drama needs to be kept in clear view if a positive working environment is to be maintained.

Forcing emotional depth in role taking can result in embarrassment and loss of confidence in the teacher. A willingness to understand the concerns and interests of the group is essential. Using approaches (satire and parody for example) which tolerate stereotype and exaggeration as a necessary step towards more subtle learning will reap rewards. Being aware of the reasons why students respond so positively to the messages of *Australia You're Standing in It*, or *Not the Nine O'clock News*, gives us a clue as to how to achieve creative, collaborative interactions with the group. Before long the protection of humour and caricature will be less important. More serious drama will be used to analyse and explore aspects of human relationships.

The expressive role model, according to Seely, occurs naturally in middle and later adolescence. There is now a much easier relationship between actors and audience; individuals are less likely to lose concentration and commitment to role because of the presence of an audience. The nature of dramatic communication resembles that of Brechtian theatre, where the social/political meanings of the drama are as important to the actors as the audience. Entertainment, persuasion and change are functions of the communication. In this sense the drama has a revolutionary emphasis. Content, and the way in which it is presented is heavily stamped with the individuality of the group. All kinds of issues related to adolescence, personal relationships, authority, sexual values, legal rights of students and young people, are likely to become the subject matter of the drama. The teacher as director has a role to play in keeping the messages of the drama sufficiently objectified to avoid overindulgence in subjectivity and self-expression. Historical and cultural perspectives can broaden the group's knowledge and experience in this respect.

One particular piece of student-devised theatre (a year 11 group) consisted, in part, of images which effectively persuaded its audience of the contradictions and absurdities surrounding attitudes towards sex and sex education. In preparing the theatre, historical medical information, legal documents and magazine articles had been used alongside current research into the effects of television on adolescent sexual attitudes. Questionnaires had been carefully prepared and interviews conducted with parents and a range of other adults. Results were used to gain a greater understanding of the group's own feelings about the issues. In a somewhat daring move, doubtless designed to shock as well as entertain, students made a theatrical statement about masturbation which was handled with artistic mastery and intellectual maturity. A balance between subjectivity and objectivity had been struck.

Because the message and the medium of its communication are important to actor and audience, the teacher as director accepts responsibility for guiding the search for 'truth'. This applies not only to the subject matter being explored, but to the artistic expression of its meanings. Reading, research and talking with people provide important background material for the search, but it is through the dramatic exploration and experience of material that personal meanings must be found. When knowledge in the drama has been synthesised, its theatrical form can then be tried and tested through workshops and rehearsal. The teacher continues to focus the group on the meaning of the drama and to find ways of leading the actors into an expression of their meaning in clear artistic images for the benefit of the audience.

Although the audience is a necessary element in the drama at this stage, care needs to be exercised in deciding who the audience will be. As the students are in a very early stage of their performance development, and because the theatre has a specifically didactic function, the audience needs to be small, supportive and interested. Fellow students, friends and family are obvious choices.

As the students mature into later adolescence their personal and dramatic development leads them into drama that now challenges with its variety and depth of roles, and its subtleties of meaning. There is a new confidence of self and a willingness to try out all manner of behaviour as it relates to characters. Formal scripts and the discipline of creating a character whose life is embedded in the language of the play become a new dramatic challenge. The plays of Shakespeare and the ancient Greeks can appeal to students whose love of language and imagery invites them into the play with its age-old messages and modern-day truths. Other students will be attracted by the plays of Williamson, Romeril or Dickens, in which the language and message is distinctly Australian.

Workshopping a range of material helps students to develop an understanding of the different demands made by playwrights on their character development skills.

If performance of a full-length scripted play is to be attempted, the teacher as director needs to understand the implications of the play for the dramatic development of the students — particularly when the wider community and other school populations are to be a part of the audience. In this respect the teacher aims to ensure that the overall experience will not only be a developing one, but pleasurable as well. It is sad to see students lose their confidence and self-esteem after performances which highlighted that their skills were simply not sufficiently developed to allow them to establish adequate, meaningful communication with the audience. If handled intelligently and responsibly, however, the presence of an audience functions positively in deepening the learning experience for the students.

This discussion of role taking and its relationship with audience indicates some generally accepted patterns of role behaviour in the developing individual. Ways in which the teacher as director can use this knowledge to inform classroom actions have also been suggested. The comments and suggestions offered should be seen as a starting point for work with various groups. Obviously the specific nature of the group will then indicate appropriate further directions.

Creating the Role

Characterisation is the development and expression of character — of a dramatic role — by the actor and, of course, the playwright. It is the means by which the playwright distinguishes one character from another in the drama.

An actor's ability to develop and express roles lies at the centre of the drama/theatre event. During the process of characterisation, the words and gestures of characters (dramatic actions) combine to give expression to the plot of the drama. Characterisation is therefore central to the artificial reality of drama and the creation of personal, symbolic meaning.

Defining Character

Much of the role taking that happens in drama does not need elaborately defined character traits. Indeed this kind of elaboration may hinder progression of the action and its learning potential. Information for character definition can be taken from four different characterisation levels (Brockett, 1964): physical, social, psychological and moral.

Physical

Concerned only with details such as sex of character, age, size, colour etc. In terms of dramatic action these details in themselves are not likely to be of much use to the drama.
Character: thirty-year-old, suntanned, slim, blonde female.
  Such a description doesn't really take us anywhere.

Social

Gives us details such as family relationships, business/personal relationships, economic status, occupation, profession, religion, living conditions. The character now has a meaningful context and this is essential to understanding her actions. There is still little chance however of the drama developing significantly.
Character: Female lawyer. Wealthy, unmarried, lives alone in
  tasteful appartment. Aged thirty. Slim, tanned, blonde.

Psychological

Information from this level exposes the character's patterns of thinking and feeling — attitudes, needs, likes, dislikes, motivations, aspirations. Since thoughts and feelings motivate actions, this psychological level is essential to the drama's meaning.
Character: As above, and interested in social justice; has strong
  political ambitions; regards life as dreary and burdensome.

Moral

Moral and ethical principles which underpin character actions usually have the effect of casting a serious, deliberative atmosphere over the drama. If searching at this moral level for a course of action, the character identifies those values which are essential to his/her being. In *A Man for all Seasons*, Thomas More's actions stem from deep moral principles to do with the relationship between God and man. Such principles are voluntarily held and action which tests the strengths of these beliefs can lead serious drama to tragedy.
Character. As above, and believes that women must demonstrate their strength and power to society.
During the drama, such beliefs often highlight contradictions in the character's actions, thereby complicating the plot/s.

Simple Characterisation

A great deal of the drama we set up in classrooms uses simple characterisation as a means of exploring issues. Students select or are given information that is primarily to do with

social details of character. Thus the building of role com-
mences with the concept of scientist, guide, builder, mother,
mercenary, feminist, each of which suggests a range of char-
acteristic behaviours. As a guide I'm obviously going to be
dealing with maps, compasses, people; I can instantly throw
myself into some action — getting maps organised, for example.

If I'm not careful, however, I may find myself involved in
a lot of doing without much meaning. To add that meaning,
detail from the psychological level of characterisation is
needed. The map-reader now has a thinking and feeling level
to inform all actions — 'People depend on me; I can't afford
to make mistakes.' Gavin Bolton (1981) stresses the importance of working from an attitude if the dramatic action is to
be purposeful and understanding is to be changed. Too often
students work in drama with physical and social details of
character only; the resulting drama is sloppy and superficial.
There is plenty of noise and action but the experience is basically empty. Energy goes into the external details of character
and action, and inner motivation for actions is ignored. Some
students may intuitively find their own psychological details
but this can't be guaranteed. How many 'busy' party, market,
or airport scenes have we witnessed where action was insincere and the drama unfocussed? At the conclusion everyone
wonders what there is to reflect on.

Characters and Names
It is handy if characters have names which can be readily
drawn on; 'Hey you', is obviously difficult! Given the opportunity, students often incorrectly select 'interesting' names for
their characters; Harry Butler, or John Leyland — map-
reader and guide; Dr John Jeckel — scientist; Mainey Greer
— feminist. The associations produce interest and hilarity,
but in doing so the focus of the drama is lost. A whole range
of irrelevant business has now been introduced which makes
everyone's job within the drama much more difficult. An important part of the student's learning in drama has to do with
the actors' concepts of economy and efficiency in role taking.
Only those details necessary to the drama's particular moment and meaning are used, otherwise we find ourselves di-
verted from the real purpose of the play. To avoid the
problems of a Dr Jeckel and Mr Hyde, it is better that students use their own names. Despite some teachers' reservations about this practice there really is no cause for concern.
Creating roles and participating in drama means that there
is always an awareness of 'the me' and 'not me'. I know that

I take my name and use it as part of the life of my character.

This simple level of characterisation is often referred to as 'role playing' by drama teachers. Because participants are essentially trying out a range of social roles and learning about their responses within them, they distinguish this aspect of role from notions of characterisation. Such a distinction seems more likely to confuse than clarify the teacher's understanding of learning in drama. A simple level of characterisation is being used, regardless of the learning objectives which may dictate that either experiential, communicative, or expressive dramatic action is emphasised. Obviously it is the level of characterisation that is easiest to use and therefore likely to be the starting point for work in drama. Whilst it is often used in association with spontaneous dramatic playing, this is by no means its natural place. And remember, it is not an end in itself, merely the way into an experience of other dramatic meaning.

Complex Characterisation

The more information the actor has about a character the more difficult creation of role is likely to be. If physical and social details are interwined with psychological attitudes and philosophical beliefs, the character becomes more complex and is capable of responding with far greater subtlety.

Teachers often use role cards as an efficient way of assigning character details, and getting the drama going. Insufficient thought at this early stage, however, can undermine the drama. Care is needed to ensure that the students is not overloaded with details or given too specific details. Sometimes characters are assigned particular involvement in events which have supposedly taken place before the present dramatic situation. The teacher attempts to playwright a background which gives the character insight into the present moment. What happens instead is that the details of prior incidents and actions actually inhibit the drama. When this occurs dramatic actions are likely to be tentative and insincere as the student struggles to remember details and make decisions about character behaviour.

Similar results are likely also if the character has aspirations and/or deep moral convictions which the student has no understanding of. The teacher's directing skills are needed to make the necessary connections between the student's experiences and the attitudes of the character. Some details may need to be modified, others removed. Watching actions and listening to the students' difficulties are essential if teacher and student are to achieve successful characterisation.

A simple way of achieving complex characters is to subtly contrast social and psychological details. Such details offer a solid base from which to work but allow maximum opportunity for the student to build creatively from that point. Of course contrasting personalities between characters will serve to complicate the dramatic action by highlighting specific details of character. In this sense chatacterisation is deepened as the drama progresses.

Some students wrongly assume that their character must doggedly cling to specific attitudes throughout the drama. Although consistency of behaviour is necessary, characters must also respond to the actions of other characters and the events of the drama. A confident, articulate political leader might become anxious and inarticulate in a situation in which a he/she feels threatened. When and if changes occur, they must be truthful responses to the dramatic situation, for they provide the opportunity to learn about the complex nature of human behaviour. A change that is too easily accomplished threatens the credibility of the character and of the drama.

Emotion and Role Taking

When it comes to the business of developing roles in drama, the place of emotion in the event has been hotly debated. Some have been ready to declare that if the individual has 'had an emotional experience', then they've been involved in psychodrama! Others have claimed that unless there has been emotional invovement, then the drama has been a waste of time! The former attitude has resulted in teachers being hesitant about 'using role play' so their classes have been a series of group-devised, humourous skits and a range of communication games. The second belief often resulted in a preoccupation with activities designed to give students practice in experiencing and expressing different emotions. The following example illustrates this point.

A group of year 10 students was told that the lesson was to be spent exploring emotional states — anger, joy fear and pain. Subdued lighting with coloured spots was organised, quiet but appropriately evocative music selected. Students lay on the floor, were talked into a relaxed state and then led through a mental exploration of each emotion. At the end of some forty minutes, the teacher concluded the exercise and asked the students to sit up. Three students, however, had concentrated very well! They remained on the floor in a semi-hypnotic state believing that they were suffering pain to the extent that they couldn't move.

Fortunately such an extreme situation is not common. But there is a range of activities used that place emotions at the centre of the experience. Most of us have been guilty in various ways at some stage in our teaching — movement in music designed to evoke emotional states, walking around the room feeling happy, sad, angry . . . or using an object onto which a range of emotions are projected — joy, frustration, love. Is it any wonder that students feel apprehensive and fellow teachers suspicious about these tasks? What is exposed in these approaches is a misunderstanding of the relationship between role, feelings and actions.

Task, Action and Emotion in Role Development

Stanislavsky aimed to have his actors fully identify and empathise with their characters. To achieve this an actor had to have a range of moods and feelings at his command. Emotional recall was an important step in the role-building process. But what he made very clear in his teaching and directing was that attention should not be focused on the emotion. Instead the concentration had to be on what is to be done and why, on the action and the desire, or motivation for it. Concentration on feelings in general, as in the above examples, will only result in over-acting and untruthful expressions of feelings. In reality, the concepts of pain, joy, fear, etc, will manifest themselves in such a variety of ways in different instances that it is fruitless to engage in generalised expression. Who I am, what my temperament is, whether I am alone, all affect my actions and emotional responses.

Let's look at an example given by Rapaport (Cole, 1947, p. 53) of this relationship between actions and emotions.

> '. . . I am in a hurry to catch a train, my things are in my room, packed and ready; I come for them, but the door is locked and I cannot find the key. In this case a purely physical object confronts me — a locked door, which I have to open to get my things.
>
> The more difficult it is to overcome the obstacle, the more actively the task will develop and the feelings which result from fulfilment of the task will become deeper and more expressive. I shall be upset, angry, annoyed at my absent-mindedness (as I mislaid the key), etc; in a word, I shall experience the same sequence of feelings as would have been aroused if such an accident had happened in real life.'

External tasks were
- (a) to catch the train
- (b) to get the luggage
- (c) to unlock the door
- (d) to find the key

The unlocked door and lost keys became obstacles which made it more difficult to complete the task. At an internal level the task was,
- (a) to will actions not to use up vital time;
- (b) to chastise self for absent-mindedness.

Another example will further highlight the internal nature of the task. I sit outside the principal's office, inwardly working at willing the principal to be merciful and consider my previous good record. Outwardly, my actions may be almost negligible but the internal actions (the counter-action, or what Liv Ullmann referred to as the countermotion) will be reflected in my eyes, the hesitancy or sharpness of certain moves, the general appearance of my body. What I am certainly not doing is concentrating on a particular emotion, fear, for example. That may manifest itself in some way, just as anger, or humiliation may, but it is the internal task, or actions, that produces the feelings. This is why we think of other things in the dentist's waiting room, when thoughts about the coming event result in anxiety and fear. We can turn to the internal task of deciding which movie to go to later, or which shop might offer the most buying pleasure. The action is to sit and wait for your turn in the dentist's chair; the counter-action is to avoid the reality by deciding which movie to see. Conflicting actions will struggle with one another and from the tension a range of emotions will result.

Obviously, in this process of action and counter-action the experience of emotion is inevitable and productive. I have the experience, I understand what motivated my actions and how this affected my emotions. I know more about my character, and more about myself. Both are pre-requisites for expression and communication of character within the drama. If I am guided to reflect upon the experience, the expressive behaviour that was part of it and its meaning, I can move into a process of refining actions for the purpose of theatrical communication. Without this basic knowledge, however, my gestures and intended meaning will be unconvincing. I wring my hands in anxiety, my eyes grow larger and my mouth opens in fear; I skip and smile broadly with joy. In fact I protect myself fully from the experience of genuine emotion and in the process I learn nothing of the subtle realities of human behaviour — the first principle for meaningful drama experiences. Some actors and trained drama teachers admit they cannot use role as a means of exploring and understanding the human condition. Their knowledge comes through other avenues, (observation, reading, discussion) but it remains intellectual and objective; it has never been synthesised and internalised through the dramatic experience. The direct learning power of drama remains a mystery. Dramatic action is viewed, and used, as a purely mechanical technique for 'theatrical' communication or, within the school, as a means of developing positive interpersonal relationships.

If we're working with children, adolescents and young adults in drama, this focus on task and its associated actions is absolutely crucial to healthy personal and dramatic growth. It is fundamental to the individual making contact with his inner self, and to allowing his actions and their associated feelings to be self-generating.

> 'The actor bases ... his understanding on the character's behaviour ... upon the uniquely personal connection which he has made between his unconscious and that of the character. This aspect of characterisation therefore requires the actor to project his deepest feelings into those of the character; this is a necessary aspect of the growth of the role, but one which must be approached with great care and patience.'
>
> (Benedetti, 1976, p. 223)

The task is the legitimate base for the development and expression of feeling in drama. We are surely not wanting to teach the self-indulgent habit of trumping up emotional states at whim.

Sensitivity and common sense are needed, of course, when working at this emotional level with students in early adolescence.

The basis of everything in drama must be this task-orientated action, internal task/external task — action and counter-action. Character, dramatic situation and task. Feelings will naturally take care of themselves.

The teacher as director, in collaboration with the student, holds the key to creative, meaningful drama. By understanding how to achieve a relationship between the individual's personal experiences and the separate artistic identity of the character, a wealth of learning can be contacted. In *The Actor at Work*, Benedetti (1976) comments on the actor's development through the experience of the dramatic event. His words also tell us why we believe that drama is a necessary subject in the school curriculum.

> '... the actor is continually expanding himself, continually having experiences that are inaccessible to the average person. By feeling what it is to live in past ages, in other places, and

inside of people quite different from ourselves, actors find their own lives continually challenged and expanded. The actor who looks only within himself for the materials of creation is robbing himself of vast riches of experience . . . the actor who, on the other hand, refuses to involve himself in his creation, will remain unaffected by the experiences he merely pretends to be having.'　　　　　　　　　　　　　　　　　　　(p. 245)

This book is about acknowledging the relationshop between drama and theatre, between students and actors, teachers and directors. It is about the learning that is embedded for us all in contacting those realities rather than avoiding them.

9 The Teacher as Actor

In theatre the actor is the prime agent in the dramatic, communicative experience. The extent to which the audience identifies with and understands the symbolic artifice of the event rests with the skill and sensitivity of the actors.

In the classroom, the teacher is the central agent in the interactive, educational experience. If students are to be engaged in significant learning encounters, teaching skills must be sufficiently developed to motivate the individual's pursuit of meaning.

Both the dramatic and teaching processes are artificial interventions in the natural course of human development. They are specific attempts to overtly manipulate human encounters for the purpose of promoting individual growth and learning. Any classroom teacher can effectively use the actor's communicative skills as a means of heightening the learning experience. For example, careful attention is paid to vocal and physical gesture, to delivering the same subject material with freshness and vitality, to the skill of improvising productively from the responses and interactions of students.

It doesn't seem unreasonable to expect that the teacher who is also trained in drama is most adequately equipped to use the skills of the actor to achieve good teaching and vitality of learning. The teacher as actor constantly and implicitly applies techniques which allow him/her to capture the class's attention and focus it on the exploration of specific meanings.

The Teacher as Actor (Implicit)

1 Is directly responsible for establishing a creative communicative relationship between teacher, student and subject matter. This requires a thorough knowledge of the lesson script, its 'super objective' and its specific contributing meanings.

2 Uses controlled, discreet, and artificial devices for the purpose of adding impact and liveliness to the learning processes.

3 Is aware that the classroom 'performance' is merely the means to an educational end. Self-centred teaching, like acting, undermines the overall purpose of the event.

4 Chooses a style of communication appropriate to the subject matter. Exaggeration, humour and entertainment may be used alongside a serious, deliberate appeal to the intellect or the emotions.

5 Uses improvisation and exploration as a predominant style of working. Confident input and specific selected offerings from the teacher are as important as the ability to receive, and yield to, the responses and feedback from students. Spontaneously building from interactions towards the exploration of learning objectives is the essence of this improvisation in teaching.

6 Controls, manipulates and varies the use of space and organisation of objects within it (desks, people, aids) to aid the interactive communication process. A teacher 'monologue' delivered from the front of a class is as appropriate and effective in pursuing specific meanings as a circle of students and teacher informally discussing ideas. To vary the proximity of teacher to particular individuals, small groups or objects can capture attention and/or emphasise meaning.

7 Understands the language of physical movement and exploits this in the communication process — a very important aspect of classroom presence and the ability to motivate and stimulate learning.

8 Is skilled in using variety and contrast of vocal gesture to enhance communication, exploration of meaning and management of the group. Variation in volume and pitch, use of pauses and silence, nuance of tone and intonation are essential aids to effective teaching.

9 Uses vocal and bodily gesture —

to enthuse	to focus	to persuade
to coax	to startle	to encourage
to lead	to follow	to chastise
to hypothesise	to support	to evoke
to instruct	to highlight	to negotiate
to criticise	to analyse	to ponder
to inspire	to storytell	to liberate
to evaluate	to search	

10 Never loses sight of the fact that the role of teacher comes before that of actor. Egocentrism, emotional investment, entertainment and applause are words that should not apply to acting skills in the classroom. The less attractive language of teaching duty, pedagogy, educative process and leadership distance should be kept well in mind.

The Teacher as Actor (Explicit)

The teacher's explicit use of the actor's role has become a popular strategy for controlling, upgrading and protecting the quality of the dramatic experience. Sometimes it is used simply as an interesting and evocative means of getting the drama started. Sensitively and intelligently used, this method of intervention can become a forceful, creative aid to dramatic learning.

To achieve this function, the teacher as actor adopts a role which is appropriate to the content and meaning of the drama. The teacher/character is then able to subtly manipulate learning from within the action. Rather than having the teacher constantly interrupt the drama to raise levels of commitment or belief, this can be achieved by the teacher as actor without stopping the natural flow of the students' work. Having the teacher repeatedly control the drama from the outside can become irritating and frustrating for students, even though they may be fully aware that intervention is needed if the drama is to be of a satisfying quality. It is not unusual, when the drama is floundering, for students to quietly signal for help in the hope that some minor intervention by the teacher will solve the problem. It is often appropriate for the teacher to quickly and efficiently intervene directly as actor.

The Nature of the Acting Role

Drama-in-education theorists and practitioners have been careful to discuss the value of 'teaching in role' without emphasising its relationship with acting. Rosemary Linnell (1982) particularly stresses that teaching in role is not acting, but simply a teaching tool. This begs the question somewhat, although of course it is also true. One of the weaknesses of the use of this teaching tool, however, is that it often fails, through lack of 'acting', to serve its function successfully. Any notion of character is deliberately buried, the normal social role — the teacher (confusing, but stay with it) — is so dominant that the dramatic role — the character — is insufficiently developed to achieve the required focus. The dramatic images are blurred and lifeless, the students respond with confusion to teacher authority rather than character actions.

Propping the Role

To make the distinction between teacher and character clear, teachers often enlist the aid of a piece of costume (hat or coat) or a prop of some kind (brief case, walking stick). They explain to the student that when they are wearing or carrying the particular thing, they will be someone else in the drama and not the teacher.

This approach has obvious advantages. Students quickly recognise the external signs of the teacher as character and adjust their responses accordingly. At the same time the teacher feels more confident in entering the drama when supported by these aids.

There are also distinct disadvantages in working this way, however. If the students are expected to communicate their dramatic images without the aid of costume or props, it will seem a little unjust that teacher is allowed this privilege — can't he/she do it alone? The fact is that the teacher's acting becomes a model for the group, whether we like it or not, and this carries certain implications. Whatever the acting role, it has to be efficiently and effectively presented — crisp, clear and believable. It must be capable of adding impact, increasing commitment and intensifying belief. It is an exciting way of implicitly demonstrating the convention of 'I am making it happen, it is happening to me.'

When the teacher relies on aids to promote acceptance of the character, it is very easy to fall into the habit of doing little else. Vocal gesture and movements can remain distinctly 'teacherish' and the vitality that should be brought to the drama is lost. Let's be very clear, however, that it is not being suggested that the teacher has to suddenly deliver some exotic, overplayed performance! That is just bad acting anyway and does nothing more than startle the students and change their participation from actors to audience. The expression of the role will only be developed far enough to efficiently contribute to the direction and meaning of the drama. In theatre one does not expect the telegram boy with two lines of dialogue to overact and upstage the rest of the actors and action; actors and audience, however, must believe in the truth of the moment! Clarity and efficiency should be the hallmark of the actor's role, as it must be for the teacher acting a role.

Another weakness associated with the use of costume/props is that the transition from teacher to character can be cumbersome. If the drama has to be stopped by teacher, the coat or hat must be removed so that the teacher is once again revealed, the article is then replaced to allow the drama to begin again. Not so much of a problem perhaps, when the drama is running well, but awkward when the going is more difficult.

Emphasising acting and character in relation to this teaching strategy is done so that the integrity of the drama will be preserved. The teacher is equally conscious of the teaching and the acting role. A creative, balanced relationship exists between the teaching function and the acting function. The teaching purpose is firmly embedded in the clear dramatic images of the character. Too great a pre-occupation with characterisation and the teacher gets lost to the character and the action of the drama. Too dominant a focus on the teaching role and the intervention is likely to result in pseudo-dramatic teacher direction — indigestion drama, if you like!

When working in the secondary school (and in the greater part of the primary school as well), we tend to underestimate the sensitivity and intelligence of the students when we assume that these added signals of costume or prop are necessary. Greater confidence is needed in the students and in the teacher's ability to give dramatic expression to the selected role. With a little thought, the teacher's speech and body language can be modified sufficiently to characterise the part. This in itself will clearly indicate when the teacher's role in the classroom has changed to actor within the drama.

Playing the Part

Mostly the teacher will find that simple characterisation is all that is required. A social role and a psychological attitude will serve most drama needs very well — the Mayor who wants to keep votes; the engineer who gives his skills only as they are paid for; the elderly citizen who seeks respect and dignity; the misfit who fights for group acceptance. Sometimes a deeply-held conviction can challenge the group into dealing with problems that they would be unlikely to encounter on their own — a stranger warns the group that a curse on the ancient house brings death and ruin to anyone who enters;

an aged citizen refuses to leave his home because this would mean that in death his soul is damned. Physical attributes of the character, age, sex, build, are only important in so far as they may arise from the social details of the role. The Mayor may be young and therefore inexperienced, for example.

When roles of authority are chosen by the teacher, extra care is needed to ensure that words and gestures are different from those normally used in the everyday interactions of the classroom. As chairperson of a conference, for example, it is relatively easy to fall into the trap of using organisational and instructional language that is more appropriate to the classroom situation than the dramatic one. 'This conference is about . . ., you are all here for a purpose . . . there are jobs to be done . . . break into small groups and work out your ideas, prepare a report . . . I'll hand out some paper and textas.' Much greater clarity and impact will be achieved if more formal speech and specialised words are used. 'Welcome to the first national conference on . . . as elected representatives, your ideas and your votes . . . we are charged with the responsibility of . . . small group seminars will discuss agenda items . . . delegates will prepare statements . . . writing materials are available . . .'

What the teacher's character says and does and the manner in which it is done have a powerful influence on the mood of the drama and the quality of the student interactions. If they are challenged to spontaneously interact with a fellow actor, rather than teacher and leader, new dimensions of exploration and extension are possible. Interactions in the drama won't be curtailed because students feel the teacher is looking for a particular answer or response. They will have to find the most appropriate way of dealing with this new personality; there will be no set rules of classroom behaviour, only the conventions of the drama to guide them. It is therefore vital that when the teacher plays the part of an authority figure, the acting is sufficiently pronounced to invite creative freedom. John Norman (1982) suggests that if roles are selected which are very different in status from the accepted teacher authority, students have more chance of being liberated within the drama. Thus characters who are weak, who do not know, who ask naive questions or who lack courage can place new responsibilities and dilemmas at the feet of the student actors. Of course characters who have power and respect because of their social or economic status, can complicate matters by assuming psychological attitudes which reduce their personal status. A king may not be able to make decisions on his own; an army officer is unable to muster the courage needed for the final attack.

At times the teacher's choice of character or manner of presentation is such that students find it difficult to constructively handle the intervention. Outrageous or sensational characters and actions can startle and/or embarrass the students; their commitment to and belief in the drama is lost. In one particular lesson, year 9 students wanted to act out a party scene. During the drama, the teacher sensed that something needed to happen for the drama to become significant. Suddenly, teacher appeared as a 'one-legged' character dragging himself confidently towards the rest of the group — 'Hi, I've only got one leg but I've come to join the party . . .'

The incongruity of the character's physical state combined with the surprise of teacher playing such a part spelled disaster and the drama disintegrated. What the teacher had hoped to achieve was a deepening of the superficial, stereotyped interactions of 'the party'. In this case, intervention of a different kind was needed.

Taking the First Step

Sometimes teachers are reluctant to play a part in the drama because they fear the negative reactions of the students — the initial giggling, the self-consciousness, the withdrawal or, alternatively, the precocious, over-confident response. Quite obviously, the experience of seeing teacher from this new perspective is unusual and it may take time for some groups to learn how to cope productively with the idea. If this is so, the teacher may find it less problematic if authority roles are chosen, and teacher's character spends a considerable amount of time within the drama. Playing judge in a court trial, or a government official on a research mission offers scope for giving focus to the drama, as well as managing the group. Such roles allow the teacher to hand over the action and direction of the drama for differing periods of time but always with the possibility of quickly exerting authority and control when needed. As the group experiences the satisfaction of building exciting, focussed drama with their teacher, this way of working becomes easily accepted. Once this stage is reached, the teacher will have little difficulty in moving in and out of the drama using a range of characters for different teaching reasons.

A gentle and effective way of introducing the idea of teacher as actor is to begin the drama session with a short piece of character work. The teacher simply explains that today he/she will briefly appear as a character and what happens will be important for the rest of the drama. All the group has to do is watch and listen, to remain as themselves, and respond as an audience to the action. Discussion will then follow. Thoughts and feelings evoked by the drama provide the basis for the rest of the lesson. The possibilities are limitless; the teacher's selection of character and situation will be suggested by the aims and content of the lesson script.

- A crime boss might make a telephone call to a partner in a respected government position . . .
- A commonwealth official speaks to the group of the aims and responsibilities of the secret space mission . . .
- 'Emily Pankhurst' delivers a short speech to a band of suffragettes . . .
- An elderly person who lives alone communicates something of the pride and loneliness of old age . . .

An advantage of working this way to begin the drama is that the teacher can endow the group with general roles and feelings. These are then made more specific in the ensuing drama as particular characters are chosen and situations explored. For the students, there is a sense of participating in a game, an adventure with unknown consequences. Because of this, their attention is easily gained and a dramatic focus is established from the outset.

Should there be initial giggles in response to the action, the teacher's character has the opportunity to deal with them if the concentration of others is affected. Sensitivity is needed, however, because often the giggles quickly subside as the drama continues and individuals begin to identify with the character and the situation. The 'crime boss' may suddenly wish to cut short the telephone call because voices can be heard. The teacher/actor listens, looks to find the source of sound, and in doing so gives the student/s time to settle into the action. If this doesn't happen, the phone call is ended and the drama stops. When the incident is discussed, the group may decide that they would like to hear more of the phone call to see if they can pick up some clues as to what is going on. The drama recommences and a significant piece of information is communicated which adds interest to the drama and rewards the group for its attention! Sometimes the character may talk directly to the student group, chastising them for their lack of sensitivity to the character, or the situation. As the comments are made within the context of the drama, the group is invited to respond as players in the game, and more often than not they do so.

Enlisting the help of one or two students can also be an easy and interesting way of getting started with teacher as character.

- Soldiers (the students) may get caught by a sentry (the teacher) as they attempt to plan a seige. The consequences of the action are made clear.
- Gang members swear oaths of secrecy and carry out deeds of allegiance for their leaders.

Whatever happens, the drama must be believable. The teacher's acting must therefore be sufficiently focussed and truthful to draw the same quality responses from the students.

The Direction of the Drama

When the group discusses this introductory action as preparation for the drama that follows, comments should focus on:

1 *Facts clearly stated in the drama.* These will have been purposefully fed into the action by the teacher, according to the content and aims of the lesson. Dates, times, characters, details of situation may be important.
2 *Things inferred by the action.* Two or more details which make suggestions at a sub-plot level, for example. Students will need to be aware of the more subtle details of characterisation and their implied meanings. Establishing the relationship between these meanings is also a necessary part of this process.
3 *What is not yet known.* By using the known or inferred facts as a starting point, those things which need to be known for the situation to be more fully understood can be isolated. Different perspectives and viewpoints can be identified as possible avenues for exploration in the drama. Background details in relation to characters or the situation may provide access to the motives or circumstances that lead to human behaviour.

The Teacher as Actor/Demonstrator

To conclude this chapter, it is worthwhile cautioning against the use of teacher's acting as a demonstration technique during rehearsal. Directors sometimes find that an actor is not giving expression to a character in a satisfactory way and resort to demonstration as a means of achieving success. 'Do it like this' or 'Watch me' is hardly conducive to creative problem solving or development in professional actors or students. Puppet-like imitation of the teacher's characterisation only inhibits and retards the student's role creation. A more fruitful approach is for the teacher to adopt a character (perhaps one outside of the text) and improvise a situation with the student which approximates that of the play. Hopefully, teacher's character can challenge and goad the student into exploring at a level which exposes important aspects of the character's behaviour.

Despite this caution, there is no doubt that the teacher as character has enormous potential for promoting students' learning and development in drama. As an aid to experiential dramatic action it could well be argued that it is an essential teaching tool. It is most productive to use this strategy from the very start, before ideas are fixed about what happens in drama and what part the teacher will play in the process. The longer that students accept that the teacher is the leader or director but never an actor, the more difficult it will be to confidently apply the teaching technique.

10   Knowing What to Say

It is clearly impossible to do drama without learning about language. Tone of voice, the use of particular words and the way we use our bodies as we speak are all part of the equipment being tested and sharpened in drama; attention to these details exposes the subtle meanings of the dramatic event. And because the individual experiences a range of different roles and situations, knowledge is also gained about the appropriateness of language in particular circumstances. Good drama can teach effectively about language because its use is tied to personal experience and action.

Characterisation and Language

Sometimes students find themselves unsuccessfully trying to build roles. They take on, or are given, a role for which they cannot match language. A struggle begins, belief in the drama wavers and the role breaks down. Let's look at the following example.

A year 9 girl is attempting to play a 'union boss' in a drama about factory working conditions. She finds herself needing to address a group of agitated 'workers', but nothing happens. She stands self-consciously before the group, struggling to grab hold of words which would allow the drama to flow. The role is abandoned and she pleads for help, 'I don't know what to say.' Teacher appropriately stops the drama and although others are volunteering to take on the role this does not happen. Through questions, discussion and suggestions, the group helps to solve the problem. Fairly quickly, a way of identifying with the role is found as someone suggests being a union boss is a bit like being a footy coach. It suits well, a spark of recognition lights up the girl's face and she is quickly making connections with her attempts in role. Back in the drama she finds the language of force and persuasion. She now deals with the questions and statements from the group — she gets a hard time of it, but she holds the role.

Knowing what to say in role is not always easy, especially in roles of high responsibility and leadership. When students are keen to attempt such roles, the teacher may have to work very hard to find ways of making the experience achievable and meaningful. Quite concrete suggestions may need to be made about 'possible things to say'. If necessary the 'prepared speech' technique can be used within the improvised drama. To achieve this, students out of role take time to think about what is to happen next. In the above drama, the workers could be asked to think about their attitudes and personal positions, and to prepare a range of questions and statements that they may want to use. The union boss works with teacher (and a couple of union representatives, if appropriate) to prepare an official address. Responses to possible questions are discussed and ways of avoiding difficult comments are considered.

A golden opportunity now exists for the students' language to be extended. Whilst it is important that the speech is thoroughly understood by the student, phrases likely to be used in a particular context can be selected — 'a log of claims', 'over-award payments', 'picket lines', 'work to regulations', 'solidarity', 'scabs', etc. At times appropriate support material can be found and used to help students with the language of drama. A newspaper report on union strife is just one example. Excerpts from a range of literary sources can provide stimulus for the use of a particular language style or vocabulary selection. The language of historical novels, for example, or words that define particular religious or social beliefs — Christianity, feminism, conservation, aboriginal mythology. Patterns of behaviour are suggested by the language, a mood is cast and the drama takes on vitality and wholeness.

Words and phrases from particular literary sources can be used as basic information upon which roles and situations can be built. Similes and metaphors provide excellent stimulus for making drama and extending language skills. Detailed suggestions for developing drama in this way are found in Part Three.

By carefully selecting stimulus material of high quality (and this may include paintings, photographs, or actual objects), it becomes relatively easy to move the language of the group into levels of formality and precision not normally experienced. So often drama is structured so that it requires only the informal colloquial words and gestures of everyday interactions.

If we take the task of students creating a ritual in drama, the formalising of speech and gesture is easily illustrated. Movements, words and objects used must be carefully selected for their symbolic power. Used in conjunction with an exploration of myths, legends and the functioning of groups in society, the drama explicitly challenges and extends the students' facility in language and their understanding of the power and function of language.

The teacher as character offers another important strategy for helping students with the language and meaning of the drama. A simple but formal, perhaps quiet, 'Why do we do such a thing?', rather than the usual, 'What are we doing that for?' creates significant impact in the drama. The pace is interrupted, the moment is heightened, focus on the event is sharpened and the implications of actions are called into question. Students respond to the impact, their language and movements will be changed with the effect of the words. The teacher need do very little else.

Drama Vocabulary

Because the relationship between drama in education and theatre has been somewhat mysterious and confusing, many teachers have felt very apprehensive about using language that implied that a relationship clearly existed. When junior students talked about acting and making up plays, teachers felt anxious lest the focus of drama be taken from the individual's 'personal and social' development. Although the subject on the timetable was still called drama, and that was another problematic question, actors, characters and plays never seemed to get a mention. Amongst the games and exercises, students could be asked to 'imagine that they were a gang leader' or 'see what might happen if . . .'

Such foundation attitudes in a subject take a long time to change. But in the eighties it is time for drama to acknowledge its meaning and its function in the growth of the individual. Part of that acknowledgement entails the use of a specific vocabulary.

If we want our students to develop to their fullest capacity, part of our task in teaching drama is to teach about drama. We are obliged to find ways to demystify the dramatic process so that students know how to gain access to it. Any area of study is characterised by a vocabulary that describes particular aspects of its processes. Establishing an understanding of this language is simply a quick and appropriate way of working efficiently; the vocabulary teaches directly about the subject.

Teaching drama's specific vocabulary is not something that needs to be handled like a spelling list, however. If the need for vocabulary springs from the action of the drama itself a much healthier relationship between the words and their function will be established in the students' minds. As the students' knowledge and skills in drama increase, added demands are made for vocabulary which describes them. What is required at year 7 will obviously differ from year 10.

Let's take an example of the first drama class with a year 7 group. The administrative preliminaries of roles have been dealt with, organisational details of where to put bags and shoes and how to sit in a circle have been completed. You've introduced yourself and the children have done the same. Maybe you've played a name game and already you and the group have begun the process of settling in together. It is now time to talk about drama. Your students need to know what this particular subject is all about, and you need to know what they think it is all about. The knowledge and expectations that they bring to drama will be an important consideration in the way you approach your teaching.

Teacher: O.K. Now that we have started to find something out about each other, let's see if we can find out something about drama. Hands up and tell me anything you can about drama. (Depending on the school's context, and the particular group, you may need to do more prompting and coaxing than this.)

Students: (A range of responses something along these lines usually follows.) It's acting . . . in plays . . . like Cop Shop . . . miming . . . playing games . . . singing and dancing . . . like Fame . . . Paul Hogan . . . being embarrassed doing stupid things . . . acting out scripts . . . having fun . . . using your imagination.

Mostly what has been offered by the students can be used to build upon. Out of the initial discussion the teacher is able to quickly isolate the important basic ideas for the students' understanding of drama.

1 Drama is making plays.
2 People (actors) create imaginary people (characters) and act out different situations as if they were really happening. They 'step into' other people's shoes and behave 'as if they were those people.

3 When we watch the play (like *A Country Practice*) we make believe it is really happening, although at the same time we understand that it is Penny Cook or Grant Dodswell who are acting as though they are Vicki Dean and Doctor Bowen. When actors play other people they learn about what it's like to be those people. When we watch the characters we also learn what it is like to be those people.

Teacher: When you're doing drama then you're in a make-believe world. It's something like telling someone a huge joke, or a made-up story, and trying to get them to believe in it. The difference is that in drama everyone knows it's really made up, so that can make it harder. I'm going to tell you a story now and I want you to ask me questions or make comments of your own as though you really believe what I'm saying . . .

'About 10 o'clock last night, I received, by special courier, a letter with the government's red seal on it . . . etc . . .' (It's important that as the story is told, teacher assumes the role of someone else; a spy, for example.)

After this, a quick discussion of what made the make-believe successful can take place. Through comments and questions you can isolate the following as essential to doing drama.

Concentration

(or **focus**, if you prefer to disassociate the term from what students are constantly being asked to do)

In language which is appropriate to the group, emphasise the nature of concentration and focus. For example, in real life we can choose to focus our attention on a particular thing (reading a book) or it can be focussed without us being aware of it — a sudden loud noise grabs our attention, for example. When this happens, we lose concentration on the book and it becomes hard to keep reading. When our attention is distracted while we're doing drama, what we do and say isn't as convincing; it's hard to believe in what's going on because we're only half doing it.

When we concentrate all our attention and we're fully focussed (like getting a clear picture through a focussed camera), the drama happens easily and seems believable.

Support

Everyone has to co-operate to help keep attention focussed on what is happening in the drama. If an actor forgets what he/she is supposed to be doing or breaks into a fit of giggles, the drama breaks down and has to start again. (Some of the students will know of Peter Seller's notoriety for messing up scenes by laughing). Sometimes outlandish ideas or 'red herrings' are introduced which make it difficult for the drama to continue so that it is believable. Talking about why the drama breaks down helps everyone understand how to offer appropriate support.

Fun

Have you ever heard actors say they didn't love what they do? Although they might work hard at it, they seem to have more fun than most other people . . .

Enough talking — it's time to get the students applying what they have learnt.

Task

Students find a partner and spread out around the room so that there is plenty of space to work in. This helps to keep attention focussed on what you are doing, rather than other people. One person has to make up a 'tall' story and the other will ask questions or make comments about it as we did before. And remember that you have to help each other to believe in what is being said. During the task, teacher keeps a close eye on the interactions and helps where needed to get a story going, or to focus attention.

The above examples are given merely to illustrate how important drama concepts are introduced at the outset. Students are given access to some of the tools that help them understand and create in drama. The concepts and the vocabulary will change as experience in drama develops.

The Language of Reflection

Drama is as much about thought processes and intellectual development as it is about feelings and aesthetic development. The two cannot be separated. Students, like actors, directors and playwrights, need to understand the many parts of the drama experience if they are to comprehend and control the whole.

In life our ability to make sense of experience, to order, categorise, build meaningful connections, is a major factor in healthy psychological and intellectual development. The process of reflection, and the skills of analysis and interpretation are therefore essential companions to experience.

In drama, teachers and students are often at a loss to know how to enter into the reflective process. After the drama everyone seems confused about what to say. Of course, sometimes there may not have been a great deal happening that needs discussion! On the other hand an experience that has been significant is often followed by spontaneous discussion which helps to clarify meanings. Other experiences leave students feeling puzzled as to what things were really all about anyway. The teacher is then needed to lead discussion which demystifies and crystallises the experience.

Knowing what questions to ask during reflection and discussion is often problematic for teachers. Vague questions and comments are tossed about the group, never really finding the concrete focus needed for clear learning, or heavy, laboured discussions result. The drama has obviously not provided sufficient stimulus for a meaningful discussion but the teacher is nevertheless intent on seeing that 'connections' are made with the objectives of the particular tasks.

Successful reflection and discussion needs to operate from a framework which is solid and clear.

1 Lesson objectives — that is, the purpose of the drama experiences — need to be clearly understood by the teacher. If adequate thought and preparation has occurred, then this will be so. Changes of direction in the running of the lesson may happen, but the teaching justification for this must be kept clearly in mind.
(a) What are we doing?
(b) Why are we doing it?
(c) How are we doing it? (This asks questions about the motivation and focus of the group, as well as the drama methods and strategies being used to pursue the learning. It results from a consideration of (a) and (b).
2 Learning objectives must be capable of challenging and extending. If students are merely experiencing simple concepts already understood, then the need for reflection and discussion is removed.
3 Questions must be specific enough to evoke insights and meaningful responses. If the teacher is working at vague, abstract levels of meaning, the students' ability to reflect on the event is inhibited.
4 Connections need to be clearly made between concrete responses and abstract concepts. Discussing the differences and similarities between ideas and experiences within the drama helps establish basic links necessary for such connections and clarity of understanding.
5 The language used by the teacher needs to be appropriate; difficult abstract vocabulary should be avoided. The teacher needs to be able to translate all abstractions into concrete examples, and vice versa. The nature of the

question and the thought processes demanded of the students in answering it need to be understood if discussions are to be fruitful in clarifying and extending the students' learning. Some brief examples of questions and their function in the drama follow.

Timing Questions

Before and during the drama	to	clarify details, find direction, explore perspectives, deepen and extend ideas, build character, deepen commitment
After the drama	to	objectify experiences, crystallise meaning, broaden understanding

Framing Questions

It is vital that questions are sufficiently open to evoke responses rather than impose them. Closed questions invite yes or no responses.

e.g. Do you think the play was good?
       Do you feel the leader was cruel?
       Were the aliens fair in their treatment of the prisoner?
       Did you notice how well they used the space?
       Did you like the special way they talked?

Open questions are more efficient in finding meaning, and more satisfying to respond to. They ask for considered, deliberate choices to be made.

e.g How would you describe the leader's behaviour?
      Why do you think the aliens treated the prisoner that way?
      In what way do you think things might have changed had the leader been willing to listen to the aliens?
      What effect was created by the use of a special language?
      What effect did the long silence have when the aliens approached the leader?
      What did the play teach us about people's behaviour in unknown situations?

Analysis

These questions relate to concrete, specific details of the drama. They are simple comprehension questions that relate directly to what can be seen and heard — **facts** that have been clearly established during the action.
These questions test
— that at a simple level perceptions are valid and undistorted;

— the extent to which what is offered in the drama is absorbed rather than blocked;

— sensitivity to detail and thereby encourage and increase awareness.

Questions are typically of the who, what, where, when, why and how variety.

e.g. Who suggested they wag school?
Why did John decide they should ask Dick to join them?
What reason was given for the wagging?
Where were they when the idea was first mentioned?
When did Harry decide that they would forge notes to explain their absence?
How did the group react to this idea?

Synthesis

These questions are more difficult. They ask the students to find, amongst the detail, the main idea or focus of the drama — the 'super objective' in Stanislavskian terms. Depending on the degree of complexity within the drama, such a broad question may well be the first question asked. Care is needed, however. Students often have difficulty in understanding meanings at this level, because they have not understood details of the drama at the simple comprehension level. A typical question would be,

What do you think this scene/play was about?
What main idea do you think this group was trying to get across to us?

(To broaden understanding and elevate language; the answer can be moved into the abstract!)

'It was about injustice and suffering.'
'They were trying to show that students must make decisions about their own educational programmes.'

If this is the first question asked, the simple analytical details which support the response can then be brought to light.

On refining and polishing a piece of work for an audience, students must know the main focus of the work if they are to decide what can be emphasised or disregarded.

Inference

These questions can require students to be aware of very subtle actions within the drama. Questions relate to:

(a) Ideas intentionally implied but not made explicit. For example, 'Can you tell us what gave you the feeling that Tom had an inferiority complex?'

(b) Judgements or deductions (two or more) which grow logically from the drama — the facts or details seen or stated. For example, 'What makes you think that the boys aren't very good at Maths? . . . are afraid of getting poor results?'

Analogy

Questions need to be firmly linked to the lesson objectives. They broaden and deepen learning by asking for connections to be made at a personal, social, historical, cultural and universal level. If questions are moved into the abstract, general level, students can be protected from the pressure to relate specific incidents from their own lives. 'Can you think of other situations:

— where rules are broken because responsibilities can't be faced?

— where boredom leads to anti-social behaviour?

— where self-interest harms innocent people?

— where apathy has led to evil?'

Hypothesis

Discussions which reflect on the drama allow past experiences to be brought to the present moment so that sense can be made of what has been seen/heard/felt. It is then possible to hypothesise about the future.

— 'What might have happened if Dick had refused to join the group?'

— 'What is likely to happen if the teacher finds the notes are forged?'

— 'In what ways was the drama the same as/different from real life?'

— 'What part of the drama do you feel was the most true to life?'

Form and Organisation of the Medium

These questions deal with how the ideas or information were organised and presented. They are concerned with identifying elements of the art form and dramatic principles, and examining the extent to which dramatic meaning was highlighted. For example,

— 'What was it about the action that made us feel the leader's strength?'

— 'What effect did it have when Frank moved right across to the window before he spoke?'
— 'What could have been done to make us feel the prisoner's desperation/helpessness/isolation/more? The terror of waiting more? The sense of hope more?'
— 'What changes of mood were noticeable during the scene?'
— 'What are the different parts that we could divide the play/scene into?'

Feedback and Evaluation

Specific questions sometimes need to be asked to give the teacher clear feedback about the progress and achievement of the lesson. Responses allow the teacher to gain insight into the effectiveness of the specific strategies adopted. They also help students to crystallise their experiences and learning within the role and the drama situation. As dramatic action is both intellectual and emotional in nature, questions focus on:

Feelings

Students may be asked to identify the range of emotions experienced as a result of the action — the strongest emotion, any unexpected or surprising feelings, etc. Words which express these emotions are sought; for example, frustration anger, fear, confusion, exhilaration. Many students find the task difficult and want to tell you what they were trying to achieve in the drama instead. Time and patience is needed — both aspects need to be understood, that is, the motive for action in the specific situation and the feelings evoked.

Thoughts and Ideas

So that the emotional experience of the drama is tied to its cause and related to the learning objectives, a statement that objectifies the experience is called for. A general question may be sufficient; for example,

— 'What do you think you learned from your experience in the drama?'

A more specific question, however, may focus attention more effectively.

— 'What did you/we learn about, courage/justice/deprivation?'
— 'Name one thing that you feel the drama told/showed you about the notion of family, guilt, revenge.'

The important aspect of these questions is that each individual is given an opportunity to respond. If the teacher is to further understand the drama medium and the effectiveness of various structures and strategies in highlighting learning, a broad range of individual responses must be gained. Of course this process of evaluation also helps students to isolate the strengths and weaknesses of their own participation and commitment to the drama. Honest interpretation of actions and motives is also a pre-requisite for positive evaluation of the drama experience.

Students help teachers just as much as teachers help their students in knowing what to say to make good drama happen.

PART THREE:

The Drama Lesson.

Introduction: Guide to Part Three

Note to Teachers

1 It is important that the following lessons are approached in conjunction with an understanding of the concepts discussed in Parts One and Two. The role of the teacher as director in collaborating with students in the making of the drama is of particular importance. Clearly, modifications to lessons may occur in response to the needs of teacher and students.

2 In presenting the lessons a range of content and styles has been selected so as to meet the needs of both beginning and experienced teachers in drama.

3 Although year levels and age groups are prescribed, in many instances the lessons can be readily adapted for other age groups.

4 The first lesson example provides a comprehensive description of the way in which the concepts discussed in Parts One and Two are applied to the lesson script. This description will be a useful guide for implementing other lessons presented in Part Three.

11   Drama Lessons for Year 7

VOYAGE TO A DISTANT PLANET

*Teacher as playwright —
unity*

Approximate age: 11/12 Years.
Time: 100 minutes (2 × 50 minutes)
Topic: Voyage to a Distant Planet
Focus: Place

Specific Objectives

*Human development
objective*
Art form objective

1 To examine the effects of a specific dilemma on a range of individual characters.
2 To develop the expressive skill of movement in order to add meaning to the
  drama.

Materials

1 Council record sheet (see below)
2 Pens
3 Exploration party instruction sheet.

*Teacher as director —
Levels of characterisation*

Physical
Physical
Social
Social

Council Record Sheet

1 Name ....
2 Age ....
3 Nationality ....
4 Names of other family members
  ....
  ....
  ....

Social
Psychological

5 Occupation ....
6 What do you value most in your life?
  ....

Psychological

7 Circle *one* or more words which best discribe how you feel about this voyage. This information is confidential and will be used only in the event of extreme crisis.

terrified   excited   shocked
nervous   sad   proud
resentful   afraid   other ....

8 Last Will and Testament:
In case of fatal accident or non-return, list possessions and to whom you wish to leave them.

....
....
....
....
....

Signed ....

Conducting the Lesson

Complementary drama — preparing the event — surprise beginning to create initial impact. Teacher as leader selects five students according to perceived degree of likely co-operation in achieving appropriate atmosphere.

Introduction: The Gathering (naturalistic style — see chapter 7) Students are seated in rows on floor in middle of room. Teacher selects five students to sit on chairs on raised rostra at end of room. Teacher explains that he/she will enter as a character and this will begin the drama. Teacher as character enters and joins group of five on rostra.

Teacher as actor and verbal playwright — sets direction of drama.

Says, 'Welcome! As you know, I am the Chairman of the Earth Council in this year, 1993. You are probably wondering why you have been brought to the Council meeting chambers. My Council members (points to the five students) and I will be accompanying you on a voyage to a distant planet in order to determine whether we can establish a settlement for Earth people there. The landscape and climate on this planet are similar to Earth's and settling there would greatly help Earth's over-population problems.

Teacher as actor — uses repetition and solemn tone to heighten signifiance of the event.

'*You have* been selected for your excellent organisational abilities. *You have* been selected for your good health. *You have* been selected for your pleasant personalities and your courage. *You have* no choice but to accompany us. This is a government order. Your families here on Earth will be well looked after. The voyage will take five months only. Here is your opportunity to do something significant for the survival of Earth. It is important that we keep accurate records of you on our files. My Council members will now distribute the council record sheets. Fill them in accurately.

The five selected Council members distribute pens and paper, collect them when completed and submit to Chairman.

Teacher as leader — identifies facts clearly stated, things inferred and things not yet known about the drama.

Reflection and Discussion

Individual responses to the beginning of the drama.

Key Questions
1 Who were the most important members of the group?
2 How was the space in the room used to make this clear?
3 Why do you think the Council would want to keep the word you circled a secret?
4 What dangers might exist for such a journey?

Teacher as director

Movement Exercise (Skill Development)

Side-coaches for appropriate commitment and movement expression using internal and external tasks as basis for action.

Students practise the way they will have to move on distant planet:
gravity slightly less than Earth.
movements are slightly slower than on Earth, but faster than on Moon.
does not affect speed of speech.
Don't allow 'astronaut' movements or slow-motion movements. Set students specific external tasks to do slowly; eg.

1 Internal task — ensure care taken not to damage contents.

1 Unpacking a crate.

2 Internal task — hope soil selected will offer important findings.
3 Internal task — hope that photos will be better than everybody else's.

The drama event. Teacher as leader/director explains task and collaborates with students to set up room as spaceship and planet environment. Use of space important for future student engagement in the drama. Collaborate with students regarding exploration party groupings and tasks on board ship and during exploration. Random selection of groups or as dictated by special needs of class.

Teacher as actor/playwright — to heighten dramatic tension, mention that exploration parties must include a range of experts in case any one group does not survive. Students in role must be given time to respond. If this proves difficult, the drama is stopped, possible occurrences are discussed, and the drama recommences. Internal task — determined to be courageous and worthy. Teacher as actor/playwright designates new direction for drama.

Internal task — musn't show fear. Hope that no danger emerges.

2 Collecting soil samples in a bag.
3 Taking a photograph of the landscape.

Whole Group Improvisation: The Planet

(Naturalistic Style — See chapter 7)

Characters
A Teacher
B, C, D, E, and **F** Council members. Authoritative, enjoy leadership role — fear of the unknown.

Others: Characters described on Council record sheet. Determined to be courageous and worthy of selection.

Situation
All seated in spaceship. Safely arrived on planet.

1 Chairman addresses explorers, explaining that they don't really know what will happen once they step outside ship. To record the details of the voyage so far, each explorer is asked to state one important event that has happened during the journey. The five Council members are asked to record these statements on the Space Log Tape.

2 Alighting from the spaceship and exploring the planet. Chairman emphasises the unknown about to be explored and warns the explorers of the need for care-

ful and quiet actions. Announces that
one Council worker will accompany each
exploration party of five people.

Exploration parties will set off in different
directions. Council members have a list of
instructions. Need to return before night-
fall, as temperatures drop considerably
when sun goes down. Names each party
and tells them a direction to explore.
(Reinforce necessary slow movements.)

Exploration Party Instruction Sheet
1 The Councillor is in charge of the party,
  and has all necessary equipment.
2 Collect various soil samples in bags.
3 Photograph surrounding landscape.
4 Collect various plant samples.
5 Collect water samples (if there are any).
6 Write a list of any unusual observations.
7 One member will act as timekeeper.

*Teacher as actor/director —
responsive to students
playwrighting the drama.
Teacher as playwright —
depending on student
characters. Alternative to
lesson script may need to
evolve. What, why and how
of new drama directions
need to be kept clearly in
mind.*

(Allow sufficient time (five to ten minutes)
for task completion. Teacher as character
oversees all operations, questioning the
group members and leaders about details
of their findings.)

*Teacher as actor/playwright
— dilemma of time used to
heighten impact.*

When appropriate, Chairman announces
that they have forgotten the time, and will
not make it back to the ship in time. Each
party has to find a way to survive the night.
Councillors still in charge. Remind students of the slower movements in the
gravity.
Out of role, teacher and students discuss
implications of surviving the night.

Teacher as director in collaboration with students. Suggestions for direction of drama made. Alternatively, teacher introduces surprise, e.g. one party member missing, strange message left in sample jar.

Suggestions

1 Findings must be protected? Night watch may be needed.
2 A way to protect against cold found; e.g. building a shelter, huddling together, lighting a fire.
3 One explorer disappears . . .
4 Footprints discovered leading to a tunnel . . .

Teacher as actor/playwright

Reporting Back: The Next Day

(naturalistic style) Chairman asks each group to plan a report on the night's events and any implications for the success of the voyage and the safety of the group as a whole. A member (not Council member) of each exploration party is selected to present a short report, giving initial impressions of planet environment, etc.

Teacher as director — language theatrics (see chapter 8) to create impact. May have to stop drama to help students find appropriate use of the art form elements to communicate the atmosphere implied by their report.

Language Theatrics

Students sum up how they managed to survive, in two or three sentences only, as tape space aboard ship is extremely limited. The manner in which the sentences are delivered should convey the atmosphere of the situation.

Situation. Safely back in the spaceship. Parties seated in rows before Chairman. Each representative gives a verbal report to the Chairman.

Complementary drama Teacher as leader — encourage the less vocal participants in the drama to offer response.

Reflection and Discussion

Discuss thoughts and feelings within the drama events.

Key Questions

1 What effect did the moments of silence have on the making of the drama? The behaviour of the characters?
2 To what extent did the slower movements help you to believe in what happened in the drama?
3 What effect did the problem of surviving the night have on the behaviour of the individual characters?

Teacher as leader/playwright — Helps group find possible new directions for the drama.

4 What might happen next in the drama?

THE ORIGIN OF THE AUSTRALIAN CONVICTS — Lesson 1

Approximate age: 11/12 years
Times: 100 minutes (2 × 50 minutes)
Topic: The Origin of the Australian Convicts — Lesson 1
Focus: Event

Specific Objectives

1 To explore the influence of greed and self-interest on human behaviour.
2 To examine the cause and effects of criminal behaviour.

Materials

Description of origins of transportation (see below) The 1839 Constabulary Commissioners' Report on Vagabondism of the Young (see below)

Conducting the Lesson

Complementary drama

Introduction. Teacher reads description of origins of transportation (below). Discussion — some students may have seen *Oliver Twist.*

A Description of the Origins of Transportation

In England in the eighteenth century, jails were extremely overcrowded and the crime rate was ever-increasing. The British government believed that convict labour in Australia would be an inexpensive way to establish the new colony. Before this time, criminals in England had been given the choice of a death penalty or exile (being banished from the country) to the West Indies or other colonial parts. In those days over 250 separate offences carried the death penalty. There was no police force in England in the eighteenth century and the death penalty was applied to even small crimes such as pickpocketing or stealing small amounts of money. Members of the public could apprehend criminals and turn them in to the officials.

Many people were extremely poor in those times. There were no unemployment benefits and very few people had any education, so many people were forced to steal in order to feed their families. Many criminals were young children, aged 14 or 15 years. Many of these children were transported to Australia in the late eighteenth century.

Many of these children were vagabonds — living in the streets, either running away from or being neglected by their parents and struggling to survive.

Teacher reads 1839 Constabulary Report:

Vagabondism of the Young

Government Reports 1839 Constabulary Commissioners

The causes from which the vagabondism of the young indirectly proceeds are: —

1 The neglect or tyranny of parents or masters . . .
2 Bad companions.
3 Bad books, which act like the bad companions in depraving the taste, and teaching the youth to consider that approvable which . . . is morally loathesome.
4 Bad amusements — as penny-theatres, where the scenes and characters described in the bad books are represented in a still more attractive form . . .

● Question class for understanding and clarification.

- The first two causes are extracted and discussed.

The drama event

Pair Improvisations: Inciting Theft

(Whole class working in pairs simultaneously)

Characters
A Single parent living in filthy, poor conditions in London in 1780. Not really concerned for child's welfare. Selfish.
B 14-year-old son/daughter. Badly mistreated by parent. Fears parent and fears arrest.

Situation
Parent has to persuade child to go to the market place to steal food and money. Child tries to find excuses for not going.
(Do not allow parent's character to become violent. Parent's emphasis should be on cajoling child to steal, and a threat rather than direct action.)

Complementary drama

Reflection and Discussion

Key Questions
1 What effect did the parent's greed have on the way the child was treated?
2 Why did child agree to the task in the end?

The drama event

The discovery

Characters
As before.

Situation
Child has returned. Parent suspects that the child is hiding money and questions child regarding details of the theft. Child proudly displays takings (trying to hide fear of being caught). Describes theft in great detail.
(Mid-way through the improvisation, announce that the child notices the purse peeking out from beneath the clothes, in order to introduce suspense.)

Complementary drama

Reflection and Discussion

Key Questions
1 What effect did the realisation that the purse was showing have on the character's behaviour?
2 How did parent react to the discovery of the purse?
3 Why did he/she react in this way?

The drama event

The Professional Pickpocket

Characters
A 17 year old leader of a professional pickpocket gang. Uses gang members to get more money for self.
B As before.

Situation
Child wants to be accepted as one of the gang — for protection and friendship. Pretends to be brave but is terrifed of leader. Leader is conducting child's gang initiation test in a pickpocketing task to be decided by students.

Complementary drama

Reflection and Discussion

Key Questions
1 What did you learn about leader's character?
2 What did child learn about leader?
3 In what ways was child's behaviour affected by his/her fear of the leader?

The drama event

The Arrest

Characters
A Middle-aged milliner, a 'respectable' Londoner (a pickpocket in his/her youth). Gains respect of authorities by turning in pickpockets to authorities.
B As before.

Situation
Child has stolen a purse in market-place. Milliner discovers child and threatens to turn child in to authorities for pickpocketing.

Child finds a way to get out of the situation whilst attempting to remain cool and calm. Milliner finds a way to get the purse for self.

Complementary drama

Reflection and Discussion

Key Questions
1 What effect did milliner's past have on his/her attitude to child?
2 What effect did the need to remain cool and calm have on child's behaviour?

The drama event

Small Group Scenes: The Hearing
(Naturalistic)

Characters
A Government official, authoritative, busy, disinterested. Has been pickpocketed several times.
B As before.
C Middle-aged milliner (description as before).
D 17-year-old gang leader (description as before) Will protect self at all costs.

Situation
A Government hearing. Official to question others. Milliner and leader are intent on proving that child is guilty. Official has only a few minutes to hear the case.

Members of groups to prepare scene for performance to rest of class.

Performance

Audience Task
Observe and decide which character is the 'most' guilty, and deserving conviction and transportation to Australia.

Brief discussion at conclusion of each scene.

Complementary drama

Reflection and Discussion

Key Questions
1 What do you feel was the main cause of criminal behaviour of

(a) Child
(b) Parent
(c) Gang Leader
(d) Milliner
(e) Official?

2 To what extent was the result of the hearing fair?

3 Can you think of other situations where children are used for other people's selfish motives?

4 Can you think of other situations where poverty and/or hardship result in undesirable or criminal behaviour?

THE ORIGINS OF THE AUSTRALIAN CONVICTS — Lesson 2

Approximate age: 11/12 years
Time: 100 minutes (2 × 50 minutes)
Topic: The Origin of the Australian Convicts — Lesson 2.
Focus: Place

Specific Objectives

1 To explore the prison environment and its effects on character interaction.
2 To examine the effects of a common desire on several different characters.
3 To explore public reaction to the penal system.

Materials

1 A description of the 'hulks' on the Thames river
2 Convict role sheets
3 A description of public reaction to conditions aboard the hulks
4 Pens, paper

Conducting the Lesson

Complementary drama

Discussion of the imprisonment of convicts awaiting transportation to Australia (recap on previous lesson). The following points need to be identified:

- Many convicts were young children.
- Many convicts were housed in hulks awaiting transportation to Australia.
- Hulks were old, run-down, unseaworthy tubs.
- Convicts were crammed together, diseases commonplace.
- Convicts wore chains on hands and feet to restrict movement and keep them under control.

Preparation for Role-building

Students complete the convict role sheet.

Convict Role Sheet

Name:
Age: (14–18 years)
Offence: Pickpocketing
Description of Stolen goods:
  (e.g. food, lace handkerchief, coins, etc.)
Length of sentence: Life

Students must decide whether their character is guilty or not guilty of the above crime.

The drama event

Whole Group Improvisation: Entering the Hulks

(Class to work together creating small cell spaces around room.) Before improvisation begins, students are told:

1 Description of cells: No room to move around, only to stand or sit. One small hole in one wall is the only light source and the Thames can be seen in the distance.

2 Task: Upon entering cell, convicts quietly introduce themselves, briefly describe their crime and how they were caught. Try to work out whether you are being told truth by other convicts.

Teacher assumes character as official overseer of the hulks — a highly authoritative role.

Situation

Convicts are lined up silently in chains, outside the hulk. The overseer randomly selects convicts, instructing them to state their name, age and offence committed. Convicts are divided into groups of four or five, led to small cell and locked in.

Allow students a few minutes to respond to the environment of the cell and complete the task.

Complementary drama

Reflection and Discussion

Key Questions

1 How did the cell environment affect the way the characters introduced themselves?
2 What judgements were you able to make about your cell-mates?

The drama event

Small Group Improvisations: In the Cells

More specific character details will be added. Character cards defining personal attributes are distributed by teacher to cell groups, who allocate one of these roles to each convict.

Character Card

Convict **A** You miss your friends and brothers and sisters. You tend to only speak when spoken to.

Convict **B** You think you are better than the other convicts in your cell. You are proud of the crimes you committed.

Convict **C** You were caught for a crime one of your friends committed. Your friend was not caught. You don't like being in the same cell with 'real' criminals.

Convict **D** You have smuggled in a little money. You think that you might be able to bribe the overseer to set you free, but you need the help of the other convicts. Your only hope is to convince them to help you to make up a plan.

Convict **E** You are terrified of the other convicts. You desperately need someone to protect you and help you.

Situation
Evening. Dark. Convicts returned from work gang, tired. Settling in cell for the night.

Teacher in character as overseer:
● Patrols outside cells.
● Keeps convicts quiet.
● Warns of punishment for unruly behaviour.
● Hints at concessions for good behaviour or information about trouble makers.
(Teacher needs to watch action and give students appropriate chances to develop the situation).

Extending the Situation
● Teacher in role as overseer authoritatively informs convicts that he/she is aware of plans being made to escape. Overseer asks menacingly or coaxingly for any convict to stand and come forward to the cell door window if they have anything they wish to tell the overseer.
(Use element of surprise to punish convict who volunteers information about cell-mate to 'save their own skin').
● If no one volunteers, overseer selects individual convicts and attempts to seek information from them.

Complementary drama

Reflection and Discussion

Key Questions
1 How did the cell environment affect the characters' attitude to the task?

2 In what ways did the convicts' common desire to improve their situation influence their behaviour?
3 In what ways did the overseer influence the behaviour of the convicts?

A New Perspective: Public Opinion

Teacher initiates discussion about how the public might react to the conditions aboard the hulks. For example, families and friends of convicts, business people, government officials, charity organisations, the Church, pickpockets and other criminals.

The teacher describes from own research public reaction to the hulks. For example: Many people in London were shocked by the conditions aboard the 'hulks' and were determined to do something about it. Many approached government members to attempt to persuade them that clean, large jails would help the criminals reform. These people thought that the criminals were a bad influence on the other young people in London, and that they spread diseases to innocent people. If the criminals were removed to a large jail in the countryside everyone would be better off. However, the government was not prepared to spend any money on 'good-for-nothings' and refused to build better jails.

Small Group Improvisation: The Public Fight

Characters:
A Ageing government official in charge of prisons. Due to retire next month. Determined not to spend any money on jails. Insensitive to convict conditions.
B Hulk overseer. An acquaintance of the official.
C A doctor who believes that unless better conditions for convicts are provided, disease will spread quickly to the rest of the population. His/her nephew is one of the convicts aboard the hulks.

D A member of the 'respectable' London populace determined to remove the hulks as they are a bad influence on London youth. Headstrong and determined.

The drama event

Situation
Officials, waiting room. Doctor and 'respectable' person discuss ways to approach official. Official and overseer sit in office plotting how to convince the public that conditions aboard hulks are good. When they have mapped out the story, the deputation is invited into the office.

Allow pairs a few minutes to plan their approach. When group is ready, begin improvisation.

Complementary drama

Reflection and Discussion

Key Questions
1 What were the strongest feelings experienced by your character during the visit?
2 Was there anything you could have done but didn't during the visit to help influence the government's stance?
3 Have you been in other situations where you have experienced those feelings?

Possible Lesson Extensions
1 Doctor and respectable person are taken on a tour of the hulks to speak to the convicts.
2 Public debate in the local town hall.
3 One convict escapes and attempts to influence public opinion.
4 Convicts en route to Australia.
5 Establishing the new colony.

THE SHOPPING CENTRE

Approximate age: 11/12 years
Time: 100 minutes (2 × 50 minutes)
Topic: The Shopping Centre

Specific Objectives

1 To use character and situation as stimulus for language acquisition and extension.
2 To use the drama as a means of promoting peer group interaction and co-operation.

Materials

1 Taped sounds of a busy shopping complex
2 Pens, paper (cut up for shopping lists and shopkeepers' records)

Conducting the Lesson

Complementary drama

Introduction
The leader explains that in today's lesson the students will be setting up a shopping centre and taking on roles of shoppers, shopkeepers and news reporters.

Movement Exercise

The following movement activities should help the students determine appropriate movements for the later role work.

Character
Students to select a character. Teacher ensures that social and psychological levels of characterisation are used. For example, a floor walker, suspicious of school-age children; a housewife, loves to spend money on presents; a truckdriver, likes chatting to everybody in shops.
Class move around room in the following situations, freezing at instruction from the teacher.

Situation
1 Walking to the shops as if wearing a heavy leather coat.
2 Walking around the record shop carrying many parcels.
3 Pushing a heavy shopping trolley around the supermarket.
4 Racing to get to a shop before it closes.

5 One-way conversations returning shirt to
clothing shop because it's too small, returning electric kettle which does not
work, returning transistor radio because
the tuning dial is broken.

Sound Stimulus

Students sit in a space of their own. The
teacher plays a short tape of the sounds of
a busy shopping complex. The students are
instructed to listen carefully to the sounds
and to try and identify several distinct
sounds, and to remember as many different
noises as possible. Questioning at the end
of the tape should isolate the various activities which occur in a shopping complex.

Role Preparation

The teacher questions students as to what
shops one would be likely to find in a shopping mall, and who would run them. The
class is then divided into three groups: the
shoppers, the shopkeepers and news reporters. The groups are given the following
information on cards:

Group 1. The shoppers. You each have
$200 to spend. Before the drama begins
you need to decide what type of character you want to play. Do you want to be
old, young, a mother, a father? Do you
have a job? How would you speak and
walk? You also need to decide what you
want to buy — a gift, food, clothes, cos-
metics, sporting goods, etc. Perhaps you
are shopping with one other person. You
will need to keep a list of what was
bought, and how much you have spent.

Group 2. The shopkeepers. Decide what
type of shop you want to run — is it a

sporting goods store, a shoe shop, a general store, a chemist, a take-away food shop, or a jewellers, for example? You need to set up a counter. You will also need to decide what sort of shopkeeper you are. Choose one word which best describes your character — for example, grouchy, pleasant, mean, suspicious, pushy. You need to make a sign or signs to show what you are selling. You keep a list of all the things you sell.

Group 3. The news reporters. Your newspaper editor has decided to produce a feature story on the local shopping mall. You will have to briefly interview the shoppers and the shopkeepers. You need to find out what people are buying, how business is going in the various shops, what goods are available and any other information your readers will find interesting. You will need to take notes to write the story later.

Allow about five minutes for the students to prepare the work.

Situation
The shopping centre. Shopkeepers stand in their shops. Shoppers wait in centre of shopping mall (room). Reporters wait to one side and initially observe what happens in the shopping centre. One by one the shopkeepers introduce themselves and describe the shop and the type of character they are. The shoppers and news reporters do likewise.

The drama event

Whole Group Improvisation: Spending the Money

Allow the improvisation to proceed. It may be necessary to stop the work and question the students in order to deepen their role commitment. Allow some time for the completion of this activity, certainly enough for the shoppers to visit each store and talk to the reporters.

Complementary drama

Reflection and Discussion

Discuss shopping lists, shopkeepers' records and reporters' notes for consistencies.

1 The shopkeepers briefly described their roles before the drama began. How do you feel they behaved when you visited their shop?
2 How would the news reporters describe the type of people who shop in this mall?
3 Describe which customers you found the most pleasant to serve.
4 What tactics did the shopkeepers use to get you to spend your money?
5 If you had £500 to spend, what other items would you have bought?

NOSTRADAMUS

Approximate age: 11/12 years
Time: 100 minutes 92 × 50 minutes)
Topic: Nostradamus
Focus: Character

Specific Objectives

1 To use the work of Nostradamus as a means of exploring public fear and suspicion.
2 To experience the effect of language theatrics on the communication of meaning.

Materials

1 A description of the life of Nostradamus (see below).
2 A selected list of Nostradamus' predictions and their interpretations (see below).

A Description of the Life of Nostradamus
Michelle de Nostradamie was born in the
south of France in 1503. His parents soon
became aware of his extraordinary
intelligence and placed his education in the
hands of Juan, his grandfather. Juan was a
doctor who taught him Greek, Latin,
Hebrew, Mathematics and Astrology.
When Nostradamus was twenty-two, he
graduated in medicine and began practising
in the French countryside. He tried to heal
the victims of the Black Death, and was
highly successful. He moved to Salon and
settled there. He converted the attic of his
house, and it was here that, at night-time,
he studied black art and the occult. In 1555
he completed ten books called *The Centuries.*
Each book contained 100 verses written in
an obscure language which was a mixture of
French, Latin and Greek. The verses
contained prediction from his time to the
end of the world.

*A Selected List of Nostradamus' Predictions and
their Interpretations*
(Transcript Keilor Heights High School.
Excerpts from 3XY Radio broadcast.)

The Great Fire of London
'The blood of the just will be damned at
London and burnt by fire in three times
twenty plus six.'

The 'three times twenty plus six' equals
sixty-six and the only major fire in recorded
history was in London in 1666. Nostradamus was right. Predicting *exactly* the Great
Fire of London — 100 years after his death.

First and Second World Wars
'Beasts wild with hunger will cross the
rivers. The great part of the battlefield
will be against *Hister.* He will drag the
leader in a cage of iron when the trial of
Germany observes no law.'

Another of Nostradamus' most famous verses and with the name being given in the quote as HISTER, there can be little doubt that HITLER is really implied. Who can be so well described by the last line? — 'the German who observes no law' Even Hitler recognised himself in these verses and together with Goebels and the propaganda ministry had Nostradamus' predictions printed (bending the facts slightly), using bombers to drop them all over Europe in the form of propaganda leaflets.

1986 — And the Arab/Israeli War

'In the year that Saturn and Mars are equally firey the air is very dry. A long meteor from hidden fires, a great place burns with heat and little rain. Hot winds, wars and raids.'

Another interesting quatrain because it gives us a day. 'Saturn and Mars are equally firey' means when they are in conjunction which is the 17th February, 1986 — the exact time that Hayley's Comet is forecast to pass the earth. Also around this period, Nostradamus foresees Mars and Saturn combining their malignant powers to influence world history with great natural disasters — like the earthquakes mentioned in the previous verse; then wars, drought and invasions.

'The king enters foix wearing a blue turbin [sic]. He will reign for less than a revolution of Saturn. The king with the white turbin — his heart banished to Byzantium — not far from when the sun, Mars and Mercury are near Aquarius.

Here, Nostradamus is decribing an Eastern War — maybe the Arabs and the Israelis — because of the turbans. 'Foix' is understood to belong to a 'Blue Turbinned Man' — maybe the President of Egypt — Anwar Sadat — elected in 1970 because Nostradamus says he will reign for less than a revolution of Saturn — less than thirty years.

A date consistent with others given by Nostradamus. And then there's the last line in the verse. The next time the sun, Mars and Mercury are in Aquarius is in 1986. In another verse Nostradamus gives an even more specific date for the start of this war.

'The Arab Prince. Mars and the sun, Venus and Leo, tears, cries and wailing, an inhuman cruel heart. Black and gold. Lake Geneva. The islands. The people of Genoa. Blood pours. Hunger for wheat. Mercy to none.'

According to the experts the next time we have a conjunction of Mars, the sun and Venus is the 21st August, 1987. This war will eventually spread right throughout Europe. And the last line, 'hunger for wheat' ... Maybe plague caused by the fallout from nuclear warfare.

'No-one left alive in nineteen hundred and eighty five will ever do ...'

'There will be a dreadful destruction of people and animals. Suddenly vengeance will be revealed a hundred hands. Thirst and hunger when the comet will pass.'

Again in reference to Hayley's Comet — and what about the second line in the verse when Nostradamus forecasts death and destruction to people and animals. Interesting because Nostradamus as a doctor would know that most diseases do not kill people as well as animals. Yet in his verse, he specifically says it will happen. Another reference to atomic fallout which kills all living creatures equally.

Finally, Nostradamus foresees America assisting in the liberation of Europe. A counter offensive will be made from Portugal and the Arabs will be defeated.

'The barbarian fights. Bloodshed. The Great Ishmael, America, will make his promentory [sic]. Frogs tremble under aid from Portugal. They will take aim against the barbarian fleet. The barbarian driven as far back as Tunis.

Conducting the Lesson

Complementary drama

Introduction
Teacher reads the description of the life of Nostradamus, then evokes student response and asks those who have read the book to comment. Discuss why he wrote in 'code' and the general topic of belief in the occult.

Then the teacher reads the selected lists of Nostradamus' predictions and their interpretations, evokes student response, discusses the accuracy of his predictions and of other predictions students are aware of. Let's imagine the scene:
(Teacher and student build together detailed scene of Nostradamus at work).
Students sit alone.

Teacher: 'I am now going to describe Nostradamus' surroundings. Try to picture the attic as clearly as you can. Nostradamus is sitting alone in his attic. It is late at night. His wife is asleep. The room is lit by one candle. There is one table and one chair only in the room. There are many dusty books on black art and the occult lying around the room. Nostradamus is reading one of these books. He turns the pages over slowly. Next to the table a large bowl of water stands on a pedestal. He looks into the water. It is from this water that he sees visions of the past and of the future. A picture becomes more clear in the bowl of water. It is a vision of the Great Fire of London. He is scared by this vision, and glances away. Slowly he turns back to the water and the vision is still there, even more precise than before. It is so clear and vivid that he feels he must tell his wife. He knows he must be quiet, as the neighbours are suspicious of his activities at night. If he is exposed as a prophet, he will be sentenced to death. This is why he writes in code. He is terribly afraid of being caught.'

The drama event

Pair Improvisations: The Fear

Characters

A Nostradamus. Mid-way through the completion of *The Centuries*. Extremely afraid that someone will discover the water — excited by the predictions. Wants to to protect wife.

B Nostradamus' wife. Aware of husband's work but wants him to stop and to continue practising as a doctor only. Has seen a neighbour snooping around outside the house at night.

Situation

Nostradamus tells wife of vision. Wife is intent on persuading Nostradamus to abandon his work to protect their lives. They talk in whispers to avoid detection.

Complementary drama

Reflection and Discussion

Key Question

What was the most persuasive moment during the improvisation? (Specific words or gestures used.)

Small Group Improvisations

(To be prepared and performed. Each group is given a different improvisation task).

The drama event

Group 1: The Bookstore

(Four students)

Characters

A   Owner of the bookstore. Has heard of Nostradamus but never met him. Sells books on many topics. Lives in the next town. Tries to keep the fact that he/she sells books on the occult a secret.

B   Nostradamus (as before). Has to keep the reason for the books' purchase a secret to avoid suspicion.

C & D   Townspeople. Middle-aged. Work in the bakery. Friends with bookstore owner. Believe Nostradamus is a sorceror.

Situation

Townspeople are talking to owner in the bookstore. Nostradamus enters to purchase several books on black art and the occult. Townspeople attempt to overhear the order and carefully discuss the occult with Nostradamus. Townspeople must not accuse Nostradamus of being a sorcerer; they must gain their information carefully.

Group 2: The Neighbours

(Four or five students)

Characters

A   Father. He is the one whom Nostradamus' wife has seen snooping around at night. Works as a farmer. Doesn't want to frighten children.

B   Mother likes to make up stories about Nostradamus to appear knowledgeable in the eyes of the family.

C,D,E Children, varying ages between eight and seventeen. Work on the farm. Try to appear brave in front of parents. Terrified of Nostradamus and black magic.

Situation

After dinner, in the farm-house. Mother initiates discussion by telling the family about one of her friends who was healed by Nostradamus in his house and told of the terrifying objects in the house.

Group 3: The Patient

(Four students)

Characters

A Nostradamus (as before)
Knows he could cure the patient with magic potion but scared of exposure.

B Nostradamus' wife (as before). Knows that Nostradamus's verses are lying all around the house.

C The patient, a blacksmith from next village, has a bad knee — very painful. Told that Nostradamus can cure it. Knows all the dreadful stories about Nostradamus' black art.

D The patient's friend. Has brought the patient to Nostradamus. Wants to search the house for evidence of black magic. Doesn't want to frighten friend.

Situation

Nostradamus' house. Midnight. Patient and friend arrive.

Group 4: The Spies

(Four students)

Characters

A,B Fourteen or fifteen-year-old children who live a short distance from Nostradamus. Terrified of being turned into frogs by Nostradamus.

C Eight-year-old child. Fears being caught because his/her elder brothers and sisters will be punished instead of her.

D Nostradamus or wife (as before).

Situation

Late at night. Parents asleep. Children meet to plan way to prove their courage by gaining an object from Nostradamus' house.

Group 5: The Investigation

(Four or five students)

Characters

A The town clerk. A stern official who has to keep law and order. Scared to set foot in Nostradamus's house.

B,C The town clerk's younger helpers. Ambitious. Want to make the town clerk appear foolish so that the public will no longer respect him/her.

D Nostradamus (as before). Tries to appear pleasant and normal'

E His wife (as before). Believes that if Nostradamus can be frightened by the three visitors then he may give up his work.

Situation
Officials visit the house to question Nostradamus and his wife. (Officials need to plan strategies for gathering evidence).

Performance: The Village Comes to Life

The five improvisations are performed without interruption in a 'village-like' atmosphere.

Audience Task
Villagers observe the differences between the reality of Nostradamus' activities and the villagers' fears of him.

Complementary drama

Reflection and Discussion

Key Questions
1 Why was public interest in Nostradamus so high?
2 What does this interest tell us about the way people regard prophets?
3 How did Nostradamus cope with the public suspicion? What hints did he give about his great fear of exposure?
4 What effect would all this public suspicion have had on his work?

The drama event

Whole Group Language Theatrics

Class is organised as follows:
1 Nostradamus stands in centre of room.
2 A narrator/interpreter stands to one side of the room.
3 A chorus of four or five students stands on the other side.
4 The remaining students stand in a semi-circle around Nostradamus.

Task

The large group standing in a semi-circle prepare one sentence each, which tries to sum up the public suspicions of Nostradamus; for example, 'You see visions in a bowl of water', 'You turn children into frogs', 'You would never be allowed to cure my children', 'You read books about magic', etc.

The chorus read the verses in a chanting style, one by one. (This has been discussed at the beginning of the lesson.)

The narrator reads an abbreviated version of the interpretation.

Nostradamus remains standing silently. (The verses and their interpretations are interspersed throughout the public statements.)

Preparation

1 Allow the large group a couple of minutes to prepare the sentences. Move around the group checking the statements and suggesting possibilities to those in difficulties.
2 Allow the chorus and narrator to quietly practise their speeches.
3 Stand everyone in place quietly before beginning. Point to each student you wish to speak, then the chorus, then the narrator.

Complementary drama

Reflection and Discussion

1 List words that describe your feelings/thoughts about Nostradamus and his accusers. (Relate to art form concepts where appropriate).
2 In what ways was your attitude towards Nostradamus the same as/different from the previous drama?
3 What do we call people who attempt to work in ways which are considered suspect? (palmist, clairvoyant, herbalist acupuncturist, etc.)
4 What influence does public fear or suspicion have on the work and lives of these people?

12   Drama Lessons for Year 8

THE CITY

Approximate age: 12/13 years
Time: 100 minutes (2 × 50 minutes)
Topic: The City — Lesson 1
Focus: Place

Specific Objectives

1 To clarify and crystallise attitudes towards city living.
2 To emphasise motivation as an important element in dramatic action.
3 To develop the skill of focus as a means of creating a clear dramatic image.

Materials

Photographs of city: skyscraper buildings, market place, eccentric faces, alley-ways, slums.

Conducting the Lesson

Complementary drama

Introduction
Discussion related to photographs. General discussion using students' experience of city life-style.

Pair and Small Group Sculptures

(Students prepare and, spaced evenly around room, present sculptures one by one. Discussion occurs only where image is unclear.)

Students, in pairs, create frozen images depicting some aspect of city life.

Students in groups of four create three frozen images depicting a new aspect of city life, or extended pair image.

The drama event

Small Group Improvisations: City Living

Groups plan and rehearse scenes for presentation to class, depicting:
1 Positive aspects of city life (two groups).
2 Negative aspects of city life (two groups).

Groups asked to ensure that their improvisation conveys the *reason* for activities within their scenes; for example, (a) lunch at a restaurant — a birthday celebration or business meeting or (b) a mugging — theft to purchase drugs.

Performance

Audience task: Observe and identify the reason/s for character's action.

Performance Reflection and Discussion

Key Questions
1 How clearly did the drama reflect your thoughts and feelings about city life?
2 What other scenes would be necessary for the drama to show the most important aspects of city life?
3 To what extent are these scenes representative of city life throughout the world?

VICTIMS

Approximate age: 12/13 years
Time: 100 minutes (2 × 50 minutes)
Topic: Victims
Focus: Character

Specific Objectives

1 To gain insight into the consequences of aggression and violence in society from a victim's perspective.

2 To use aspects of epic and naturalistic style in order to heighten dramatic experience.

Materials

Teacher stimulus — Connexions *Violence*, by C. Ward, Penguin, 1970.

Conducting the Lesson

Complementary drama

Introduction
Teacher initiates discussion about the victims of aggression and violence, which were emphasised in the drama of the last lesson, 'The City'.

Discuss the concept of a victim.

Clarify through discussion the notion of an immediate victim (person killed, raped, bashed, etc.) and of an associated victim (friends, family, etc. of immediate victim).

The drama event

Narrative Profile

(Prepared Speech and Frozen Image) Students work in small groups and develop a victim profile. Presentation of profiles to occur in context of live T.V. studio exposé. Teacher adopts character of T.V. floor manager.

Profile Example
Group 1.
Student **A**: 'John Bilkins died 10th January, 1984, victim of fatal assault with .22 rifle.'
Student **B**: 'Jane Bilkins, 26-year-old wife and mother of three children, underwent emergency treatment for shock.'
Student **C**: 'Children were given to foster home to ensure proper care that mother was unable to provide.'
Student **D**: 'Jane Bilkins did not respond to treatment and is now in a psychiatric hospital.'
Student **E**: adopts frozen pose of disoriented Jane Bilkins sitting in hospital room.

When profiles are prepared, teacher emphasises T.V. studio context. Groups are spaced appropriately around edge of room. 'Floor manager' asks for silence on the set, gives 'On Air' signal and groups in pre-arranged sequence present profiles.

Complementary drama

Reflection and Discussion

General discussion to clarify any unclear frozen images or blurred verbal details. Discussion about effect on audience of style of presentation.

The drama event

Small Group Improvisations: The Victim (Naturalistic)

Students work in same groups to develop a 'slice of life' scene which elaborates on the victim profile. (e.g. Group 1 — develop scene about children's separation from mother.)

Performance

(T.V. Studio context as before)

Complementary drama

Audience Task

Observe the ways in which the scene helped us understand more about the extent of the victim's plight.

Performance Reflection and Discussions

Key Questions.

1 If you were watching this T.V. exposé, what reactions might you have towards aggression and violence in society?
2 Which parts of the drama had the most impact on you?

THE PRANK

Approximate age: 12/13 years
Time: 100 minutes (2 × 50 minutes)
Topic: The Prank
Focus: Event

Specific Objectives

To gain insight into the motivation and consequences of one aspect of adolescent non-violent aggression.

Materials

Butcher's paper
Texta pens
Poem, 'My Parents Kept Me From Children Who Were Rough', by Stephen Spender (see below).

My Parents Kept Me From Children Who Were Rough

My parents kept me from children who were rough,
Who threw words like stones and who wore torn clothes.
Their thighs showed through rags. They ran in the street
And climbed cliffs and stripped by the country streams.

I feared more than tigers their muscles like iron,
Their jerking hands and their knees tight on my arms,
I feared the salt coarse pointing of these boys
Who copied my lisp behind me on the road.

They were lithe, they sprang out behind hedges
Like dogs to bark at my world. They threw mud
While I looked the other way, pretending to smile,
I longed to forgive them, but they never smiled.

                                                Stephen Spender

---

Complementary drama

Introduction
Discussion about victims and non-violent aggression. Poem is read and class isolates victim and type of non-violent aggression.

Discussion focuses on pranks as major illustrations of non-violent aggression.

List on paper examples of non-violent pranks (for example, shoplifting, free rides on buses, sneaking into movies without paying, knick-knocking on doors, throwing stones on roof).

List on paper likely victims of pranks (for example, old people, young children, handicapped people.)

Discuss motivation for pranks.

The drama event

Small Group Improvisations: The Prank

Each of the following scenes is allocated to the various groups:
(Time is allowed for planning and rehearsing the scene.)

Old People
Group selects specific characters and situation. Drama shows a particular prank being played on elderly citizens.

Young People
Group selects specific characters and situation. Drama shows a particular prank being played on young people.

The Backfire
Group selects specific characters and situation. Drama shows a prank which backfires and causes harm to the pranksters.

The Mistake
Group select specific characters and situation. Drama shows a prank which results in serious consequences for the victim.

Complementary drama

Performance Reflection on Character Action

List on paper words or phrases that isolate thoughts and feelings of:

(a) Victims	(b) Aggressors (Pranksters)
e.g. angry	e.g. terrific fun
confused	excited
frustrated	superior/powerful
frightened	'a great joke'
want revenge	

Reflection and Discussion

1 Imagine you are writing a lead article in a daily newspaper about the victims of adolescent pranks. Decide on a headline for the article, based on the experiences of the drama.

THE CONFERENCE

Approximate age: 12/13 years
Time: 100 minutes (2 × 50 minutes)
Topic: The Conference
Focus: Event

Specific Objectives

To gain insight into the range of attitudes in relation to the protection of the individual against violence and aggression.

Materials

1 Newspaper Article: 'Bad guys are better off than the good, says Police Commissioner', by Andrew Rule, chief police reporter, from the *Age*, Melbourne, 18 February 1984 (see opposite).
2 Paper, Texta pens
3 Character cards:
   Group 1 — five social workers
   Group 2 — five policemen
   Group 3 — five citizens
   Group 4 — five victims (three immediate, two associated)
   Group 5 — five aggressors (three ex-prisoners, two juvenile delinquents)
4 Conference Agenda (see below)

National Conference for the Protection of Victims in Society

1 Opening welcome and address.
2 Group seminars.
3 Presentation of delegates' proposals.
4 Key note address, Dr Werffeli (Swiss Sociologist).
5 Conference submission to parliament.
6 Closing address.

Bad guys are better off than the good, says Police Commissioner

By ANDREW RULE, chief police reporter

The Chief Police Commissioner, Mr Mick Miller, has called for more stringent laws just three weeks after the Minister for Police and Emergency Services, Mr Mathews, warned senior police against publicly commenting on any aspect of Government policy.

Writing in the latest issue of 'Police Life', published last night, Mr Miller said: "As it stands, the law does not protect us from the criminally disposed . . . the bad guys are better off than the good guys.

"The crime rate continues to rise, armed robbery is an accepted fact of everyday life, everyone's home is vulnerable to burglary, it's not uncommon for women to be raped in their own homes, elderly women are routinely victims of handbag snatchers, it's becoming increasingly unsafe to walk the streets at night and the motoring mayhem continues on our roads."

Late last month, Mr Mathews rebuked senior police for publicly commenting on what they described as defects in Victorian law which hindered proper investigation of crimes.

Mr Mathews said police were prohibited under Section 95 of the Constitution Act from commenting on any aspect of Government policy or adminstration.

This provoked an angry response from the police union, which, at a protest meeting on 1 February, unanimously passed a vote of no confidence in the Premier, Mr Cain, over what union spokesmen described as the erosion of police powers.

Since then Mr Miller has asked Mr Mathews for talks on guidelines proposed by the Government which would prohibit police comment on virtually any public issue.

In the article published yesterday, Mr Miller obliquely attacked what many senior police see as the State Government's soft attitude towards law enforcement.

He said that if crime increased at its present annual rate, within five years one in four Victorians would be the victim of crime.

More than 200,000 people in Victoria had become victims of crime in 1983, Mr Miller said, 'Of these crimes, only 22.8 per cent were solved,' he wrote.

'Not even the most ardent libertarian could suggest that the rights of wrongdoers are being violated or even threatened at the same alarming rate.

'It seems that, in this respect, the bad guys are better off than the good guys. In a free society the law-abiding majority deserve better than this.'

Mr Miller said the law's protection of the rights of those accused of crime should not outweigh the rights of crime's victims.

'If George Orwell was alive today, he would perceive that the greatest threat to his civil liberties would be in becoming a victim of crime . . . as a free spirit, he might well agitate for a Big Brother to protect him from the criminally disposed,' wrote Mr Miller,

He said he feared that pre-occupation with the rights of individuals overrode the citizen's responsibility to contribute to the common good.

'As 1984 unfolds, our freedom will not be assailed by the spectre of totalitarian tyranny, but all of us will be confronted by the very real threat of victimisation by increasing crime,' said Mr Miller.

'It would be better for us all if the scales of justice were more equitably balanced.'

Mr Mathews was not available for comment last night.

Conducting the Lesson

Complementary drama

Introduction
General discussion to ensure that the group is familiar with the ideas explored in the previous lessons (e.g. immediate and associated victims, serious crimes, pranks, etc.).

Discuss role of social workers, ordinary citizens and police in relation to violence and aggression.

Character cards distributed according to numbers in group, ensuring that each group (e.g. citizens) is adequately represented.

Students instructed to wait outside room for commencement of drama.

The drama event

Whole Group Improvisation: The Conference

(a) Teacher as Chairman of conference welcomes delegates, stressing significance of conference, responsibility of delegates to prepare parliamentary submission and explaining registration and accommodation details and conference agenda.
(b) Teacher as Chairman delivers opening address, using newspaper article as stimulus.
(c) Teacher as Chairman organises groups (as per character cards) and explains task.

Task
Discuss group's views on protecting society from violence and aggression. Decide on three possible solutions to the problem.

Select one solution and plan and rehearse a scene which illustrates the solution (for example, social workers act out a situation where they approach Mayor re building of a local recreation centre.)
(d) Chairman assembles delegates for viewing proposals. As proposals are presented Chairman lists each group's proposal on a large sheet of paper (for example, more facilities for adolescents).

(e) Chairman apologises for embarrassing situation of Dr Werffeli's non-attendance. Chairman instructs delegates that their parliamentary submission will have to be prepared without Dr Werffeli's expert advice.

(f) Chairman instructs delegates to form new groups so that a variety of opinions can be exchanged. Groups to determine and list which two proposals they consider the most likely to protect society.

(g) One spokesperson from each group presents their findings, briefly stating reasons for decisions. Chairman lists findings on large sheet of paper.

(h) Delegates vote on the order in which the proposals should be submitted to parliament.

(i) Chairman closes conference, thanking delegates for attendance and hard work, and expresses confidence in parliament's acceptance of the proposals.

Complementary drama

Reflection and Discussion

General discussion concerning problems and complexity of determining solutions to the problem of violence and aggression in society.

Possible Extensions

Expressive Skills Development

The drama event

Focus: Event.

1 Emphasise exaggeration, caricature and humour.

2 Hugely exaggerate the contrast between victim's actions and emotions and aggressor's actions and emotions.

3 Students and teacher decide on situation; for example:
— dentist and patient;
— school nurse and student;
— high pressure salesperson and client;
— over-protective parent and timid child.

4 Workshop individual skills in exaggeration. Small groups can use this work to build scenes for performance.

The drama event

Famous Victims
Focus: Character.
Materials
Assassinations: The Murders That Changed History, Marshall, Cavendish Ltd, London, 1975.

Students research historical details of violent acts against famous people; for example, John Kennedy, Dr Martin Luther King, John Paul Marat, Arch Duke Ferdinand, etc.

The groups work together over three double sessions to find ways of presenting their famous victim profile.

The drama event

Aggressors as Victims
Focus: Character.
Students research historical details of the aggressors; for example, Lee Harvey Oswald, Charlotte Corday, Ned Kelly, etc.

The group work together over three double sessions to find ways of presenting their famous aggressor's profile.

13   Drama Lessons for
Year 9

A FEATURE PROGRAMME FOR
PERFORMANCE: GROWING UP

Approximate age: 14 years
Duration of unit: 10–13 weeks (150 minutes
per week)
Content: Growing up
In this unit of work the class will be working intensively on a small group devised
performance on the theme of growing up.
A feature programme describes a performance resulting from the exploration through
drama of a particular theme. The group's
ideas about the theme are performed to a
small audience and the students' separate
sections are linked together by a narrator.

The aim of this method of working is for
the students to build up a comment of their
own, as dramatically varied as they please,
on the theme. The various comments or
sections would include improvised scenes,
movement or dance drama and work produced from various stimulus materials such
as newspaper cuttings, music, photographs,
prose or poetry.

The theme of growing up is selected for
its accessibility, wide scope and interest,
yet may be changed if the class wishes to
pursue another topic. The teacher selects
some aspects of growing up that present
problems for students, such as:
— the importance of belonging to a peer
   group;

— changing attitudes towards authority figures;
— making decisions about the future;
— self-image and sexuality.

This provides a concrete starting point for discussion and planning.

Drama Objectives

1 To explore the theme of growing up.
2 To develop the expressive skills of voice, movement and improvisation in order to communicate meaning to an audience.
3 To develop the expressive skills of voice, movement and improvisation in order to explore and express human experience.
4 To develop appropriate dramatic images to explore and extend the drama.
5 To select and use appropriate elements of the art form in order to work towards meaning.
6 To develop the ability to sustain and extend commitment to role within different dramatic structures.
7 To reflect, analyse and articulate an understanding of self in relation to the ideas and experiences of others.
8 To select relevant and appropriate data in order to extend the theme and use the data in the drama.
9 To describe and analyse the extent to which the product fulfills its particular aim or function.

Specific Objectives for Lesson 1 (3 × 50 minutes)

1 To introduce the concept of a feature programme.
2 To use students' experiences of growing up as a basis for the drama.
3 To express individual feelings and ideas about growing ᵗp through movement.

Materials

A flow chart on the theme of growing up (Figure 8 on page 183). Paper, cards, textas.

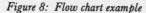

Figure 8: Flow chart example

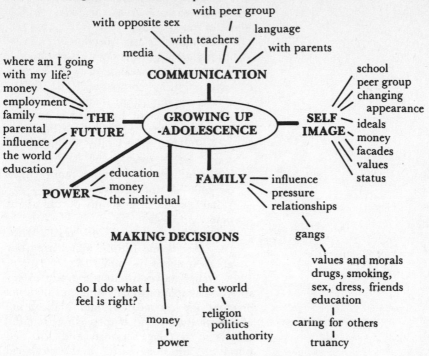

Conducting the Lesson

Complementary drama

Introduction

Introduce content and nature of the programme. Teacher explains the details of the programme, outlining purpose of the work in terms of the personal, human development and dramatic art form meanings to be explored in the topic. If the class is motivated and agrees to pursue the topic, the teacher indicates that they will need to look at many other aspects of growing up apart from those already highlighted by the teacher, and that will be the first task of the lesson. Show class flow chart (Figure 8) as an example of how to brainstorm topic ideas on paper.

Small Group Planning Activity

The class is divided into groups of three or four. Each group is given a large sheet of card and texta pens. Class members are instructed to write down all their ideas on the theme of growing up.

Some comments and questions to stimulate thoughts might be:

— Remember the way you were several years ago as compared with today. What was important then/now?
— What influence do friends have on you?
— What thoughts do you have about the future? Has the world changed as you've been growing up?
— What influence does your family have on your life and future?
— What is good/bad/exciting/boring about being your age?
— What fears and hopes do you have for the present and future? What are your greatest needs just now?

The teacher moves about the group to ensure task is spontaneously and quickly done probing for clarification and elaboration where necessary and emphasising that the task is to be taken seriously and not used purely as an imaginative and fantastical journey.

Whole Group Planning Activity

— Groups return to the centre of the room to share and record their ideas. Teacher (or student scribe) will record ideas on master sheet of butcher's paper under appropriate headings.
— A spokesperson is selected from each group. One aspect of their brainstorming is isolated and briefly explained. This is given a place on the master flow chart.
— Each group is asked to offer a new aspect for consideration, or to add important ideas to areas already identified.
— The group establishes the interrelationship of ideas by instructing the scribe to use circles, lines, arrows, etc.
— Discussion for clarification occurs, and to allow the teacher to understand what

attitudes offer the starting point for the drama experiences.

The flow chart is pinned on the board or wall and a large blank sheet is placed beside it. A record of ideas explored and understanding reached will be kept here as possibilities for inclusion in the Feature Programme performance.

The class is asked to collect resources that may be used in exploring the theme — newspaper clippings, poems, photos, stories, songs, etc.

Individual Sculptures

Students are spaced around the room and develop quick, frozen body sculptures which express aspects of growing up. Suggested focus:

1 Small child playing marbles
   Child climbing tree
   Children playing 'house'
   Children building with blocks
2 Adolescent waiting for bus
   Adolescent arriving at disco
   Adolescent talking with parent/peer.
3 Parent   coaching   child   at
   football/basketball
   Parent discussing homework
   Parent greeting son/daughter's new friend

Small Group Movement Performance

— Allow students time to plan and rehearse
— Groups of three or four
— Select *two* frozen images per student from 1,2 and 3 above.
— Develop and rehearse a continuous movement sequence based on these images.
— Repeat the sequence. Teacher stops the sequence when images have been clearly conveyed.

Reflection and Discussion

General discussion about feelings and thoughts evoked by the movement images.

Which images were the most powerful or created a lasting impression?

THE IDEAL PARENT AND CHILD

Approximate age: 14 years
Time: 150 minutes (3 × 50 minutes)
Topic: The Ideal Parent and Child
Focus: Character

Specific Objectives

1 To explore concepts of conflict, resolution and harmony in parent/child relationships.
2 To experiment with the element of contrast in creating meaning.
3 To use exaggeration, caricature and humour as a means of exploring and communicating meaning.

Materials

1 Ideal Parent and Child Questionnaires (Appendix 1a and 1b)
2 The Flow Chart.
3 Pens, paper.
4 A 'Dear Dorothy' letter (Appendix 2)

Complementary drama

Conducting the Lesson

1 Class discussion of the qualities of the 'ideal' or 'perfect' parent and child.
Focus on media portrayal of the ideal family: *The Brady Bunch, Eight is Enough, Little Women.*
List attributes on the board; for example:

Ideal Parent	Ideal Child
never tired or irritable	never misbehaves
generous, warm	tidy, polite
cheerful, patient	conscientious

The teacher attempts to draw out the extreme, fantastical image of the perfect parent and child and directs students to think about the relationship that might exist between them. This is an attempt to focus students' attention on the critical as-pects of a parent/child relationship; for example, authority, freedom, control, influence, co-operation.

Preparation for Character Development

Explain that the next task will provide the basis for some small group improvisations. Each student is given a copy of the Questionnaire in Search of the Ideal Parent' (see below). Students organised into individual spaces. Teacher takes question 2 from questionnaire and illustrates task by asking for responses.

Questionnaire in Search of the Ideal Parent*

Who is the Ideal Parent from a child's perspective?

Note: Circle **one** letter only.

Question 1:

The Ideal Parent is aged between . . .

A 25 to 30 years
B 30 to 40 years
C 40 to 50 years
D over 70 years

Question 2:

The Ideal Parent will earn an income of . . .

A less than $2000 per year
B $5000 to $6000 per year
C $10 000 to $18 000 per year
D over $200 000 per year

Question 3:

The Ideal Parent will make you attend school . . .

A everyday, even when you are in an iron lung

* This questionnaire is reproduced by courtesy of David McKernan.

B every day that you are well enough to
   go
C every alternate week
D will not worry at all about you going
   to school

Question 4:
The Ideal Parent will give you pocket
money of . . .
A no pocket money at all
B 95 cents each week
C $5 to $8 each week
D over $25 each week

Question 5:
The Ideal Parent will expect you to wash
the dishes . . .
A after every single meal
B twice a day
C three times each week
D only on public holidays

Question 6:
The Ideal Parent will expect you to mow
the lawn . . .
A once a day
B once every third day
C once a week
D once a month

Question 7:
The Ideal Parent will encourage you to
bring your friends home . . .
A not at all
B only on Tuesday evenings between 5–6
   pm.
C only on the weekends
D all the time

Question 8:
The Ideal Parent will allow you to drink
and smoke at home . . .
A never
B only after dinner at night
C at anytime they are out of the house
D without any restrictions, and will even
   buy your cigarettes and alcohol

Question 9:

The Ideal Parent will allow you to have your own bedroom . . .

A only after you leave home
B once you become a teenager
C from the age of five onwards
D will never make you share with a brother or sister

Question 10:

The Ideal Parent will allow you to be lazy around the house . . .

A at all times
B only on weekends
C for one week of each year
D will not let you be lazy at all

Question 11:

The Ideal Parent reads your school reports . . .

A never
B only when they are excellent
C only when you have failed badly
D reads every report

Question 12:

The Ideal Parent will buy you your own car when you become eighteen . . .

A Yes?
B No?

Questionnaire in Search of the Ideal Child*

Who is the Ideal Child from a parent's perspective?

Note: Circle **one** letter only.

Question 1:

The Ideal Child is aged . . .

A under five years of age
B seven to twelve years of age
C thirteen to sixteen years of age
D over sixteen years of age

* This questionnaire is reproduced by courtesy of David McKernan.

Question 2:
The Ideal Child will expect pocket money
to the value of . . .
A over $25 each week
B between $5 and $8 each week
C less than $2 each week
D only what you can afford to give
  him/her each week

Question 3:
The Ideal Child will go to school each day
. . .
A without any disagreements
B only when you continually 'nag'
  him/her to go
C only when you bribe him/her to go
D only when he/she wishes to go

Question 4:
The Ideal Child will wash the dishes . . .
A after every meal without being asked
B after the evening meal only after a fight
  with you each night
C three times a week
D will **not** wash the dishes

Question 5:
The Ideal Child will mow the lawn . . .
A every day
B each week after a fight with you about
  doing it
C once a month without being asked
D will **not** mow the lawn

Question 6:
The Ideal Child will be courteous and re-
spectful to you at all times . . .
A Yes?
B No?

Question 7:
The Ideal Child will **not** drink and smoke
. . .
A at any time
B without your permission
C will drink and smoke behind your back
D will drink and smoke whenever he/she
  wants to

Question 8:

The Ideal Child will demand his/her own bedroom . . .

A at no stage in his/her life

B once he/she is a teenager

C as soon as he/she can talk

D only to keep the family unhappy and not because he/she wants his/her bedroom

Question 9:

The Ideal Child will be lazy around the home . . .

A at **no** time

B only when you continually 'nag' him/her

C only during school holidays

D at **all** times

Question 10:

The Ideal Child will work hard at school so that his/her report is . . .

A excellent

B as good as you (as parent) can expect

C as good as he/she thinks it should be

D will not worry about his/her report or what you think

Question 11:

The Ideal Child will expect a car from you the moment he/she becomes eighteen

A Yes?

B No?

Question 12:

The Ideal Child will remember your birthday and . . .

A spend all his/her pocket money that he/she has been saving for five months

B wish you a very happy birthday and give you an appropriate little gift

C will wish you a happy birthday and spend all the week's pocket money on himself/herself

Ask students to select most outrageously idealistic characteristics for 'the ideal parent' and 'the ideal child'.

Questionnaires are then quickly completed, collected, discussed and related to the list of attributes on board.

The drama event

Pair Improvisation (Exaggeration)

1 Pairs plan short, polished improvisation using three attributes from the board list of the ideal parent and child.

Situation
This can be extracted from questionnaires and/or use students' own ideas.

The teacher moves about the room, watching and promoting the focus of each group, and clarifing the task; encourages appropriate actor/audience relationship; and helps with the dramatic expression of character, emphasising exaggeration and caricature.

2 Students present scenes to the class, organising audience seating as they wish.

Audience Task
1 to observe and decide which three attributes each character portrays;
2 to observe how the attributes are communicated (voice gesture/body gesture);
3 to list on the board specific gestures used to communicate attributes. (See below.)

	Ideal Parent	**Ideal Child**
Voice Gesture	Sweet, gentle, soft, warm	enthusiastic, bright, fast, bubbly
Body Gesture	flowing, graceful, controlled	bouncy, upright, physical contact with parent

Possible Extension: Language Theatrics

Half the class works on the same scene, using restricted language and gesture.

The other half works on elaborated language to highlight character attributes and to extend experience in voice and movement skills.

Notes: Audience task (3) should be completed as quickly and efficiently as possible.

The humour and fun of the drama should be encouraged and supported.

Spontaneous, Naturalistic Improvisation

Preparation

The teacher reads the Dear Dorothy letter (see below) to stimulate a more serious focus on the topic. Responses to the letter are linked with aspects of the parent/child relationship described on the flow chart on page 183. Then discuss briefly Julia's attitudes towards parent/child relationships, for example:

What — angry   resentful   hostile

Why — treated like a child   not trusted

Dear Dorothy

Can you help me? I am fifteen years old but I look much older than I am. All my friends are seventeen or eighteen years old and many don't go to school anymore. They are great fun to be with and like to go out a lot. They never cause any trouble, and I believe they are genuine, honest people. My problem is that my father doesn't see it my way. He thinks I am far too young to have friends this age and that I see too much of them.

Whenever I come home I am put through the third degree. Where have I been? Why am I home ten minutes late when I should have been home at

midnight? Who was I with? Why haven't I done my homework? Why didn't I do the dishes before I went out? It's always the same. It's getting to the point where it is easier to stay at home. How can I get them to understand that I can look after myself and that I am only having fun?
Julia

Improvisation

(a) Two volunteers (parent and child) enact scene whilst group watches. Those aspects of parent and child relationships that could cause friction are highlighted in discussion.

(b) Audience observes and decides what realistic attributes each character portrays, and notes how attributes are communicated (voice gesture/body gesture) at the conclusion of the improvisations. List on the board the specific gestures used to communicate attributes.

The drama event

Situation

Students decide on scene to be explored:

1 Julia (from letter) is questioned by her father when she returns home at 10.30 pm.

2 A sixteen-year-old boy with his mother. He wants to visit friends; she wants him to do homework.

Note: It is essential that in offering the students the freedom of playwrighting these scenes, the drama remains at an artificial and imaginative level. State this openly to your students so that they understand that the artistic medium must be appropriately controlled. The teacher ensures that the task and the action are appropriate for deeper understanding of the characters and of parent/child relationships; for example, in 2 above prescribe external task and inner action:

Boy — to get to friends quickly;
— to remain calm and in control.

Mother — to get boy to do homework;
— to avoid preaching and threatening punishment.

The teacher can sidecoach for focus on task, commitment to role and the dramatic situation, and encourage naturalistic expression of response.

3 New situations and characters can be used in subsequent improvisations to explore a range of parent/child conflicts.

4 When the drama has exposed meanings about the causes of conflicts, scenes are replayed to find realistic resolutions to the conflicts.

Students and the teacher make suggestions to student actors as to how the conflict might be resolved. To do this, changes must be made to the characters' inner tasks and attitudes.

Complementary drama

5 Through reflection and discussion, quickly note the audience's awareness of:
— how gesture was used to add meaning to the drama;

Gesture	Realistic Parent	Realistic Child
Voice	sarcastic, loud/slow, quiet/slow, pleading, coaxing	cool, casual, unconcerned, light, polite
Body	clenched hand, fingers stroked temple and lips, moved about a lot	Rolled eyes, sighed (when not being watched), tapped foot occasionally

— the causes of conflict and possible ways of avoiding or resolving it.

Contrast and Impact in Drama

Preparation and Motivation
The teacher refers to the effect of the contrasts listed in the improvisation on page

195 (for example, loud/slow, quiet/fast vocal gestures). The teacher and students discuss the way the media uses contrast (for example, the before and after pictures in weight loss advertising) and the effects of differences being placed side by side — that the differences are magnified and therefore made clearer.

The drama event

Small Group Polished Improvisation

This aims to crystallise and communicate understanding of contrast and its impact on meaning. Students divide into groups of four.

Characters

One pair	**A**	Realistic Parent
	B	Ideal Parent
Other pair	**C**	Realistic Child
	D	Ideal Child

Order of dialogue — **A. B. C. D.**
              A. B. C. D., etc.

A The Realistic Parent opens the scene by greeting the Realistic Child then freezes.

B The Ideal Parent speaks next, greets the Ideal Child in an appropriate 'ideal' manner and freezes.

C The Realistic Child responds to the Realistic Parent and freezes.

D The Ideal Child responds to the Ideal Parent and freezes.

Dialogue and freezes then continue in this order. A. B. C. D. etc. The teacher helps the students find appropriate task and inner action for character; provides examples of how dialogue may happen and uses teacher as character to demonstrate the opening lines of the scenes. There should be constant interaction and collaboration with small groups and individuals to reinforce style, task and structure. Support and patience are needed as this activity places high demands on the students' skills and commitment. The setting chosen for the scene should be such that students work closely together; for example, in the kitchen, the lounge, the bedroom, etc.

Presentation of Scenes

(*All* scenes are viewed before final discussion.)

Audience Task
1 To observe the effect of differences in highlighting details of parent/child relationships.
2 To identify those interactions they found to be most effective in communicating the ideas of the drama.

Complementary drama

Reflection

Key Questions
1 What have we discovered about conflict between parents and children? (For example, that everybody seems to experience some degree of conflict in their relationships.)
2 What have we discovered about resolution and harmony between children and parents? (For example, that the mood we're in affects the extent to which the conflict is resolved happily.)
3 What have we learnt about the use of the element of **contrast** in communicating meaning? (For example, that greater the contrast the more obvious and powerful the scene may become.)

Conclusion

On the card next to the flow chart, list anything you might want to include in the feature programme.

THE BLIND DATE

Approximate Age: 14 years
Time: 150 minutes (3 × 50 minutes)
Topic: The Blind Date
Focus: Character

Specific Objectives

1 To experience the influence of peers on trust and honesty in parent/child relationships.

2 To experience, communicate and express thoughts and feelings about self-image, peer influence and conformity.
3 To experiment with theatrical 'style' and explore its expressive ability to manipulate audience response.

Complementary drama

Conducting the Lesson

Re-cap last week's work and learning. The teacher consults the master flow chart and explains that these lessons will explore some aspects of self-image and peer group influence.

The drama event

Pair Improvisation

These should be spontaneous and naturalistic, with the whole class working at the same time. Emphasise the importance of character focus on tasks and attitudes during the short improvisation. Work for commitment to role, support in improvisation and artistic truthfulness of interactions.

1 Characters
A A fifteen year old
B A parent

Situation
A wants to go to a party on Friday night, although **A** has formerly promised **B** that he/she will babysit younger brother while parents go out. **A** must 'sell' the party to **B**, and be allowed to go.

2 Characters
A fifteen year old
B A close friend

Situation
A tells **B** about the party on Friday night; for example, who's going, what might happen, etc.
(This description may be somewhat different to the one in in the first improvisation.)

3 Characters
A fifteen year old
B A member of the opposite sex, of a similar age to **A**.

Situation
B has to ask and persuade **A** to go to the party.

4 Characters
A The member of the opposite sex from the previous improvisation.
A friend of **A**'s of the same sex.

Situation
A has to explain to a hostile **B** why they aren't going to the party together. In explaining, **A** must state what hopes he holds for the night with his date.

Complementary drama

Reflection and Discussion

Key Questions
1 How did the parents in the first scene feel about son/daughter's approach to 'selling the party'?
2 What did this and the following scenes tell us about parent/child relationships? (refer back to Julia's 'Dear Dorothy' letter for connections)
3 What influence did friends have on actions in the drama?
4 What effect, if any, did the events of the drama have on self-image?

The drama event

Whole Group Drama: The 'Let us Transform You' Company

Preparation
Divide the group in half. Each half will take on the roles of company members specialising in preparing the 'perfect blind date'; that is, transforming any adolescent into a highly desirable person. (Note that the company and its clientele are highly respected and moral. This reputation is rigidly guarded.)

Both groups choose a member who is willing to act as the person to be transformed. (A girl from one group and a boy from the other.)

Company members, in consultation with this person, discuss the 'perfect blind date' and decide what characteristics and personal attributes the blind date will be endowed with. (Personality, values, philosophical attitudes and interests should be focussed on, rather than physical details.)

The characteristics which the adolescent held before are also decided upon. The 'blind date' selects two company spokespersons who will promote his/her transformation.

Prepared speech technique. Some members help in the preparation of 'Before and After' accounts of the transformation. Other members of the group help the clientele with details of conversation or attitudes to be displayed during the blind date meeting.

'Let us Transform You' Promotion

Company members line up to present and view the dates. Spokesperson 1 steps forward and describes the 'Before' characteristics of the client. For example:

'When this person first came to us, he/she was underweight, anxious and very shy. The hands quivered when the mouth had to speak . . . the bright purple and green clothes hid the grey mouse beneath . . .'

Spokesperson 2 then steps forward with the client and describes what the company has now achieved in this 'perfect blind date'. Both groups complete their promotion.

Company members should work from attitudes of high status and pride in achievement. Clients should work from attitudes of 'I must live up to what they expect of me.'

Whole Group Drama: The Proof of the Pudding

Situation

A party or disco scene. Two blind dates must find a way to meet and talk together in a way that is appropriate for their 'transformed' characters.

Characters
Two perfect blind dates. Adolescent, other party goers.
All party goers have a responsibility to help the dates meet, but must do so without causing embarrassment.
Allow a brief moment for students to focus energy and commit themselves to role. For convenience, students need only play an 'adolescent party goer'. Individuals may select a specific attitude toward the party and the 'dates', but must work from this point towards ensuring the success of the Company's transformation.

Allow several minutes for the drama to work towards its aims. Stop the drama if focus and belief is inadequate. Use the teacher as a character, the 'company director', to give personal support if needed. A disc jockey, drink waiter or bouncer can thwart interactions that are too hasty or superficial, for example. Conclude the action before it 'plays itself out'!

Complementary drama

Reflection and Discussion

Key Points
1 Differences and similarities between the company's 'perfect date' characteristics.
2 The attributes which help make the meeting of the dates easier or more difficult to handle:
   — The topics discussed?
   — The values stated or played down?
   — The outer gestures and inner feelings.
3 The extent to which the 'transformation process' helped or hindered self-image and confidence.
4 In the light of the experiences of the 'Let's Transform You' drama, how do you feel about the existence of computer dating services, advertising for companions, etc?

ON TRIAL

Approximate Age: 14 years
Time: 150 minutes (3 × 50 minutes)
Topic: On Trial
Focus: Event

Specific Objectives

1 To use research material as a basis for developing the drama.
2 To use the trial situation as a means of objectifying and evaluating peer group and family relationships.
3 To explore a range of communication techniques to create impact in the drama.

Materials

Newspaper clippings, statistics, brief case studies, magazine articles, etc. related to teenagers and self-image. (Resources can be collected by the students as part of their research responsibilities.)

Complementary drama

Conducting the Lesson

Introduction
Brief discussion of previous work.

Sculptured Tableau: I, Me and You

Groups of three or four quickly prepare a frozen tableau, paying particular attention to the use of contrast and gesture. The tableau should present one image of the drama lesson which held particular impact and meaning for your group.

Half the class freezes into tableau whilst others view the images, and vice versa. Discuss only to clarify unclear images.

Peer Group Influence, Conformity and Self-image

Have a brief discussion to isolate what 'appearances' are important to self-image or group acceptance (the two may coincide).

This naturally leads to a discussion of values and attitudes which are important to self-image and group acceptance. (Try to emphasise what is actually so, rather than what is stereotypically accepted!)

The drama event

Small Group Planned and Rehearsed Scenes

'The darker side of peer group influence and conformity'. Students in groups of four or five plan scenes about the above topic.

The newspaper clippings, statistics, brief case studies and photographs which have been collected by the group will now form the basis of the drama.

Groups are given about twenty minutes in which to carefully consider the material, their responses to it and the style of drama they will present.

— Restricted language and gesture may be used.
— A narrator or chorus may comment objectively on action.
— Contrast of exaggeration and naturalism may be used (similar to the Ideal Parent/Realistic Parent improvisation).
— Caricature and satire may be used.

The teacher explains that the style of presentation will reflect the group's attitude towards the content of the scene. How they want the jury/audience to react and judge will need to be considered, since the style selected must be capable of effectively communicating their views.

The drama event

Whole Group Improvisation:The State Versus the Peer Group
Situation
A court scene where filmic evidence (the prepared scenes) will be presented to a judge — the teacher as character!

Characters
According to small group scenes. When not presenting scenes, students become members of the jury.

Small group members are cross-examined by the jury after the presentation of scenes. The judge may disallow questions if they are irrelevant, hostile or unfair. When all evidence has been presented, the jury considers its verdict. The charge is that 'The group destructively manipulates self-image and selfishly enslaves its peers.'

For ease of discussion and deliberation, small groups may need to be assigned the task of passing judgement on each of the groups and reaching a final verdict. When the groups return one by one, the jury leader delivers the judgement of guilty or not guilty.

Complementary drama

Reflection and Discussion

Key Questions
1 In specific terms, what aspects of behaviour did the peer group attempt to influence in the drama?
2 To what extent did the drama reflect the situation in real life?
3 What pieces of evidence most influenced the jury's decision?
4 What differences and similarities existed between male and female peer groups and conformity?
5 To what extent were the 'victims' of the peer groups merely weak or stupid?
6 How accurately did you think the drama showed the influence of the peer group on self-image?
7 Given your experiences in the drama, and what you know of real life, find a statement that sums up how you feel about peer group influence, conformity and self-image. Put it in the form of a magazine article headline, if you like; for example, 'Peer Group Influence A Myth', 'Inner Strength Must Be Developed From Childhood'.

Conclusion
The group decides what parts of this drama they want to consider for use in the feature

programme, and this is written on the programme performance list. Students are reminded to gather further data that relates
to the drama so far, or that may be used
in future lessons.

THE GANG

Approximate age: 14 years
Time: 150 minutes (3 × 50 minutes)
Topic: The Gang
Focus: Place

Specific Objectives

1 To use a poem to explore the relationship
between self-image and facade.
2 To use poetic imagery as the stimulus for
expressive skills development.
3 To extend students' understanding of the
use of space and movement to create artistic meaning.

Materials

'Leather-Jackets, Bikes and Birds' by Robert Davis, Sufficient copies for the group.

Leather Jackets, Bikies and Birds

The streets are noisy
with the movement of passing motors.
The coffee bars get fuller.
The leather-jacket groups begin to gather,
stand, and listen, pretending they are
looking for trouble.
The juke box plays its continuous
tune, music appreciated by most.
The aroma of espresso
coffee fills the nostrils and
the night.
Motorbikes pull up.
Riders dismount and join
their friends in the gang.
They stand, smoking, swearing,

playing with the girls;
making a teenage row.
They pretend not to notice the drizzle
falling out of the dark,
because you've got to be hard to
be a leather-jacket.
A couple
in a corner, snogging,
hope the motor lights will not be
dipped too much,
so that the others will see them.
They must all have recognition;
there must always be enough
leather-jackets around them,
the same as theirs.
The street lamp on the side
of the street shows the rain
for what it is — wet and cold.
But it does not show their faces
for what they are.

Robert Davies

Conducting the Lesson

Complementary drama

Introduction
The teacher explains that the lesson will
explore a poem found by one of the class.
The student feels that 'bikies' are a good
example of peer group pressure and conformity. The teacher reads the poem to the
class, allowing the full impact of the images
to work for the students. The poem is distributed for discussion.

Discussion

Responses to images are shared and meaning or vocabulary are clarified. Images of
conformity are listed on the board. Note the
absence of images which directly descibe
bikies. Compile a list of bikies' characteristics; for example:

What observers see	What they are
Teenage row	Insecure
Smoking, swearing	Needing friendship

   Discussion of poem is linked with pre-vious drama and ideas are listed on flow chart.

Movement, Gesture, Space and Image: Skill Development and Art Form Exploration

Students are given the task of developing a bikie walk that will express 'pretend' toughness, and 'group recognition'.

Situation
'The leather jacket groups begin to gather,
   stand and listen,
pretending they are looking for trouble.'
The students walk around the perimeter of the room then, in ever decreasing circles, towards the centre, where the 'gang' will gather. When in the centre, they 'stand and listen', and are 'looking for trouble'. Watch the focus of the group, and freeze when the achievement is appropriate. The teacher comments on the visual effect of the 'grouped gang'. Students comment on their feeling responses to the action of the 'grouped gang'. Repeat the exercise with more concentration and consideration of grouping image; for example, one bikie may place hand on another's shoulders. (The exercise can be repeated with half groups watching so that they understand the visual effect of the movement and spacial grouping and can make suggestions about how to improve the images.)

Improvisation and Dialogue

Still frozen, students are reminded of the phrases 'they stand, smoking, swearing', 'you've got to be hard to be a leatherjacket', and 'They must all have recognition ... there must always be enough leather-jackets around them, the same as theirs.'

Students now think of what they may talk about in a bikie gang. On a given cue, the 'grouped gang' comes to life, improvising dialogue. The students remain grouped together but on another cue, they turn and begin a new conversation. Sidecoaching is used carefully during the improvisation; for example, 'Yes, it is raining, but pretend not to notice', 'There are pedestrians about ... watch the image you want them to see.'

(If the dialogue isn't flowing stop the drama and discuss possible things to talk about — your bike, girlfriend or boyfriend or last night's 'rage'.)

Repeat the exercise until skill development and dramatic images have reached a satisfying level of artistic turthfulness.

Reflection and Discussion

Key Questions
1 What topics of conversation did you feel were most appropriate to the 'grouped gang','leather jacket' images?
2 In what ways did other gang members respond to you?
3 What were the most marked similarities between the group members?
4 Isolate some of the feelings you had as part of the leather-jacket gang.

The drama event

Small Group Performances: 'For Who They Are'

Role Preparation
Brief discussion of 'For Who They Are'.Comments are already listed on the board. Use these comments to suggest how bikies may behave away from other gang members, at work, school, home, etc. List the suggestion on the board.

Scene Preparation
Class divides into groups of four or five.

Characters
One group member plays a bikie character; the others play family members, co-workers, school friends, etc. The group decides on the key characteristics they want the bikie to have.

Situation
The groups choose a situation which will best highlight the bikie's characteristics as suggested by the statement 'For Who They Are.'

Complementary drama

Performance

Work is shared and discussed.

Key Questions
1 What characteristics were portrayed and how clearly did the drama communicate them?
2 How do you think other gang members would react if these characteristics were displayed?
3 What purpose does the bikie's facade have?
4 To what extent do individuals use facades in everyday life?

The drama event

Improvisation 'Faces Don't Show What They Are'

The students return to the perimeter of the room as before. The exercise is repeated as before, but this time when the group improvise their dialogue, each gang member will allow one of the 'for who they are' characteristics to be exhibited. (For example, one bikie may feel sympathy for a handicapped pedestrian, but blocks the response before it can be fully observed by others.)

Allow several minutes for the improvisation to proceed. Where unsubtlety of expression results, establish inner tasks for students so that meaning and expression of it is clear and sincere.

When the group's achievement is satisfactory, the teacher may freeze the action
and ask pairs or small groups to 'replay'
their interactions and dialogue, while the
rest of the group remains still and listens.
Continue this process until all the gang
members have run through their dialogue.

Complementary drama

Brief Discussion

1 The ways in which key characteristics
were exhibited.
2 Responses from other gang members.
3 How students avoided over-acting and obvious portrayal of characteristics.
4 The difference between self-image and
personal facade.

The drama event

Image Building

The class is now asked to apply the skills
learnt and understanding gained through
the drama experiences to a theatrical presentation of the whole poem.

Students work in groups of four or five.
For each of the following sections of the
poem they are to prepare a frozen group
image which will clearly communicate the
feelings and attitudes of the bikies.

Section 1
'The leather-jacket groups begin to
gather,
stand, and listen, pretending they are
looking for trouble.'
Section 2
'Riders dismount and join
their friends in the gang.
They stand, smoking, swearing,
playing with the girls
making a teenage row.'
Section 3
'They pretend not to notice the drizzle
falling out of the dark,
because you've got to be hard to
be a leather-jacket.'

Section 4
'They must all have recognition
there must always be enough
leather-jackets around them,
the same as theirs.'

Organisation

One member of the group will read the whole poem aloud while the others move from one frozen position to the next.

After the last two lines are read, present a thirty-second condensed version of one of the improvisations you did about 'For Who They Really Are.'

At the end of this section, the last four lines of the poem will be repeated, and each group member will take up a new frozen position representing the 'For Who They Really Are' characteristics.

Allow ten or fifteen minutes for this work to be prepared.

Note: Offering a concrete example of how to approach the poem readily crystallises the learning of the drama to date. At the same time the programme goal is likely to be achieved with efficiency and a great deal of satisfaction. Experiential, communicative and dramatic action have provided a range of insights into the art form and the content.

Complementary drama

Performance and Reflection

Discussion should focus on the power of the frozen images, the effect these images have on the words of the poem and the contrast between the facade and the 'real' person.

Key Questions

1 Which were the most powerful frozen images?
2 How did the images highlight the different characteristics of the bikies?
3 How was the element of contrast used to create impact and meaning during the drama?

Conclusion

The class discusses all the work so far and decide which scenes they want to include in the feature programme. This is recorded on the list next to the flow chart. Those aspects of the topic already explored are circled on the flow chart. Students identify any other aspects they wish to explore before rehearsal for performance.

Rehearsal and Performance

Narration and scenes are prepared and rehearsed for performance.

14 Drama Lessons for Year 10

Whole Year Course Outline

Four units taking thirty-two weeks (150 minutes per week)

Unit 1: Exploring a Variety of Themes (six weeks)

Unit 2: Myth, Legend and Ritual for Performance (ten weeks)

Unit 3: Performance on a Theme/ Documentary Theatre (sixteen weeks)

Unit 4: Theatre Visits (concurrent)

Unit 1: Exploring a Variety of Themes

(Six weeks)
1 Students and teacher decide on a variety of issues for exploration; for example, 'The World of the Child', 'Conformity', 'The Unknown'.
2 Students will use a variety of dramatic experiences and skills to explore the issues.

Unit 2: Myth, Legend and Ritual for Performance

(Ten weeks)
1 Students will research a myth, legend or ritual, and prepare a brief report for the rest of the class.
2 Students will participate in a series of workshops led by the teacher in which

aspects of myth, legend and ritual are explored.

3 Students will explore the notion of formal rituals in contemporary society; for example, a graduation ceremony, a twenty-first birthday, a wedding, etc. Students will also explore the concept of informal rituals in their daily living.

4 Students will develop skills in make-up, mask and costuming appropriate to the material being explored.

5 As a result of the workshop processes, students will devise a performance programme.

Unit 3: Performance on a Theme: Documentary Theatre

(Sixteen weeks)

1 Students and teacher decide on an area to be explored in workshops and prepared for performance; for example:

   (a) Significant events in Australian history.

   (b) World War 1 and its effects on Australian family life.

   (c) The world of the child.

   (d) Technology and people.

2 Students will be expected to undertake research in selected areas, and record the findings of their research,

Unit 4: Theatre Visits

(Concurrent)

1 Students will attend a minimum of three performances throughout the year and participate in discussions of each performance in order to develop a critical appreciation of theatre.

2 Refer to Guidelines for Reviewing a Theatre Performance on Page 227.

THE WORLD OF THE CHILD

Unit 1: Exploring a Variety of Themes

Approximate age: 14/15 years
Time: 150 minutes (3 × 50 minutes)

Topic: The World of the Child
Focus: Time

Specific Objectives

1 To explore aspects of early childhood.
2 To use space, light, movement and sound to add meaning to the drama.

Materials

1 'Onkerpled' — by Michael Dugan, in *Stuff and Nonsense*, Collins Australia, 1974.

Conducting the Lesson

Complementary drama

Introduction
General discussion about earliest memories of childhood.

Complementary drama

Awareness Exercise One

Students find a space of their own and lie on the floor. They close their eyes and imagine they are newly born. They are to attempt to see and feel things about them for the first time. Open eyes and begin exploration. Teacher talks students through exercise. Students are to sit up and attempt to move, but they are unable to walk or crawl. They may see and explore other people or objects in the room.

Discussion and Reflection

General discussion about their responses during the exercise; for example, wonderment.

The drama event

Awareness Exercise Two

Students find a space of their own. Now they imagine that they are at the toddler stage. Each student decides on a specific task that the toddler will be engaged in; for example, painting or building blocks. They should begin working in isolation and, if and when appropriate, join other toddlers in their activities.

Complementary drama

Discussion and Reflection

General discussion about awareness gained during exercise — e.g. freedom, innocence, spontaneity, danger, fear, etc.

The drama event

Small Group Improvision: A Child's Eye View

Students devise an improvisation which encapsulates the awarenesses discovered during the exercise. Adult characters may be used in the improvisation. The emphasis should be on concepts of distance and height to add impact to the drama. The students prepare and perform to rest of class.

Complementary drama

Reflection and Discussion

General discussion about the effectiveness of the improvisation in communicating aspects of early childhood.

Movement Exercise 'Onkerpled'

The teacher reads the poem dramatically, then holds a general discussion about the meaning of the poem and links with previous exercises. Discuss childhood fears of the dark, etc., as illustrated by the poem.

Onkerpled

If a Glomp is hiding
Beneath your bed,
Don't be afraid —
Yell 'onkerpled'.

Glomps may be scary
And their whiskers are red,
But they run away quickly
If you yell 'onkerpled'.

LOUDLY.

Michael Dugan

Students find a space on their own and imagine they are a Glomp — the scariest imaginative being they can contrive. To a slow count of ten, students rise and move silently into the shape of the Glomp and freeze. Repeat the exercise until there is maximum expressive development.

Students develop a walk and sound to extend the expression of the Glomp.

Half the class watches whilst the other half slowly rise from the floor and bring their Glomps to life in order to scare the rest of the group. Teacher and students yell 'onkerpled' at an appropriate moment and the Glomps must fade to the floor. Repeat with the other half class. (Try slow motion and fast motion, counting to ten, to add variation to the expressive development.)

The drama event

Small Group Improvisation: The Glomp

Students work in small groups to devise a scene based on the poem. (Lighting or lamps on the floor may be used to create distorted shadows for the Glomp.) Students prepare and perform their scenes for the rest of the class.

Complementary drama

Reflection and Discussion

Key Points
1 Isolate those aspects of early childhood that the group feels were most effectively experienced and communicated in the drama.
2 Discuss the impact of space, light, movement and sound within specific improvisations.

THE LEGEND OF NED KELLY

Unit 2: Myth, Legend and Ritual to Performance

Approximate Age: 14/15 years
Time: 150 minutes (3 × 50 minutes)
Topic: The Legend of Ned Kelly
Focus: Character

Specific Objectives

1 To explore the elements of legends and their function in transmitting historical events.
2 To dramatise a legend based on the life of Ned Kelly.
3 To examine the use of narration and montage to effectively communicate a narrative.

Materials

Cards with Ned Kelly details.

Conducting the Lesson

Introduction
The teacher pins large cards around room.

Card One
Ned Kelly — Born in 1855 in Victoria,
Ned's father (Red) — ex-convict from Ireland, died 1866.
Ned — A wild youth, constantly in trouble with the police.

Card Two
Ned Kelly, Aged eighteen.
Tall, powerfully built, attractive young man.
Expert horseman.
A crack shot.
Has already been imprisoned for several offences.
Has already spent three years in jail.

Card Three
The Kelly Family.
Mother, Ellen Kelly, a hardworking, determined, spirited Irishwoman, fierce protector of the family. Also spends short time in goal.

Brother, Dan Kelly, joined Ned in horse-stealing, and member of the 'Kelly gang'. Four sisters and a much younger brother.

==========

==========

Card Four

Stringybark Creek murder — the Kelly gang (Ned and Dan Kelly, Steve Hart and Joe Burn) hiding in hills.

Two policemen killed instantly in confrontation with gang. Another policeman killed shortly afterwards.

One policeman escapes to warn the authorities. Huge reward offered for capture of gang. Ned Kelly devises suits of armour to protect gang from police bullets.

==========

==========

Card Five

Glenrowan Incident — Kelly's last stand.

The Kelly gang fails in an attempt to derail a police train.

The stationmaster is captured and held with other hostages at Jones' Glenrowan Inn. A policeman escapes to warn incoming police that Kelly's gang was at the hotel with guns and armour.

Despite the armour, Ned and his gang are finally captured after a long and bloody siege. Riddled with bullets, Ned Kelly lay drenching the earth with his blood.

==========

==========

Card Six

During sentencing and upon his death, Ned Kelly made the following statements:

'My mind is as easy as the mind of any man in this world, as I am prepared to show before God and man.'

'I am not the only man who has put men to death.'

'A day will come at a bigger court than this when we shall see which is right and which is wrong.'

(To the judge) 'I will see you where I'm going.' 'Ah well, I suppose it had to come to this. Such is life.'

(Two days after Ned Kelly, aged twenty-five, was hanged in 1880, the judge who sentenced him became ill. He died ten days later.)

Complementary drama

Students are asked to read the information on the cards silently and to visualise Ned Kelly as a hero rather than a villain.

General discussion for clarification.

From their previous reading of legends, students isolate important elements of legends and their function within communities.

The drama event

Small Groups Improvisations: The Legend

Students are to use the information on the cards and their understanding of the elements and function of legend to create 'The Legend of Ned Kelly'. In creating the legend, the students are required to use both narration and 'acting out' (montage) as tools for effectively communicating the story.

Students prepare and perform the work. The audience become future generations of Australians in the year 2500. They sit in a semi-circle for community sharing of the legend.

Complementary drama

Reflection and Discussion

Key Questions

1 To what extent were the elements of legend incorporated in the work of the group?

2 Discuss the audience's response in terms of the values the legends were attempting to promote.

THE VILLAGE OF GANYTHIA

Unit 2: Myth, Legend and Ritual to Performance

Approximate age: 14/15 years
Time: 200 minutes)
Topic: The Village of Ganythia
Focus: Place

Specific Objectives

1 To explore the function of myth, legend and ritual within a tribal community.
2 To experience the effect of symbols and other ritualistic elements, as a basis for understanding cultural differences.

Materials

1 'Ceremonial' cloths.
2 Materials for making symbols — paper, scissors, objects, fabric, etc.

Conducting the Lesson

The drama event

Introduction
The teacher as character, draped in 'ceremonial' cloths, addresses the students who are gathered in semi-circle. This is used as the basis for the ensuing drama.

Using restricted language and gesture, the teacher as a tribal leader makes the following statement:

'Since the death of the Great White Bird, Onitius, our people have never regained the peace with which we have always been blessed. Our hearts and minds are troubled by the misfortunes that have befallen us. The Gods seek revenge on us for our irreverent and negligent regard for Onitius. We must speak together and find a way to repent of our actions ...'

Complementary drama

Discussion

General discussion about reactions to situations and a possible setting for such action takes place. Using details of the tribal leader's speech, students build up a brief profile of the village of Ganythia.

The drama event

Small Group Improvisations

The People of Ganythia

Students create a scene(s) which will communicate and express the nature of the tribal community. Things to be considered are relationships between members of community, leaders, etc. and the way the tribe lives — food, shelter, religion, education, etc.

The Myth of Ganythia

Students create a myth which explains how the people of Ganythia believe the 'heavenly' phenomena (sun, stars, moon, clouds, thunder, lighting, etc.) came to be.

The Legend of Onitius

Students to create a legend which the people of Ganythia have retold for many hundreds of years. The legend must somehow be linked to the worship of Onitius.

The Ritual of Repentance

Students create a ritual which all the people of Ganthia will enact to appease the Gods for their irreverance towards Onitius. Students create symbols which will be used in the ritual; for example, masks, objects, headpieces, robes, bowls, scrolls, spears, etc.

The Ceremonies of Ganythia

Students create a ceremoney which is performed in the tribal community:
1 to mark the event of birth; or
2 to mark the event of death; or
3 to mark the arrival of adulthood; or
4 to mark the harvest of the crops.

Students prepare and perform all but the Ritual of Repentance. Hold a general Discussion about the life and beliefs of Ganythia.

Whole Group Improvisation: The Ritual of Repentance

Group 4 explains the Ritual of Repentance and the whole group, as the people of Ganythia, participate in the Ritual.

Complementary drama

Discussion and Reflection

1 Discuss the feelings evoked by participation in the Ritual.
2 Discuss the link between these feelings and the students' understanding of the Ganythian community as expressed in the drama performance.
3 To what extent does the isolation of Ganythia foster the perpetuation of the people's beliefs and life-style?
4 Using your experiences of living in a multi-cultural society and considering your responses within the drama, how important is it that such beliefs are either continued or modified?

15 Senior Drama

Year 11 Whole Course Outline

Four units taking thirty-two weeks (250 minutes per week)

Unit 1: Poetry to Performance (nine weeks)

Unit 2: Performance on a Theme (sixteen weeks)

Unit 3: Theatre Styles (seven weeks)

Unit 4: Theatre Visits (concurrent)

Unit 1: Poetry to Performance

(Nine weeks)

Topic: Family Relationships

1 Students and teacher collect a variety of poems on the theme of 'The Family'.

2 Students use dramatic experience to explore the emotional and intellectual realities of the poetry.

3 Students select between three and five of the poems which best illustrate their understanding of the theme.

4 Students use workshop exploration of the selected poems as a basis for creating theatre images for performance.

5 All students will take an acting role in the performance.

Unit 2: Performance on a Theme

(Sixteen weeks)

Topic: The Future

Background Research: Resources
1 *Factual Data.* Students will gather factual information which supports predictions about the future. Students will be directed to relevant sections of reading material in order to do this. For example:

Future Shock by A. Toffler, Chapter 1.
Small is Beautiful by E. Schumacher, Chapter 1.
Will She Be Right? by Kahn and Pepper, Chapter 1.
Inventing Tomorrow by M. Allaby, Indroduction.
Confronting the Future by C. Birch, Chapter 1.
2 *Non-Factual Material.* Students will be required to read selectively from the following resources:
Novels
A Clockwork Orange by A. Burgess
Farenheit 451 by R. Bradbury
Brave New World by A. Huxley
1984 by G. Orwell
Where Late the Sweet Birds Sang by K. Wilhelm

Short Stories
'Nine Tomorrows' by I. Asimov (collected stories)
'The Pedestrian' by R. Bradbury
'Dark They Were and Golden-Eyed' by R. Bradbury
'The Machine Stops' by E.M. Forster (collected stories)

Poetry
'5 Ways to Kill a Man' by E. Brock.
'Apostrophe to Man' by E. St Vincent Millay
'The Future' by S. Milligan
'Your Attention Please' by P. Porter
'The Last Flower' by J. Thurber

Research Specialisation
Students will work in pairs or groups of three to share research in one of the following areas:

1 Population
2 Employment
3 Education
4 Food, Energy and Resources
5 Government and Politics
6 Changing Lifestyles, Family and People
    Each pair or small group will be required to submit a written assignment (not less than the equivalent of 1000 words) on their chosen research area.
    Each pair or small group will report or present their findings to the rest of the group.

Performance Preparation
1 Students use dramatic experience to explore resource material and ideas held by the group.
2 Workshop exploration is used as the basis for creating theatrical statements for performance.
3 All students will take an acting role in the performance.

Unit 3: Theatre Styles
(Seven weeks)
1 Students will explore a range of dramatic texts. Selected excerpts will be used to develop an awareness of dramatic problems inherent in different theatre styles.
2 In particular, students will examine the relationship between space, movement and objects in the communication of dramatic meaning.
3 Students will gain insight into analysis and interpretation of the material. Dramatic expression of character and a practical exploration of staging techniques will be central to the workshop process. Excerpts will be selected from each of the following theatre styles:

Naturalistic
John Romeril: *The Floating World*, David Williamson: *The Club*, Alex Buzo: *The Front Room Boys* and Tennessee Williams: *The Glass Menagerie*.

Epic
Dorothy Hewett: *The Chapel Perilous*, Bertolt Brecht: *The Caucasion Chalk Circle*, Sophocles: *Antigone* and Peter Shaffer: *The Royal Hunt of the Sun*.

Anti-theatre
Louis Nowra: *Inner Voices*, Eugene Ionesco: *The Lesson*, Jean-Claude van Italie: *America Hurrah* and other plays, and Samuel Beckett: *Happy Days*.

Unit 4: Theatre Visits

(Concurrent)
1 Students will attend a minimum of four performances throughout the year and participate in seminar/discussions of each performance in order to develop a critical appreciation of theatre.
2 Students will submit four written reviews on those performance, using the following guidelines.

Guidelines for Reviewing a Theatre Performance

Use the following seven points as a guide:

1 Personal Responses
   Did it entertain you?
   Did it challenge your ideas?
   Did it create any new understanding about the theme?
   Did it keep you interested?

2 Content
   Recall the plot.
   What was the play trying to say?
   How did they say it?

3 Character
   Which characters did you identify with and why?
   Which characters remained believable for the duration of the performance? Why?
   How would you explain the 'type' of

characters presented? What relationship did they have with each other?

4 *Theme*

How is the theme dealt with and presented in the play? Give specific examples.

5 *Technical*

What 'style' of theatre was it? E.g., proscenium arch, intimate, theatre in the round, etc.

Did this work? What were the effects of this style on the audience?

Was the set appropriate to the dialogue? Was the set effective in this sense? Why? Discuss the use of exits and entrances.

Did the lighting emphasise the mood?

Which acting performances were poor, if any? Why? Discuss the performances overall.

Were the costumes appropriate? Overdone? Did they suit the characters? How much did the actors rely on costume to help the portrayal of their characters?

6 *Structure*

Was there a climax? Where? Why? When did the mood of the play change? How? What was the most powerful scene? Why?

Did the ending work? What feeling did it leave you with?

7 *Evaluation*

Was it a good play?

Explain what effect it had on you and justify this.

Lesson Example: FAMILY RELATIONSHIP

Unit 1: Poetry to Performance

Approximate age: 16 years
Time: 150 minutes (3 × 50 minutes)
Topic: Family Relationships
Focus: Character

Specific Objectives

1 To explore guilt as an aspect of family relationships.
2 To explore the power of dramatic images as a means of making emotional/ intellectual responses.

Materials

Sufficient copies for the whole class of the poem 'My Mother in Her Latter Years' by Bruce Dawe.

My Mother In Her Latter Years

My mother·in her latter years —
the while her mind was moving
under the centrifugal force
of age, of insecurity and
damned outright neglect towards
the rim of things where the soul's speed is
    such
all's spelled out in one laconic blur,
pegged to her wilful
suffering skin by a grim
knowingness: she kept
a loaded .22 single-shot by the bed,
smelled assassination loitering like phosgene
in every shell-hole into which
privation pushed her —
still was acted upon by one centripetal
    hope:
to have sufficient money set aside
to pay for her own funeral.
Seven years dead, she still
clings phantasmagorically
to this proud irreducible concern,
her night-gown flapping in the painful wind
that teases tears from her screwed-up eyes,
a tight-lipped satisfaction on her face
not all the funeral-parlor cosmetician's
artifice could erase,
she spins forever in the wholly-bought-and-
    paid-for

coffin to call her own.
(My mind's clay crumbles round its rotten
    lid.)

Bruce Dawe

Conducting the Lesson: Introduction

Complementary drama

The teacher reads the poem twice.

The teacher emphasises the images which give expression to the poet's understanding of the woman. Clarify any images not understood.

The drama event

Small Group Improvisation: The Mother

(Based on first stanza of the poem)

Characters
A the mother
Others as decided by group

Situation
Decided by group

Task
Plan and rehearse an improvisation which communicates the group's understanding of the mother, using the poet's words as reference points for the drama. The scenes are performed.

Complementary drama

Performance Relection and Discussion

Discuss dramatic images in relation to poetic images.

The drama event

Structured Improvisation in Pairs: Mother and Son

Half the group will represent mothers. The other half will represent sons or daughters.

Space is used so that pairs sit opposite each other, about 1 m to 1.5 m apart. Space pairs evenly around the room to ensure adequate space for creating the drama.

Ask the sons, daughters and mothers to listen to the *images* in the words read by the teacher, and to *slowly* build a character in relation to them.

(*Note*: The mother and child live in separate houses as is represented by the distance between them.)

The drama and expression of it evolves from individuals building and observing images created during the improvisation.

Situation

(The characters are alone in separate houses. Their actions evolve in response to selected poetic images read by the teacher (see below):

'her mind was moving under the
   centrifugal force of age
of insecurity and damned outright neglect
towards the rim of things
pegged to her wilful suffering skin
a grim knowingness
one centripetal hope
to have sufficient money set aside
to pay for her own funeral
proud irreducible concern
the painful wind...teases tears from her
   screwed-up eyes
a tight-lipped satisfaction — wholly
   bought and paid for coffin to call her
   own!'

Tasks

1 The mothers give physical expressions of character by moving and sitting in space. The sons and daughters use the mother's images as a basis for building a relationship with her.

2 The sons and daughters give physical expression to the character by moving and sitting in space.
The mothers observe and use these images to extend understanding of their relationships with sons or daughters.

3 The mothers use space and collect an imaginary object which is significant in re-

lation to the character's life. Take time
to reflect on the object and build character memories. Find a motivation to lose
interest and replace the object.

4 One-way conversation. Sons and daughters, whilst the mothers watch their actions, telephone the mother to explain
that they cannot visit on a previously ar-
ranged day.

You know the disappointment that will
be felt so be gentle, but be aware that
you *cannot* visit. Conduct a one-way conversation — the mothers *do not* reply.

5 The mothers at last have enough money
for a coffin — so their reason for living
is gone. As a symbol of their deaths, they
stand, walk around a chair and lie in
their coffins.

Allow the sons and daughters a moment
to reflect on this.

6 The sons and daughters now imagine
they have some flowers; see them, smell
them and touch them.

They think about who they are for and
the feelings they have about placing
them at their mother's side.

They imagine that they are now at the
graveside, and place the flowers . . .

The teacher explains that final layers
of characters and relationships will be
added. Students should hold understanding of character so far and be aware that
they will now consciously extend their
drama.

7 The mothers, as an expression of their
spirits, rise slowly from where they are,
move and stand, looking at their sons
and daughters.

They give facial and physical expression
to how they feel in death.

8 *Conclusion*. The mothers, sons and daughters reflect on their relationships and
feelings at this moment. Each to find one
statement or word to express this. The
mothers make their statements first.

Complementary drama

Reflection and Discussion

1 In pairs, students talk about the *images* and *feelings created*. Isolate the strongest moments and discuss weaknesses in images or responses and the ability to consciously control the role.
2 (Whole group) One by one the students make a statement about what they learned most clearly from the experience. Refer back to the poem.

Key Questions

1 What do you think the poet's feelings towards the mother were?
2 How different from or similar to your experiences in the drama are the poet's feelings?
3 To what extent do you think guilt is a significant aspect of family relationship?

Lesson Examples: THE INSTITUTION

Unit 2: Performance on a Theme (Lesson 1)

Approximate age: 16 years
Time: 150 minutes (3 × 50 minutes)
Topic: The Institution
Focus: Place

Specific Objectives

1 To use experiential and exploratory aspects of dramatic action as the basis for creating a clear and persuasive theatrical statement.
2 To experience, through dramatic play, personal attitudes towards the institution and welfare.

Materials

1 Clipboards, paper, etc. for the teacher as a character.
2 Social welfare department form (see below).

Interview Sheet

SOCIAL WELFARE DEPARTMENT

NAME _____ DATE _____

1 Body language, verbal communication, general disposition.

2 Family background — living conditions, lifestyle, relationship with
   family members.

3 Current life — living conditions, interests, relationships with peers,
   goals, attitudes towards future in general.

4 Suitability for Community and Family Adoptive Scheme (you should
   offer clear recommendations with supporting comments)

5 Other. (Special comments for welfare attention)

SIGNED _____

Conducting the Lesson: Introduction

Complementary drama

The teacher explains the dramatic situation
and characters. The time is 1998 and society faces a crisis. The extraordinary number of unemployed and homeless youths

has resulted in an upsurge of violence, endangering the safety and health of the community. The government and the general public have instigated a 'Community and Family Adoptive Scheme' (CAFAS). All homeless, unemployed youths must be placed in foster homes for rehabilitation.

Role Preparation

Characters
Half the class are social workers. The other half are homeless youths
 The following role-building cards are distributed:

Social Workers
Professional qualifications and experience? Age (approx.) How long in this particular job?
Personal Details
 — Marital status
 — Lifestyle — interests, etc.
Emotional Recall —
1 A *personal* experience that was significant in your past, and a *personal* experience that is significant in your present.
2 A professional experience that was/is significant and rewarding; significant and unpleasant, frustrating, disappointing
 . . .

(Individuals verbally express aspect of 1. or 2. and then find appropriate stance and walk.)

Homeless Youths
Name: Age:
Family background
 — neighbourhood/lifestyle
 — relationship with family members
 — number in family

School
 — type of school; formal qualifications
 — personal strengths/weaknesses at school.
Current living conditions
 — movement since leaving home
 — reason for leaving
 — interests, goals
 — relationships with peers
 — current accommodation
Emotional Recall (Character) —

1 An experience in your distant past that is significant and happy.
2 An experience in your past — distant or immediate, that is unpleasant, traumatic, problematic.
3 An individual who currently holds special meaning for you.

The drama event

Pair Improvisation: Behind the Scenes

Situation The whole class work simultaneously.

The social workers set up interview areas. New members of staff are transferred from regions to aid the interviewing process. Social workers find a fellow worker (you don't know) and make polite, welcoming, conversation. Then use the *polite* conversation to find out something personal and something professional.

The homeless youths are awaiting interviews about placement in CAFAS. You have never met many of these people before. Find a reason to talk to one person and find out how they are feeling about their lives and about CAFAS.

Whole Group Improvisation: The Interview

Characters
 The teacher as a character — the Welfare Supervisor
 Social workers
 Homeless youth

Situation

CAFAS interviews. The welfare workers need to gain information relevant to placing the homeless youths with foster families. The homeless youths wait outside the interview area. The social workers are seated in the interviewing space.

The drama event

The teacher, as the Welfare Supervisor, welcomes the homeless youth and makes an 'occasion' of the interviews. The teacher as character stresses the importance of making an impression, watching posture, language and attitudes. The Welfare Supervisor is formal and a little abrasive and has negative attitudes towards rehabilitation and CAFAS. The Supervisor ushers youths to the interview spaces. An interview begins.

The welfare officers are to complete the interview sheets during the interview (see page 234).

Allow half an hour for the interviews. The teacher as character ends the interview and asks the homeless youths to wait in a separate area whilst interviews are considered by the welfare officers. The youths discuss their experiences in the interviews. The social workers make final recommendations.

To conclude, the welfare officers submit recommended names to the Welfare Supervisor, who then assembles the selected youths.

Complementary drama

Discussion and Reflection

The same pairs work together and discuss their thoughts, feelings and actions during the interview.

The same pairs prepare a brief statement which expresses their attitudes towards the Institution and the State, and these statements are shared with the whole group. Question and discuss to clarify viewpoints, and list the attitudes on butcher's paper.

Lesson Example: THE STATE

Unit 2: Performance on a Theme (Lesson 2)

Approximate age: 16 years
Time: 100 minutes (2 × 50 minutes)
Topic: The State
Focus: Place

Specific Objective

To engage in dramatic/theatrical problem solving as a result of the experience.

Materials

The attitudes listed on butcher's paper.

Conducting the Lesson

Complementary drama

Introduction
Teacher and students discuss the attitudes listed in the previous session.

Performance Preparation

1 Pairs prepare a movement sequence which expresses central attitudes to the State and the Institution. The sequences are rehearsed and presented.

Complementary drama/drama event

2 Small groups prepare a theatrical statement designed to persuade an audience of their particular viewpoint(s). Prepare, rehearse and perform.

Audience Task
To observe the performance and:
1 Discuss the style of presentation and its appropriateness to the drama.
2 Isolate any new insights gained about the theme or dramatic form.

Complementary drama/drama event

Performance Reflection and Discussion

Discuss the clarity and persuasiveness of the theatrical images, and the responses from students' audience task.

Lesson Example: THE CITY OF THEBES

Unit 3: Theatre Styles

Approximate age: 16 years
Time: 150 minutes (3 × 50 minutes)
Topic: The City of Thebes (Greek Tragedy)
Focus: Place

Specific Objectives

1 To communicate the notion of agony and faith.
2 To gain an emotional identification with the setting and the suffering of the people of Thebes and with the King's burden in reconciling the relationship between man, God and the elements.

Material

Situation sheets (below).

Situation Sheets*

Sheet 1: The City of Thebes
Sorrows beyond all telling
Sickness rife in our ranks
The city reeks with death in her streets
Mothers kneel at every altar
Barren agonies of birth
Pestilence
Fever grips the city
Death in the pastures
Death in the wombs of women
Death from which there is no escaping
A tide of death

Sheet 2: The People of Thebes
Why do we suffer?
Heal our pain
Ease our fear

*Note. All the details on the sheets are direct textual quotes from the opening scene.

Our children die
Make us clean
You saved us once — save us again

Sheet 3: The Theban Priests
Great King —
we seek your help
Hear the voice of your people
See the suffering of your city
We know you can save us
Wake this dying city
Save us from this fate
Find some deliverance for us

Sheet 4: Oedipus, The King
Lord and King
The first of men
Giver of life
Greatest of men
Saviour of the people

Conducting the Lesson: Introduction

Complementary drama

The teacher introduces the concepts of Greek Tragedy; for example, passion, religiosity, the emotional, spiritual relationship between Man, God and the Elements.

The theatre structure and the actor's relationship with the audience are discussed; for example, the huge open space of the Greek theatre; the nature of the masks, costuming and gesture; the audience expectation of a significant theatrical event; etc.

Role Preparation

The teacher asks the group to move around the room familiarising themselves with the situation in Thebes as described on the sheets.

The class is then divided for the drama:
1 The King is selected.
2 Three or four Theban Priests are selected.

3 The remaining students become the people of Thebes.

Task

1 The King is separated from the group (allowed to wear a robe) and asked to familiarise him/herself with the character card textual details and *director's instructions*.

The King
I grieve for my people.
I know the suffering of my city.
My heart feels my people's sorrow.

Director's Instructions for the King
You are Lord and King.
You are responsible for the people and the city.
You are wise and good.
Watch and listen
You know you've sent for help.
You await the messenger from the Oracle.
You care.
Respond as you feel appropriate.
Keep images of the King in your mind.
You may leave the drama at any time **if** you feel you have dealt appropriately (as the King) with the situation

---

Complementary drama

2 Students find a space of their own and reflect on the details of Thebes. Then they sculpture an image and devise a sound that communicates the notions of agony, suffering and grief. (Teacher and students briefly discuss agony and suffering and highlight the *quiet* nature of suffering. Students are warned *not* to use images or sounds which will over-dramatise and lack dramatic truth.)

3 In pairs or small groups the students develop images that express the agony and

suffering of the people of Thebes. Students should decide on their relationships as Theban people; for example, mother, children.

Discuss whether their images were appropriate as a theatrical expression of the situation in Thebes.

The drama event

Whole Group Improvisation: The Supplication

Characters
As above

Situation
On the steps of the King's Palace. The people of Thebes make supplication to the King to relieve their suffering. The priests act as spokespersons for the people. The King meets with his people.

The priests's task is to observe people's images of suffering and use them as a basis for appeal to the King. The priests may have dialogue with the people as appropriate.

The people's task is to use previous images as a basis for their relationship with Thebes and King Oedipus.

The Teacher sets the scene for the ensuing drama. Remind the people of their suffering and fear and of their hope and faith in the King.

Allow the drama to proceed until the King leaves, or other resolutions eventuate.

Complementary drama

Reflection and Discussion

Hold a general discussion about:

1 The power and appropriateness of images in relation to Greek Theatre.
2 The King's relationship with the people of Thebes and the Gods.
3 The way in which the drama can be used as an approach to staging the text.

Year Twelve Whole Course Outline (Example)

Unit 1: Staging a Play.
   (5 hours per week × 16 weeks)
Unit 2: Australian Theatre.
   (5 hours per week × 8 weeks)
Unit 3: Electives.
   (5 hours per week × 8 weeks)

Unit 1: Staging a Play

(5 hrs per week × 16 weeks)

Background Research

1 Students will research one of the following areas:
— The History of Australian Drama between 1950 and 1970.
— The History of Australian Drama since 1970.
— John Romeril and his theatre.

2 References
P. Holloway (ed.), *Contemporary Australian Drama*, Currency Press, Sydney, 1981.
L. Rees, *A History of Australian Drama*, Vols 1 and 2, Angus and Robertson, Sydney, 1973.
W. Fairhead (ed.) *Spotlights on Australian Drama*, MacMillan, Australia, 1979.

3 Requirements
Each student will:
Present a report on his or her selected research areas to the rest of the group in one of the following ways:
practical workshop, lecture, videotape, cassette recording, or lecture/discussion.
Write an essay on the selected research area, not exceeding 1500 words, outlining his or her major findings.
Submit his or her work folio containing evidence of research findings, any additional resource material, newspaper clippings etc.
Submit a written evaluation of the work at the conclusion of the performance project.

Staging *Chicago, Chicago*

Students will participate in workshop exploration of the text led by the teacher. Students may then work in *one* of the following areas:

Direction

Students will be responsible for the staging of scenes, their rhythm and voice work and for directing these scenes in consultation with the teacher with the appropriate acting group. The scene designs and blocking plans are to be submitted in a work folio.

Movement

Students will be responsible for the creation of particular movement passages and for directing the appropriate acting groups.
Justification for the movements in particular scenes are to be submitted in a work folio.
Note: All students will take an acting role in the performance.

Unit 2: Australian Theatre

(5 hrs per week × 8 weeks)

Theatre Visits

A minimum of six performance will be seen during Terms 1 and 2 in order to develop a critical awareness and appreciation of the various aspects of drama and theatre within Australian society. Areas which will be covered include community theatre groups, professional theatre groups, amateur theatre groups and theatre in institutions.

Group discussions and analysis of each performance will take place, and a written critique, not exceeding 800 words, is to be submitted in a work folio within two weeks of each excursion. These critiques will be used as the basis for discussion.
Refer to guidelines for reviewing a theatre performance on page 227.

Australian Playwrights

Select one or two plays by the same author from the list below, or from the works of another Australian playwright. Consult with your teacher regarding your choice.

Dorothy Hewett: *Suzanna's Dreaming, The Tatty Hollow Story, Bon Bons and Roses for Dolly, This Old Man Comes Rolling Home, The Chapel Perilous* and *Golden Oldies.*

David Williamson: *A Handful of Friends, The Club, The Department, Don's Party, The Removalists, Travelling North* and *What if I Died Tomorrow?*

Jack Hibberd: *A Toast to Melba, One of Nature's Gentlemen, The Les Darcy Show, A Stretch of the Imagination, Dimboola, Who?, White with Wire Wheels, The Overcoat* and *Sin.*

Alex Buzo: *The Front Room Boys, Martello Towers, Macquarie, Makasser Reef* and *Norm and Ahmed.*

Read the texts and complete this written assignment:

1 Write a brief summary of the plot of both texts.
2 Write a short description of the main characters in each text.
3 Describe the settings used in both plays.
4 What is the major theme or message of each play?
5 What is the style of each play?
6 What do the plays say about Australian society? Describe in detail and *justify, using examples from the text.*
7 Describe the similarities and differences between the two plays in content, theme, characters, style, etc.
8 Write your own brief evaluation of the playwright and the play as examples of contemporary Australian literature. How different is this from what other writers have to say?
9 Any other comments.

Work with one or two other students who are studying the same author. Each group will:

1 Discuss similarities and differences between different texts: in style, characters, etc.
2 Prepare a verbal report on how you see this author's work for the rest of the class.
3 Select a section from one play by the author which the group believes crystallises their understanding of the way in which the author views Australian society. Workshop and rehearse the scene for presentation to the rest of the group.
4 Students will participate in practical workshops designed by the teacher to explore selected sections from the works.

References

L. Rees, *A History of Australian Drama*, Vols 1 and 2, Angus and Robertson, Sydney, 1973.
P. Fitzpatrick, *After 'The Doll'*, Edward Arnold, Australia 1979.
G. Dutton, *The Literature of Australia*, Penguin, Harmondsworth, 1964.
P. Holloway, *Contemporary Australian Drama*, Currency Press, Sydney, 1981.
W. Fairhead, *Spotlights on Australian Drama*, Macmillan, Australia 1979.

Unit 3: Electives

(5 hrs per week × 8 weeks)
Students may choose an elective from one of the following, or may evolve their own.

Performance: Australian Playwrights
1 Students working in small groups will select either one act or several scenes of an Australian play.
2 Students will workshop their selection.
3 Students will prepare the scenes for performance to the rest of the class, and to friends and family in an evening performance.

4 Students are expected to make decisions about lighting, costuming and appropriateness of stage setting.
5 Students will submit a written record of the working process, the script excerpts, the production brief and an assessment of the strengths and weaknesses of the performance.

Poetry and Movement
1 Students will participate in a series of practical workshops designed to explore a theme through poetry. Emphasis should be placed on the use of movement and sound during these workshops.
2 Students will prepare the poetry for performance to the rest of the class, and to friends and family in an evening performance.
3 Students are to submit a written record of the working process, the selected poems, the production brief and an assessment of the strengths and weaknesses of the performance.
Note: An analysis of the statement each poem is making, *and the feelings evoked by each one*, should be included in the submission.
Reference: J. Reid, J. Ciardi *et al, Poetry, A Closer Look: Programmed Instruction with Selected Poems*, Harcourt, Brace and World, New York, 1963.

History of the Theatre
1 (a) Students will work individually, in pairs or small groups and explore one of the following:
Greek theatre
Medieval theatre
Jacobean theatre
Commedia dell'arte
Absurdist theatre
Kabuki theatre
Russian theatre
(b) Students will present a seminar to the group about their particular area of study.

Guidelines for research and seminar:
A description of the style of theatre you
have selected:
— How, where and why it began,
— How it relates to other theatre forms
  existing at the time, perhaps in other
  parts of the world.
— Examples of the theatre forms.
— Audience reaction then and now.
— A justification for the selection of plays
  for performance.
— A description of the method(s) your
  group will employ in order to work towards the performance piece.
2 Students will prepare selected scenes for
  performance to the rest of the class and
  to friends and family in an evening
  performance.
3 Students will submit a written record of
  the working process, the script excerpts,
  the production brief and an assessment
  of strengths and weaknesses of the
  performance.

General References*

A Lewis, *The Contemporary Theatre*, Crown,
New York, 1971.

M. Croydon, *Lunatics, Lovers and Poets*,
McGraw-Hill, U.S.A., 1974.

R. Williams, *Drama in Performance*, Watts,
London, 1968.

A.P. Hinchcliffe, *The Absurd*, Methuen,
London, 1969.

J. Pilling, *Samuel Beckett*, Routledge, Kegan
and Paul, London, 1976.

D. Conacher, *Euripides*, University of
Toronto Press, 1967.

K. McLeish, *The Greek Theatre*, Longman,
London, 1972.

References: Plays

Greek: Sophocles: *Electra* and other plays,
The Theban plays, *Oedipus the King, Oedipus
at Colonus*, and *Antigone*.

*Other references can be obtained from libraries after
areas are selected.

Euripides: *Medea, Hecate, Electra,* and *Heracles.*

Jacobean: Three Jacobean Tragedies and Four Jacobean City Comedies.

Absurdist: Ionesco: *Exit the King, The Motor Show, Foursome, Rhinoceros, The Chairs,* and *The Lesson.*

Jean-Claude van Itallie: *America Hurrah* and other plays.

Beckett: *Waiting for Godot, Happy Days,* and End Game.

Elizabethan: Shakespeare: *Merchant of Venice, Romeo and Juliet, Macbeth, A Midsummer Night's Dream and Hamlet.*

Appendix: The School Play

The school play has often evoked feelings of hostility and antagonism from drama teachers, trepidation from parents and sanctimonious pride from the school principal. Few school events carry such potential to create upheaval, disarray and panic as does the annual school play. Despite the many and varied criticisms of these productions, the school play persists. Producers, directors, stage managers and choreographers are fiercely protective about them and vow every year that the next one will be even bigger and better. Let us look at the elements common to most school productions before we analyse the relationship between drama, the play and learning.

Characteristics of the School Play

The annual school play usually involves a large number of students, but little consideration is given to whether these students are capable of talented performances. The plays are usually American or English musicals which run for at least three hours, of which a large part is taken up with twenty-minute scene changes. Several staff members work for months, with a totally inadequate budget in a totally inadequate performance space, and with totally inadequate actors. However, it's almost always 'alright on the night'. Several hundred parents, relatives, friends of the cast and staff 'theatre critics' enable enough profits to be made to finance the next year's production.

The Drama Teacher and the School Play

Why is it that throughout the last decade drama teachers have shied away from any involvement with the school play?

Traditionally, drama in schools was seen to have its roots in dramatic literature and the performance of these works became the school play. Often the English teacher would produce a Shakespearean play or another classic. With the increasing popularity of American Broadway musicals during the 1960s, the English teacher and the Music teacher would often work together to stage the annual production. With the advent of drama specialists in schools during the 1970s, it was logical for the school administration to assume that they should contribute to the annual school production. Yet drama teachers frequently refused to offer their services to the school play. The reason for this can be traced back to the drama/theatre debate of the 1970s.

The notion of 'free play' and 'creative play' began to usurp the 'performance' approach to drama during this time, and drama teachers felt that 'formal' performance was not the prerogative of a drama programme in schools. Performing in front of an audience, regardless of the child's age or abilities, was considered detrimental to the child's development. 'Creative self-expression by the child, for the child,' was considered a more valuable activity in drama; in fact, many drama teachers felt that 'play' and 'performance' were diametrically opposed activities. Blind adherence to this dogma was clearly not conducive to any real analysis of the relationship between play, performance and learning.

Let us now attempt to analyse this relationship from what we know of a child's social development, 'dramatic age', art form learning, the role of the teacher as director and the selection of the script.

The Social Development of the Child

The school community generally regard the school play as a major social function. The audience will rarely criticise any lack of theatrical skill and will applaud what they regard as 'team spirit', or the confident manner in which the students present themselves on stage. After a performance, there is little discussion of the theme of the play, the meaning of the script or of any symbolic interaction which occurred between the actors and the audience. Many parents see their child's involvement in the school play as a pleasant social experience where the child's peer group will be expanded, and the more important 'life skill' of self-confidence developed.

While it is hopefully true that a child's involvement with the school play is a pleasant social experience, this has little to do with learning in drama.

Our specific objectives for drama are the analytical and evaluative development and the expressive and communicative development of the student. All are directed to art form and human development learning. If any social development comes from participation in the school play, this does not mean that any drama objectives have been fulfilled.

It must also be borne in mind that a common criticism levelled at the school play is that it produces precocious 'show-offs' and self-centered 'stars'. Unless this is consciously avoided by the production team, development of the child may not be positively aided in any way.

Scripts which play down the star syndrome may be hard to find, but scripts can be modified. With some extra effort from the teachers — and students if possible — extra scenes might be added, and the roles of the stars pruned.

If we accept the benefits of the school play, what effect does the child's age have on involvement in the school play?

The 'Dramatic Age' of the Child

As was discussed in Chapter Eight, there are quite clear stages in a student's ability to take on a role, to find the appropriate means of expressing a role, and to clearly communicate this to an audience. Until students react to the 'expressive' dramatic age at fifteen or sixteen years, awareness of an audience will tend to produce self-conscious role behaviour and a lack of artistic sincerity. Younger children cannot distinguish between the character and themselves on stage. They say the line and execute the stage movements, but there is no evidence of a role relationship in the presentation of a character.

Peter Slade, when asked why acting on a normal stage is bad for young children, replied,

> 'Because it destroys child drama, and the children then merely try to copy what adults call theatre. They are not successful in this, and it is not their way of playing . . . It makes them conscious of an audience, spoils their sincerity and teaches them to show off. The logical end of all this is a bombastic little boaster who wants to go on the stage . . .' (p. 351)

Young children, when they are in the exploratory stage, tend to identify rather than characterise. This can be seen in the child who identifies with her mother and produces similar voice, stance and behaviour when engaged in exploratory play. Children's ability to characterise evolves slowly. The child must move through the imitative stage to the identification stage and then to the role-taking stage. Children, in order to characterise, must be able to incorporate objective knowledge of the role with their own felt experience, and to maintain a balance between the two. Quite simply, young children's cognitive skills are not yet refined to the extent where the oscillation between the 'me' and 'not me' can be held in stasis.

If we recall our own experiences of watching young children performing on a stage it is clear that there is little evidence of belief in the role. One particular child in a production of *Oliver* spent most of his time on stage waving to friends in the audience, trying to wipe off his stage make-up and forgetting most of his lines. When he did remember his lines, they were said in a rapid, mechanical fashion. The child had little or no idea of what playing a role in performance meant. Certainly, senior students are more readily able to adopt roles and develop characterisation skills and may achieve several drama objectives through an involvement in the school play. The crucial factors here are the choice of play and the production process, which will be discussed shortly.

John Allen sums up the difficulty of involving younger students in the school play when he describes a not uncommon experience:

> 'Some of my colleagues have suggested over the years that the evil provenance of the school play was the Nativity play in the infant school. This is usually the first occasion when children are required to go through the formal procedures of performing in front of an audience. The occasion usually involves a fairly large number of children, dressing-up, lines learnt, scenery shakily erected, and as large an audience as the hall will hold. In performance we have inaudibility, lack of involvement, angel's eyes searching for Nan in the audience and friendly smiles when contact is made — every kind of distraction that destroys the very nature of the performance that is being offered.' (p. 128)

Art Form Skills

As we have stated, many drama teachers rejected the school play, and indeed, any form of performance within their courses, in favour of personal development objectives. In doing this, they usually denied their students any overt knowledge of the art form of their medium, and the students often battled to try and find appropriate means of expression for their work. This is rather paradoxical, in that the director of the school play offered students similar experiences to that of the drama teacher: personal and social development. These drama teachers may have been quite correct in their disapproval of younger students' involvement in performance, yet neither the school play nor the personal development drama course catered for the acquisition of expressive skills needed for performance and symbolic learning.

A student's acting ability in the school play was often seen as a skill which the student possessed or not. Students would be considered an asset if they had voice projection skills. They were either capable of conveying emotion in their voices or they weren't. Students were still encouraged to be in the school play, however, regardless of their 'acting' skills. After all, if your are in a chorus of fifty or sixty, there is little need for subtle role work.

Any school play or performance usually attempts to create an apparent reality or a sense of truth for the audience, so that a role relationship between the actor and the audience can be established. The script is the filter through which an idea or image is conveyed from the actors to the audience. It there is no sense of 'truth' or a real belief in the imaginary situation on the part of the actors, then the script, or filter, becomes meaningless. The expressive skills of the actor are a vital factor in establishing believability for the audience. If a student has no real role truth, then the audience members will merely see Mary Smith of Year 8 dressed up and walking around a stage talking. The filter, the script, then carries no importance, for the actors are unable to create the necessary belief in the play.

Students need to understand and acquire proficiency in the use of art form elements so that appropriate forms of role expression are realised in the performance, or, as John Allen states, 'the private vision (can be) expressed in communicable terms.' (p. 118)

The Role of the Teacher/Director

As in a drama class, the role the teacher assumes in the school play will determine the type of learning which occurs. For purely pragmatic reasons most school play directors tend to adopt an autocratic role. This is characterised by drilling the students, shouting instructions at the actors, demonstrating what should be happening on stage, and organising the backstage crew so that they resemble an army drill team. Understandably, for many directors this may seem to be the least problematic method of producing a play with a large cast. At the very least, the performance will appear somewhat similar to the Broadway version, if only in content. The paradox here is that in deciding on this style of direction, little or no characterisation and role belief can occur.

The autocratic director would often demand little more of their actors than learning lines, entering on cue, and being heard. More often than not, the director would stand at the end of the hall, giving instructions through a megaphone such as 'louder!' or 'I don't want to see you waiting in the wings. Stand back!' The director would often demonstrate the 'correct' method of delivery of lines and expect the child to copy exactly. As a result the child's performance is not genuine, it is merely a mimickry of the adult demonstration; the role is one-dimensional, shaped to meet the adult requirements of outward form.

Usually, in this style of direction, there is no discussion of plot development or character development. The notions of rhythm, contrast or space, for example, remain covert. They are implied in the director's instructions, such as, 'Walk on more quickly!', 'That passage of speech should be spoken quietly', or 'Stand a little closer to her.' No justification for these directions are given. A clear understanding of a role is unlikely to occur in such circumstances.

What, then, is a more appropriate role for the director to assume if any learning is to occur?

Naturally it is easier to work with a small cast, but one cannot dispense with the chorus in *Oklahoma* or *Annie Get Your Gun*. The chorus is there to provide life, energy and colour to a musical production. In such circumstances, one has to contend with 100 actors who should, in the best of all possible worlds, all have strong role belief and characterisation skills. There can be little doubt that this is a time-consuming process, but both the performance benefits and long-term gains should offset this to a degree.

The first step would be a simple discussion with small groups in the cast about their characters. The actors should isolate a few key characteristics from the social and psychological levels of characterisation.

The actors could build on this by writing a full character synopsis. Once this external character manifestation has been established, then the director should link this with the personal experience of the student. A further step, before any script work begins, would be to develop the characters further by placing them in improvised scenes, where the character development can be realised and extended. It may be necessary to repeat this process a number of times until it is apparent that there is a degree of artistic truth in the students' work.

When working with the script, ask questions about the characters instead of giving detailed and specific instructions. What is the character trying to do at this moment? Why is he/she trying to do it? How is he/she trying to do it? The teacher/director must be able to help the student find the answer to these questions — to identify the external task as well as the internal action. This motivational level of awareness is essential to role development and sincerity of action. To forego this step and resort to demonstration, instruction and drilling is totally destructive.

It is also necessary to lead the student to an understanding of the way in which the art form elements are manipulated in the production. If there is to be a moment in the play where the actors are to be frozen in fear, then instead of saying, 'Freeze, hold that look on your faces for five seconds', it may be better to discuss the ways the various characters react to a shock, and the dramatic tension that they have produced by a loud sound or silence or the contrast between movement and stillness. Similarly, why a particular character always enters from the right wing and never the left, for example, will need to be made clear.

While this process is time consuming it ultimately benefits the director. As in a drama classroom, discipline and management occur in the context of the content of the work. If the actors in the school play have a belief in their role and an understanding of particular directions then the students learning is much sounder and more rewarding. There will be a greater commitment to the production and performances and learning will be of a higher quality.

Selection of the Script

The most important criterion for selection of the script for the school play is its potential for role development, characterisation and audience identification. At the middle and senior school levels, it is clear that certain scripts carry greater potential for learning than others. *The Good Woman of Setzuan* or *Under Milkwood* carry greater scope for role development and learning, for example, than *Annie Get Your Gun* or *The Wizard of Oz*.

Many producers of a senior school play tend to reject works by Eugene O'Neill, Tennessee Williams, Brecht, Shakespeare or Arthur Miller, for instance, believing that the audience will find them too difficult to understand, and therefore not entertaining. A more 'accessible' work is then selected such as Alan Hopgood's *And the Big Men Fly, The Boy Friend* or any number of contemporary American musicals. In doing so, these teachers have limited the possibility of a richer dramatic experience for both actors and audience.

If the plot, setting and theme are superficial or asinine, then the audience has little to identify with, particularly if the characterisation is also weak. If characterisation is weak then the audience will have little belief or interest in what happens to the characters, and the meaning of the play will be lost. So many plays, particularly American musicals, contain two-dimensional characters who exibit stereotypical behaviour, devoid of the subtle nuances of human emotion. Therefore, in order for a school play to be anything more than fifty students reading lines surrounded by theatrical gadgetry, the characters in the play need to be convincing enough to allow the audience to identify with them. At the same time, the roles in the script should be challenging enough so that the student can experience new human perspectives, rather than merely reproducing things already known. *Death of a Salesman*, for example, may allow the student to experience the notion of frustrated ambition and living in the past, and the effect these memories can have on present day living.

Clearly, there are several excellent pieces of dramatic literature which are unsuitable for school performance. Difficult absurdist theatre pieces, which make no attempt to present realistic characters or themes and which use illogical language leave many school age audiences perplexed and disoriented. In addition, the actors would need a broad understanding of the rationale and workings of those obscure pieces for any fruitful learning experience to occur. Similarly, Kabuki theatre and some early Greek plays can be confusing.

The decision to produce an original play instead of a scripted work can also be problematic. It is true students in the middle levels seek to express existing ideas and emotions in a form they devise. Senior students however, are capable of identifying with an author's character and ideas, even though these may be quite challenging.

The senior students often find scripted work a useful vehicle for applying and extending their art form skills and for expanding their human development knowledge. This distinction between adolescent expression and the seeking of new horizons is succinctly stated by Louis Arnaud Reid:

> 'Popular art in our culture tends to express life as felt by the adolescents of all chronological ages; serious art by its sophistication tends to probe levels of experience that the young may not yet have undergone.' (p. 300)

A senior art exhibition in a high school would seek to display works of the highest standard within the field; there appears to be no justification for drama to do otherwise. The school play need not be banal or trivial, careful and considerate selection, allowing for the development of characters with whom the audience can identify, will enable a meaningful and 'successful' production to occur.

School Politics

The drama teacher's aversion to the school play often creates feelings of hostility and antagonism amongst other staff members. Obviously there needs to be a delicate balance maintained between a teacher's ideals and those of the school. Criticism of one of the school's major social activities, the school play, is often condemned, especially if the criticism is seen in terms of theoretical psychological or pedagogical argument.

Several drama teachers have produced the school play with eighty junior students to contend with, so that their professional competence remains highly regarded, or so that the school council will release funds for the construction of a drama studio. If producing the school play will aid the development of the drama programme within a school, then so be it. Be aware, though, that in directing a musical in the five weeks allocated to the production of the school play, you are not teaching drama in a similar manner in the classroom, you are merely attempting to get eighty thirteen year olds to vaguely resemble their adult counterparts without being highly embarrassed. Perhaps after two or three years of directing the school play (if you haven't resigned) you may suggest that a senior school play would be an interesting variation to attempt. At least then you would be able to work with students who are capable of creating roles for performance.

Practical Advice on Producing the School Play

A Large-scale Scripted Production

Once the initial decision to produce a school play has been made, and the script selected, many teachers find the administration and organisation a daunting prospect, particularly if this is their first production. Ideally, a production manager should be appointed to cope with administrative aspects so the director can concentrate on the actors' preparation, but this is not always possible. Four areas which require a great deal of time are the preparation of the budget, organising the production team, preparing the rehearsal schedule and organising publicity.

Judy Carlson is a drama teacher at Mitcham High School in Melbourne. She has produced ten major musicals and two drama productions during the past ten years. Her extensive experience has made her a valuable resource for producers in schools in Victoria. The following notes are based on a lecture she delivered at a recent music teachers' conference in Melbourne.

The Budget
Income. First of all, how do you establish the show budget? We decide how many nights or performances we are going to have and then the number of seats we could possibly sell. For example, we run for five nights with an average attendance of 350. The school hall seats 450 and there are approximately 750 students in the school.

Assume the adult price is $4.50 and the student price is $2.50. Add them together ($7.00), divide by two ($3.50) then subtract 20 per cent (70¢), which gives you your average ticket price — ATP (in this case $2.80). Then, to obtain an estimate of gross income or gross profit, multiply the number of performances (five) by the average number of tickets sold per performance (350), to obtain a fairly reliable estimate of total tickets sold, i.e. $350 \times 5 = 1750$. The Average Ticket Price is $2.80 so your expected gross income is $4900. This gives you a basic figure to work with. People staging their first show could establish their budget by estimating ticket sales at approximately 50 per cent of seats available.

Expenses. A major consideration, if you're presenting a major musical, is the payment of royalties. They must be paid and are generally assessed at between $12\frac{1}{2}$ per cent and 15 per cent of the gross income. On application to produce the show the school will be sent a statement of the amount of royalties to be paid.

Generally it's a minimum of $100 per performance or $12\frac{1}{2}$ per cent to 15 per cent of the gross income, whichever is greater. Thus it is possible to estimate ahead of time approximately how much the royalties will cost. With the more stringent enforcement of the copyright laws, it is folly even to contemplate doing a show without going through the proper procedures. Royalties are payments made to the author and/or composer of the show for each performance where admission is charged. It is asking for a lot more trouble than any school can afford to even contemplate performing without obtaining the legal rights and papers.

Other costs are listed below as a percentage of the gross (before expenses) income. Remember they are approximations only and can be higher or lower depending on the show chosen.

Item	Per cent	Notes
Royalties	15	See above.
Costumes	15	These costs depend on stock in hand as well as show requirements. If costumes are made, storage after the show is a consideration.
Scripts/Vocal Scores/Orchestra Parts	10	These items can be hired or purchased as determined by the school's needs or by contract clauses.
Lighting/Sound (Hall Hire)	10	Generally school halls don't have enough of the right kinds of lights or microphones, which means you have to hire or buy if they are really necessary.
Publicity	10	Most of the publicity will not have to be paid for but even basics, like cast photos and printing of programmes and tickets, cost money.
Scenery	20	Including hardware, paint, wood, canvas, etc. depending on the show, its requirements and the school's resources. Some items may be hired but there's always the doubt

		whether the flats of backdrops will suit another stage.
Miscellaneous	10	For those totally unexpected unforseen emergencies, or something overlooked.
Estimated profit:	20	

What do you do with the money left over (and let's be positive about the success of the venture)? We've been very fortunate at Mitcham High. We've performed ten musicals and two drama shows and none has lost money. We always keep $500 in the bank which is used for starting off the next production.

The school has felt that money raised by the school productions should be channelled back into projects which would benefit the departments most involved in the shows — in our case, the drama and music departments. Some of the projects which we've spent our profits on include carpeting the drama and music rooms and a colour video porta-pak plus TV. Thus we have been able to turn our profits into very real, useful assets. Not only are you seen to have performed a good show but you have something tangible to show for the combined efforts of staff and students.

Organising the Production Team
I've been producer, director and production manager in our shows. It's difficult but after a while you begin to cope. It isn't the best way of working to have all the responsibility concentrated in one person. Coping isn't where it's at — a good show needs to be a greater team effort.
Lists. You live with lists. Keep one under your pillow because you might think of something during the night. You wake up, scribble a note and then in the morning you discover you can't read what you've written. But you carry on.

In doing a big musical, director and musical director are equals. You're the head of the team, and you must work as one. Talk together so that the questions and problems are confronted before you reach rehearsal stage. Know where you're going.

You've also got to have a choreographer, unless you're also a dancer. I know what I want with movement but I don't know how to get it. Talk to the choreographer and make sure that the dance needs are fully understood, along with the moods of the show. Communication is essential.

Design is the next major area in the concept of the show. Ideally, one person, in consultation with the director, would design costumes as well as scenery. This gives a tremendous unity to the visual side of the show. However, this is rarely possible. Nonetheless, they must be co-ordinated, within budgetary limits and appropriate to each other. The director needs to understand some of the basics of set design and construction to make the stage movements flow naturally once the scenery is in place. Set construction must be delegated once the designs are finalised.

Costumes can be handled in much the same way. Once the designs are approved, delegate. Costumes can be made by the students or their parents or the staff often volunteer to make the more fiddly, intricate items. This works for some shows while for others it's best to have costumes made by a small team of parents and teachers along with some senior students.

Front of House

Front of House (F.O.H.) management people are essential members of the production team and they're too often overlooked. Publicity gets the audience to the theatre and F.O.H. takes care of them once they arrive. If there is a symbol for the play or musical, make sure it is carried over between the posters, programmes and the dress of the F.O.H. staff. Sometimes this isn't possible or feasible, but it can add to the general ambience when it does.

Although the director shouldn't have to keep the daily accounts of the show, there should be an up-to-date knowledge of the budget limits and ongoing expenses. Mould the entire cast and crew into a unified company, working together to present the best show possible. Teach the students to have respect for the mystique of the theatre — preserve the mystery and excitement for the audience by not letting the cast members go out at interval or after the show still in costumes and make-up.

I believe as few adults as possible should be involved, because it is primarily a learning experience for the students — one which hopefully will make them want to continue being involved in productions once they have left school. This applies to cast, backstage crew and orchestra. We have a student stage manager who comes to all production meetings, takes notes and once the show starts, is completely in charge backstage. By the time students reach years 10 and 11, many have had enough stage experience to enable them to have a try at designing costumes, scenery, lighting, plots and publicity. They're usually very good at these aspects and can assume considerable responsibility for their finished products. They take pride in their efforts and results in a very mature fashion.

The Rehearsal Schedule

Liaison between staff and parents is a very delicate subject. Good rapport is essential. We always publish a rehearsal schedule at the beginning of our rehearsal period, which usually lasts eight to ten weeks. We stick to it and expect other people involved in the show to abide by it also. We have a permission slip for the show which is signed by both student and parent, saying, 'Yes, we know about the rehearsals and we will be there.' Any request for absence from rehearsals must be in writing one week beforehand. There have been times when we've had to say to the student, 'I'm sorry, you must be at rehearsal or you're out of the show.' We don't like having to say that but the students know that it's for their own sake, as well as for the sake of the whole show.

We have rehearsals at night. Generally once a week for the whole cast, and a second extra night for the principals. These rehearsals start at 5 p.m. and end at 9 p.m. We are relatively punctual. 9 p.m. is not too late for even year 7 students to be getting home once a week. We've had students from years 7 to 12 involved with shows and make every effort to ensure that their classes and homework obligations are fulfilled as a condition of their participation in school productions. Therefore the foyer of the hall is available for study so when time allows, students have a quiet area in which to work. Saturday rehearsals are from 1 to 5 p.m. while scenery construction is from 9 a.m. to 1 p.m. Generally there's a big conflict with footy matches. We can't have Sunday rehearsals because our hall is hired out for Church services. Other schools use Sunday rehearsals rather than Saturdays and this seems to work out very well.

Publicity

You must get an enthusiastic person to spearhead the publicity drive. It's very demoralising for the cast to have only a few people in the audience. They are the reason for all the long hours of rehearsal. Audiences make or break a show — and good publicity is essential. Word of mouth is good, but an actual, concentrated, publicity drive aimed at reaching beyond the local area is best of all.

Free Sources of Publicity

Local papers.

The AATT magazine will publish performance details, as will the Drama Resource Centre, Bouverie Street, Carlton and the Victorian Drama League. Write a letter to all of the councils and drama/music teachers of the local schools — primary, secondary and technical. Consider having a school matinee. It's an excellent final dress rehearsal. Have it on the Thursday afternoon with the opening on Friday night. Contact the *Age* 'Weekender' for a listing. Many of the radio stations will broadcast community service announcements free of charge.

Bibliography

H. Albright, P. Halstead & L. Mitchell, *Principles of Theatre Art*, Houghton Mifflin, Boston, 1968.

J. Allen, *Drama in Schools: Its Theory and Practice*, Heinemann Educational, London, 1979.

R. Benedetti, *The Actor at Work*, Prentice-Hall, New Jersey, 1976.

G. Bolton, *Towards a Theory of Drama in Education*, Longman, London, 1980.

O.G. Brockett, *The Theatre: An Introduction*, Holt, Rinehart & Winston, New York, 1979.

R. Burgess, H. Collins, P. Gaudry & A. Tartaro, *Drama and Theatre: A Shared Role in Learning*, Education Department of Victoria, 1982.

J. Burns, M. Cadoret & K. Cross, 'Integrated Arts' in *Mask*, vol. 7, nos 2 & 3, Education Department of Victoria, 1983.

L. Button, 'The Pastoral Curriculum' in J. Nixton (ed.), *Drama and the Whole Curriculum*, Hutchinson, London, 1982.

P. Cole, *Acting: A Handbook of the Stanislavsky Method*, Crown Publishers, New York, 1955.

P. Cook, 'Evaluating Drama' in *2D*, vol. 2, no. 1, A.B. Printers, Leicester, 1983.

R. Courtney, *The Dramatic Curriculum*, Webcom, Ontario, 1980.

M. Croydon, *Lunatics, Lovers and Poets*, McGraw Hill, 1974.

J. Deverall, 'Playing the Game: Play Games and Drama' in *National Association for Drama in Education Journal*, vol. 6, no. 2, New Era Press Pty Ltd, Brisbane, 1981.

W. Dobson (ed), *Bolton of the Barbican*, National Association of Teachers of Drama, Longman, London, 1982.

E. Eisner, 'The Mythology of Art Education' in *Curriculum Theory Network*, vol. 4, nos 2 & 3, 1974.

R. Figgins, 'Teaching as a Dramatic Performance: An Inquiry into the Application of the Stanislavsky Method to the Classroom', Ph.D. thesis, University of Michigan, 1980.

E. Goffman, *The Presentation of Self in Everyday Life*, Pelican, Harmondsworth, Middlesex, 1971.

B. Hogan, 'The Development of Drama in Victoria: A Personal View' in *Mask*, vol. 7, no. 1, Education Department of Victoria, 1983.

V. Hospers, *Understanding the Arts*, Prentice-Hall, New Jersey, 1982.

W. Lett, 'The Framing of Realities: From Actual to Virtual — Children's Thinking and Making in the Arts' in *National Association for Drama in Education Journal*, vol. 7, no. 2, Hyde Park Press, Adelaide, 1982.

R. Linnell, *Approaching Classroom Drama*, Edward Arnold, London, 1982.

J. McLeod, *A Survey of Drama in Post-Primary Schools*, Education Department of Victoria, 1978; *Drama: A Curriculum Statement*, Education Department of Victoria, 1980; and *How Do I Evaluate Drama?*, Education Department of Victoria, 1983.

D.E. Outerbridge, *Without Make-up: Liv Ullmann*, William Morrow & Co., New York, 1979.

L.A. Reid, *Meaning in the Arts*, Allen and Unwin, 1979.

K. Robinson (ed.), *Exploring Theatre and Education*, Heinemann Educational, London, 1978.

M. Ross, *The Creative Arts*, Heinemann Educational, London, 1978.

J. Norman, 'Why Does the Teacher Always Get the Best Parts?' in *London Drama*, vol. 6, no. 6, Stacey Publications, Kent, 1982.

J. Seely, *In Context: Language and Drama in the Secondary School*, Oxford University Press, London, 1954.

P. Slade, *Child Drama*, University of London Press, London, 1976.

K. Stanislavsky, *Creating a Role*, Bles, London, 1963 and *An Actor Prepares*, Bles, London, 1937.

B.J. Wagner, *Dorothy Heathcote: Drama as a Learning Medium*, National Education Association, Washington, 1976.

B. Watkins, *Drama and Education*, Batsford, London, 1981.

B. Way, *Development through Drama*, Longman, London, 1967.

J. Willet, *Brecht on Theatre*, Methuen, New York, 1964.

D.W. Winnicot, *Playing and Reality*, Tavistock, London, 1971.

R. Witkin, *The Intelligence of Feeling*, Heinemann Educational, London, 1974.

Index

Acknowledgements

We would like to thank the following for permission to reproduce copyright material:

The Age newspaper for the article, 'Bad guys are better off than the good, says Police Commissioner'; Bruce Dawe for 'My Mother in Her Latter Years' from *Sometimes Gladness, Collected Poems, 1954–1982*; Michael Dugan for 'Onkerpled' from *Stuff and Nonsense*, edited by Michael Dugan, published by William Collins, Sydney; Faber and Faber publishers, London, for 'My parents kept me from children who were rough' by Stephen Spender from *Collected Poems*; Oxford University Press, Oxford, U.K., for 'Leather-Jackets, Bikes and Birds' by Robert Davies from *Every Man Will Shout*, edited by Roger Mansfield and Isobel Armstrong, 1964.

Every effort has been made to trace and acknowledge copyright, but in some cases copyright proved untraceable. Should any infringement have occurred, the publishers tender their apologies.